BISTRO
COOKING

BISTRO

COOKING

BY PATRICIA WELLS

◆──────◆

ASSISTED BY JUDY KLEIBER JONES

First published in Great Britain by
Kyle Cathie Limited
7/8 Hatherley Street London SW1P 2QT

This paperback edition published 1993

Copyright © 1989 by Patricia Wells

ISBN 1 85626 119 0

A CIP catalogue record for this book is available from
the British Library

Acknowledgements

Page 2: *Photo Harlingue-Viollet*—Paris, Montparnasse. Interior of the café "La Coupole"
around 1930. **Page 16:** © *Harlingue-Viollet*—Interior of a Dupont café around 1930.
Page 66: © *Roger-Viollet*—Kitchen around 1930. **Page 80:** © *Roger-Viollet*—Paris's
"Chez Raoul," the cabaret "des Belles Lettres" on Rue de Richelieu in 1924. **Page 96:** ©
Roger-Viollet—Paris. Le Café de la Paix in 1921. **Page 116:** © *Roger-Viollet*—Paris
bistro scene; women at the counter of a bar. **Page 132:** © *Roger-Viollet*—The man who
opens oysters on the terrace of a restaurant, 1926. **Page 168:** © *Roger-Viollet*—Bistro.
Page 196: *Photo Harlingue-Viollet*—Basque restaurant in Paris around 1925. **Page 222:**
Photo Boyer-Viollet—Interior of a café, the "Maison du Café," Avenue de L'Opera in
1937. **Page 256:** © *Harlingue-Viollet*—Kitchen.

Book illustrations by Jewell Homad
Cover photo by Steven Rothfeld

Printed and bound by Butler & Tanner Ltd, Frome and London

DEDICATION

To my mom and dad, Vera and Joe Kleiber, who taught me the lasting value of honest home cooking.

ACKNOWLEDGMENTS

I t's amazing what open, warm-hearted enthusiasm the word "bistro" generates. Over the years, I have rarely had to persuade friends to accompany me to a simple neighborhood restaurant, and at home there is always a horde of eager eaters ready to sample the latest roast chicken, potato gratin, or apple tart.

Throughout, many people have knowingly and unknowingly assisted me in my search for authentic bistro fare. Without the cooks—ladies like Marie-Antoninette Cartet (of Paris' Cartet), Adrienne Biasin (of Paris' Chez la Vieille), Marie-Louise Auteli (of Lyons' Chez Tante Paulette), Marie-Claude Gracia (of La Belle Gasconne in Poudenas) and men like the late Antoine Magnin (of Paris' L'Ami Louis)—there would not be a book. Thanks also to the bakers, the butchers, the merchants who added

inspiration as well as recipes: I am especially grateful to Roland Henny, my butcher in Provence, who is always ready to share his vast creative talents with each and every customer. And thank you, Kermit Lynch, for helping me discover and better appreciate so many of the wonderful wines of France.

Likewise, it is my friends and editors—among them Rita and Yale Kramer, Maggie and Al Shapiro, Susy Davidson, Catherine O'Neill and Richard Reeves, Steven Rothfeld, Stuart McBride, Pamela Fiori, Malachy Duffy, Linda Wells—who over the years have accompanied me, encouraged me, allowed me to weave my work life and my play life into a most pleasurable existence.

In Paris, my assistants helped gather recipes from cooks, chefs, bakers, and restaurateurs, and tried to help me keep the ever-growing stacks of recipes, facts, quotes, and tidbits in some reasonable order. I want to thank Jane Sigal, Anne Trager, and Laura Washburn for their cheerful assistance.

Back in the U.S.A., others have worked to make sure that the recipes made sense to the home cook in America. For testing and retesting many of the recipes, I am sincerely grateful to my sister, Judy Kleiber Jones, and the friends from her weekly quilting/cooking/testing group in Ramsey, New Jersey, including Maureen Papola, Carol White, and Rose Anne Tockstein.

Likewise, thanks to Susan Herrmann Loomis, my longtime colleague and great friend, who spent many hours in her "alley-cabin" in Seattle, often coaxing scribbles into workable recipes, keeping me in line as far as fish and shellfish were concerned.

None of this could have happened without the insight, support, and encouragement of my publisher, Peter Workman, and my editor, Suzanne Rafer, who has so carefully tended to—and mended—my copy for years. I'm beginning to lose count of the number of first editions and updates we've all been through together. Thanks also goes to Mardee Haiden Regan and Shawna McCarthy for their editorial work, and to Kathleen Herlihy-Paoli for the lovely design.

Finally I thank my parents, Vera and Joe Kleiber, for allowing me the freedom to develop as I desired, and my husband, Walter, for holding my hand all along the way.

CONTENTS

INTRODUCTION: BISTRO AS A WAY OF LIFE

I like to think that this book began to take form in the fall of 1979, when my husband, Walter, and I were vacationing in France. Walking the back streets of Lyons one evening, we wandered into a little restaurant around dinnertime.

We feasted on giant salads of curly endive tossed with chunks of bacon and coated with enough vinegar to make your mouth pucker and your eyes water. There was a golden roast chicken with the crispiest of skins, a meltingly tender potato gratin, carafes of chilled Beaujolais, and then a rich, dense chocolate mousse for dessert. Much of the food came to the table in giant white bowls, and there was a marvelous sense of generosity about it all. Although the menu was traditionally French, it could just as well have been prepared by my mother back in Wauwatosa, Wisconsin, for it was all very familiar fare.

In retrospect I realize that it was the first of hundreds of authentic bistro meals to come.

We moved to Paris from New York a few months later, and restaurants big and small soon became the focus of my daily work, my passions, my life. At that time, "nouvelle cuisine" was all the rage and although we made regular pilgrimages to small, old-fashioned Parisian bistros such as L'Ami Louis, we spent the bulk of our dining hours in the more elegant, upscale restaurants.

Times changed, tastes changed, and little by little we began to favor the smaller, less fashionable spots that served very simple, traditional French home cooking.

As I gathered material for my first two books—*The Food Lover's Guide to Paris* and *The Food Lover's Guide to France*—I was very conscious of the difference between luxury restaurants and small family affairs, and made a special effort to seek out the kind of restaurants we now all know as bistros.

So when Suzanne Rafer, my editor, called one gray winter's day a few years back to say, "Write us a bistro cookbook," my heart skipped a happy little beat. Before she could elaborate, my response was out. A big, positive "Yes!"

Quite unconsciously, I'd been collecting information for this book for years—interviewing chefs and jotting down tips and recipes in their kitchens, noting the number of variations on the potato *gratin,* writing essays on *pot-au-feu* and *aïoli,* fattening my files with ideas for homemade desserts, meaty winter *daubes,* and cool summer salads.

Unlike other projects that have consumed me to the point of total distraction from all else around me, this book has been a very natural, friendly part of my life for the past few years. Some days, everywhere I turned there was a bistro clue: a tip on grilling fish, an exciting new fruit tart, a quote from a writer who tugged at my heartstrings and put me in the mood for platters of fresh, briny oysters.

BISTRO! BISTRO!

The world, I am sure, will never agree upon the exact origins of the word "bistro." The most often-quoted explanation is that "bistro! bistro!" is what Russian soldiers shouted as they made for the cafés after seizing Paris in 1815. But since the word really did not enter the French language until 1884, other explanations are more plausible. Some suggest the word comes from "bistrouille" or "bistouille," which in the north of France refers to a mixture of coffee and eau-de-vie, or to a poor quality eau-de-vie, both drinks one might find at a "bistro." Going one step further, we have the verb "bistrouiller," which refers to the preparation of an ersatz wine made with water, alcohol, and other products, which of course might be passed off as wine in a low-quality "bistro." Whatever its origins, everyone agrees that whether it's a café, a small unpretentious restaurant, or simply a place to enjoy a glass of wine and a simple yet hearty sandwich, a bistro is a place for good times with friends.

Throughout the seasons I'd test the recipes, rushing through my market on Rue Poncelet in search of the freshest scallops from Brittany, or wandering the markets of Provence to find a plump farm-raised chicken, the season's first green olives, discs of firm goat cheese for curing in oil.

And as I feasted in bistros all over France, then returned home to test and retest the discoveries in my own kitchens, I began to notice certain changes in my dining and cooking habits. The food was becoming simpler, less complicated, but no less delicious. In short, bistro had become a way of life. I am certain, for these reasons and more, that bistro fare is timeless fare.

As long as man consumes platters of *pommes frites* and thick, pan-fried steaks, while hoisting stout round glasses filled with cheap red wine, the homey, welcoming small neighborhood restaurant will continue to warm our souls with images of copious, hearty, no-nonsense meals and good times among friends.

Most simply, a bistro is a small neighborhood restaurant serving home-style, substantial fare. The china is almost always thick and plain white, the tables covered with waffled, crinkle-edged paper, the floor peppered with sawdust. The menu—often an illegible mimeographed sheet encased in clear plastic—is brief and changes infrequently, save for perhaps the ritual *plat du jour:* If this is Monday they must be serving *pot-au-feu.*

In bistros, people don't whisper, they shout, and diners are on a first-name basis with the harried waitress wrapped in a frilly white apron. In bistros, you might not even get to choose what you eat or drink. The "patron," or owner, may usurp that right. And in bistros, you will often find yourself chatting across tables with perfect strangers, sharing their platter of French fries while you wait for yours to come sizzling from the kitchen at the end of the room.

In days past, in Paris in particular, the bistro served as an extension of the family living room. Apartment kitchens were small (in fact almost nonexistent), and many Parisians took all their meals at their local café-style bistro. In some cases, they even stored their own napkins there.

Bistro food is not just a style of cooking but also a manner of presentation. Order *terrine de campagne*—usually a rustic, thick pâté of ground pork and pork liver spiced with cognac and herbs—and you are not served a thin slice on a plate. Rather, the waitress offers the entire terrine, and you're meant to eat your fill. Order a roast chicken and a whole golden bird arrives tableside, to be carved in front of you.

Bistro cuisine is French home cooking at its best, a style of cooking that demands a minimal of technical skills and does not require a professional collection of pots and pans. Ingredients aren't exotic; they come straight from the local market. And it's a way of cooking that grew out of a need to maximize every morsel in the market basket, so it's easy on the pocketbook.

What I love most about cooking

and eating bistro food at home is its sense of generosity, of wholeness, of copiousness. If I prepare a meaty beef *daube* from Provence, I bring the entire steaming, enameled cast-iron casserole directly from the kitchen so my family and guests, if any, can see just what they are about to be served. Salads are not arranged like fussy still lifes. Rather, the entire salad bowl arrives at the table, ready to be tossed and served.

Bistro fare is not afraid to be lusty and earthy, filling the air with wafts of pungent garlic or sweet bacon sizzling in a huge steel skillet, or the sweet caramel scent of a *tarte Tatin* about to be released from the oven.

What's more, it is a food without

OF HANDY TIPS AND LEFTOVERS

Just as we never seem to have enough motherly tips—on taking out pesky stains, on saving sauces that have turned—the French have turned tip-giving into a veritable art. They have a tip, or "truc" for just about every occasion, thus the book is sprinkled with tips to make the cook's life easier, more efficient and enjoyable. Likewise, I've tried to offer numerous suggestions for using leftovers, or what the French call "les restes."

pretension, a cuisine based on familiar ingredients that we can all relate to: voluminous green salads; golden potato *gratins;* inexpensive but flavorful cuts of meat marinated in purple-red wine and cooked until it is so tender it falls off the bone; and a whole array of simple desserts, such as fruit-filled flans and sweet, creamy custards.

Bistro cuisine knows no boundaries, and the roster of dishes that could seriously be labeled "authentic bistro" runs into the hundreds. Paris has its own style of bistro cooking, as do the French cities of Lyons, Strasbourg, Nice, and Marseilles. Each region of France offers its own special touch, and thus we have southwestern bistros offering confit of duck served with potatoes sautéed with a healthy dose of garlic; Alsatian bistros serving chicken cooked in the local white Riesling; Provençal bistros serving daubes with macaroni gratin.

Of course, bistro chefs are conscious of the way we like to eat today. That means they serve more salads, more fish, less meat. While charcuterie—sausages, hams, terrines and pâtés—have long played a starring role in bistro cooking, today they appear in different guises, cubed and tossed into composed salads or served in smaller portions.

Wine is as essential to a good bistro meal as a crusty baguette, and bistro cuisine demands its own style of wine. Simple, uncomplicated, unpretentious. Of course, the king of bistro wines is the all-purpose Beaujolais, but the choice is vast. Some popular bistro reds include a chilled Saumur-Champigny or Chinon from the Loire; a rustic Cahors, Madiran, or Gaillac from France's southwest; a delicate Pinot Noir from Alsace; Provence's Côtes du Rhône, Bandol, and Côtes de Provence. In whites, the favorites include Burgundy's Saint-Véran, Aligoté, and Mâcon-Villages; the Loire Valley's Sancerre and Pouilly-Fumé; as well as Muscadet from the Atlantic coast.

While traveling about France in search of authentic bistro fare, I've gathered an abundant list of favored dishes from favorite haunts. As you read this book and create the recipes in your own home, I hope that you will come to know the people who have shared their heritage with me, and that you will be inspired, no matter your roots, no matter where you live, by bistro cooking and the bistro way of life.

BISTRO
COOKING

LES HORS D'OEUVRES, POUR VOUS METTRE EN APPÉTIT

*Appetizers, First Courses,
and Palate Teasers*

Everyday bistro menus almost certainly include a series of "sure bet" first courses, such as tangy celery root in mustard sauce, soothing warm poached sausages with potato salad, and pick-me-up herring marinated in oil and herbs. Some starters, like Chez Gilbert's vibrant spread of anchovies, garlic, and olive oil, are made for hot summer days and all but send me back to the first time I sampled this most adaptable Provençal classic one sizzling August afternoon. Others, like Juveniles' Sandwich of Beef and Confit of Tomatoes, remind me of the rainy winter's day we sought shelter inside a friendly little wine bar. But perhaps the favorite, and most versatile of all, is La Boutarde's open-face sandwich, a brilliant combination of garlic-flecked pistou (pesto) spread on warm toast, then layered with smoky trout, snippets of ham, or cured duck. I've lost count of the number of times I've served this starter, which reflects most clearly the sort of creativity distinctive to modern bistro fare.

ANCHOÏADE CHEZ GILBERT

Anchovy, Garlic, and Olive Oil Spread

Chez Gilbert is a favorite Provençal bistro, set along the sun-kissed port of Cassis, on the Mediterranean coast. This delicious appetizer, also known as *quichét,* is served on tiny toast rounds, with pre-dinner drinks. I love the surprise taste of vinegar, which I find marries well with the salty hit of anchovy and the pungency of garlic. I find that anchovy fillets packed in olive oil work best here. Anchovies tend to be too salty for many palates, so for this recipe, they are soaked before using, but this is an optional step. Serve this dish with a chilled rosé, such as Domaine Tempier Bandol rosé.

2 cans (each 2 oz; 57 g) flat anchovy
　fillets in olive oil, drained, oil re-
　served
16 thin slices from a long, narrow
　French bread or baguette
2½ teaspoons best-quality red wine
　vinegar
4 garlic cloves, coarsely chopped
3 tablespoons chopped fresh parsley

1. Preheat the broiler.

2. In a small bowl, cover the anchovies with 1 cup (25 cl) of cold water. Soak for 10 minutes. Drain the anchovies and pat dry on paper towels.

3. Arrange the bread slices on a baking sheet and broil about 4 inches (5 cm) from the heat, turning once, until browned on both sides, about 1½ minutes. Set aside; leave on the broiler.

4. Mince the anchovies with the reserved oil. Add the vinegar, garlic, and parsley and chop together; the mixture should be rather coarse. Spread the anchoïade over the toasts and broil for 1 minute, just until warm. Serve immediately.

Yield: 4 servings

THE "ANCHOVY MONTE-CRISTO"

Alexandre Dumas is credited with inventing this recipe: Stuff a pitted olive with a cured anchovy fillet. Place the olive inside a black bird, the black bird inside a quail, the quail inside a pheasant, the pheasant inside a turkey, the turkey inside a pig, and roast over a roaring fire. The true gourmands eat only the anchovy.

TAPENADO RESTAURANT MAURICE BRUN

◆———◆

Restaurant Maurice Brun's Tapenade

U nlike most tapenades, which are blended to a purée, this classic Provençal blend of black olives, capers, anchovies, and herbs is very lightly mixed in a food processor, turning out a rather chunky, substantial appetizer. At the homey, museum-like Marseilles restaurant, Maurice Brun, they serve this version, which uses rum, rather than a more traditional Cognac. Madame Brun once explained to me that in the 1930s, they used to watch ships filled with barrels of rum dock right outside the restaurant, which is located on the old port of Marseilles. The rum was bottled right in the neighborhood. Thus their recipe calls for it. The Bruns serve this as a separate appetizer course, to be eaten with a fork, not spread on bread.

2 tablespoons drained capers
4 anchovy fillets
1 teaspoon fresh thyme
1 tablespoon rum
2 tablespoons extra-virgin olive oil
2 cups (½ pound; 250 g) oil-cured
    black olives, preferably from
    Nyons, pitted

1. Combine the capers, anchovies, thyme, rum, and oil in a food processor and process just until blended. Add the olives and pulse on and off about 10 times, until the mixture is fairly coarse but well combined.

2. Transfer to a bowl and serve.
Yield: 1 cup

THE PURITY OF OLIVES

"The Greeks, who attributed a divine origin to olives, venerated them so much that for a long time the only people who were employed in the cultivation of this small tree were virgin women and pure men. An oath of chastity was required by those who were charged with harvesting the crop."

—ALEXANDRE DUMAS
Dumas on Food

TARTINES DE PISTOU ET POISSON FUMÉ LA BOUTARDE

La Boutarde's Grilled Country Bread with Pesto and Smoked Trout

Of all the millions of food combinations one might dream up, this one I am sure would never have occurred to me if I hadn't sampled it one summer's evening at La Boutarde, a lively bistro near the *International Herald Tribune*'s offices on the western edge of Paris. That evening, we were served, as a sort of appetizer/first course, these lovely bright *tartines,* or open-face sandwiches: Grilled country bread was topped with a vibrant pesto sauce, then layered on top were the thinnest slices of *flétan* (whiting). I've adapted the recipe just a bit, using the more readily available smoked trout. The idea here is to use thin slices of any available lightly smoked fish, such as trout or whiting. Try this with a chilled rosé de Provence.

AH, BASIL

Today we put basil in everything. But at the turn of the century, even in Provence and along the Côte d'Azur, basil was synonymous with pistou and was used only in *soupe au pistou.* As one contemporary Provençal chef, Guy Gedda of La Tonnelle des Délices in Bormes-les-Mimosas, confesses, "I am sick for basil. I adore basil . . . I make sandwiches of basil leaves that I sprinkle with olive oil. Delicious with a touch of salt and bread rubbed with a clove of fresh garlic—it brings me to my knees."

4 tablespoons (60 g) Pistou (see Index)
4 thick slices country or whole wheat
    bread, freshly toasted
4 thin slices smoked fish, such as trout
    or whiting

Spread 1 tablespoon of pistou on each slice of toasted bread. Place a slice of smoked fish on top. Neatly trim the edges of the fish to fit the bread, and serve.
Yield: 4 servings

SAUCISSON CHAUD POMMES À L'HUILE

Warm Poached Sausage with Potato Salad

What would bistro food be without steaming, well-seasoned sausage served alongside warm potatoes bathed in oil and shallots? This dish always makes me think of one of my first visits to France, when my husband and I would sometimes just wander into places that looked interesting. It was on one of those visits, after exploring a narrow side street in Lyons, that I first sampled this dish. It's no wonder that six weeks later, we left New York and moved lock, stock, and barrel to France! With the potatoes and sausage, try a Burgundian white, such as a dry Rully, or Saint-Véran. If you prefer a red, make it Beaujolais.

½ cup (12.5 cl) extra-virgin olive oil
4 shallots, finely minced
1 large fresh country-style pork sausage, or several individual fresh pork sausage links (weighing a total of about 12 ounces, or 360 g)
1½ pounds (750 g) small new redskinned potatoes, scrubbed
¼ cup (6 cl) best-quality sherry wine vinegar
Salt and freshly ground black pepper
Small handful of fresh parsley

1. Combine the oil and shallots in a small bowl; set aside. As the shallots marinate in the oil, they will lose any bitterness.

2. Place the sausage in a saucepan, cover with cold water, and bring just to a simmer over medium-high heat. Adjust the heat and simmer gently—do not allow the water to boil or the sausage casings may burst—until the sausage is cooked through, 35 to 40 minutes. The sausage may be kept warm in its cooking liquid for up to 30 minutes.

3. While the sausage simmers, cook the potatoes in plenty of salted water, just until tender.

4. Meanwhile, whisk the vinegar into the oil and shallot mixture. Season to taste with salt and pepper.

5. Drain the potatoes. As soon as they are cool enough to handle but are still warm, cut into thin, even slices. Toss with the vinaigrette and sprinkle with the parsley. Mound in the center of a serving platter.

6. Drain the sausage. Cut into thin, even slices. Surround the potatoes with the sausage and serve.

Yield: 4 servings

CERVELAS RÉMOULADE

Pork Sausage with Mustard Sauce

T his is an old-fashioned, traditional bistro dish, typical of the char-cuterie-rich menus of days past. It's one that's a snap to put together. Buy the best quality precooked sausage you can find, and if you have the time, prepare your own mayonnaise. This can be served with a tossed green salad placed on the same plate. A few slices of crusty bread are an essential accompaniment.

1 cup (25 cl) mayonnaise, preferably homemade (see Index)
1 tablespoon imported Dijon mustard, or more to taste
8 ounces (250 g) precooked pork sausage, such as knockwurst
Several sprigs of fresh chervil, or 1 tablespoon minced fresh parsley, for garnish

1. In a small bowl, combine the mayonnaise and mustard. Taste, and add additional mustard if desired.
2. Cut the sausage into ¼-inch slices and evenly divide them among 4 dinner plates. Spoon the sauce over the edge of the sausage slices; sprinkle with the chervil. Serve, with a tossed green salad alongside.

Yield: 4 servings

CÉLERI RÉMOULADE

Celery Root in Mustard Sauce

T his is a simple, wonderfully piquant version of one of my favorite bistro salads. I love the tang of celery root—also known as celeriac—one of France's most traditional vegetables. And when it's combined with a palate-stinging mustard sauce, zow! Try to find fresh celery root (older roots turn bitter), and use a good, hot imported Dijon mustard. Make the dressing first, and toss the celery root as soon as it is grated, to keep it from darkening. While most classic versions of this dish are dressed with a mustardy mayonnaise, I find this sauce less cloying and a bit lighter. By the way, even though celery root appears to be very hard, it will grate easily in a food processor.

2 tablespoons freshly squeezed lemon
  juice
2 tablespoons imported Dijon mustard
  or to taste
1 cup (25 cl) crème fraîche (see Index)
  or heavy cream
Salt and freshly ground black pepper
1 celery root (about 1 pound; 500 g)

1. In a large mixing bowl, combine the lemon juice, mustard, crème fraîche, and salt and pepper to taste; mix thoroughly. Taste and adjust the seasoning.

2. Quarter the celery root and peel it. Grate coarsely, in a food processor or on a Mouli grater. Immediately add it to the mustard sauce and toss to coat. Season to taste. Serve as a first course.

Yield: 4 to 6 servings

THE MONTH IS DECEMBER, TIME TO VISIT A PARIS BISTRO

A classic menu, simply made, to warm the soul on dark, gray days. Uncork a bottle of young Bordeaux, and think of warmer days to come.

CÉLERI RÉMOULADE
Celery Root in Mustard Sauce

◆

TENDRONS DE VEAU LE CAMÉLÉON
Le Caméléon's Braised Veal with Fresh Pasta

◆

CRÈME CARAMEL
Caramel Cream

HARENGS MARINÉS

◆

Herring Marinated in Oil and Herbs

This is one of my all-time favorite bistro preparations, and one that's a five-minute wonder to prepare at home. At many old-time bistros, the herring is marinated in oil with onions, carrots, and herbs and served out of a huge white porcelain terrine. The entire terrine is brought to the table (meaning you're welcome to take seconds, or thirds) and served with warm, sliced potatoes tossed with vinaigrette and parsley.

At home, herring marinated in oil serves as a great luncheon dish, or as a first course for a more elaborate meal. The oil reacts in a lovely way with the sweet, smoked herring, serving to soften and enrich it, while also softening and tenderizing the onions. We've found that the best brand of herring to use in the United States is King Oscar canned smoked herring or fresh-cured unsmoked matjes herring from a delicatessen. For this dish, you'll need about four 3½-ounce cans. Don't worry if the herring tends to fall apart as you take it out of the can. It's inevitable, but won't alter the flavors of this marvelous dish!

16 small herring fillets (about 12 ounces: 360 g)
2 onions, sliced into thin rounds
2 carrots, peeled and sliced into thin rounds
2 lemons, sliced into thin rounds
2 bay leaves
1 teaspoon dried thyme
12 whole black peppercorns
2 to 3 cups (50 to 75 cl) peanut oil

1. In a 1-quart (1 l) oval or rectangular terrine, layer half of each of the ingredients in this order: herring, onions, carrots, lemon, bay leaf, thyme, and peppercorns. Add a second layer, in the same order. Pour on enough peanut oil to thoroughly cover all of the ingredients; cover securely and refrigerate. Marinate for 2 to 4 days before serving. (You might want to sample it after 2 days, to see how the flavors are developing.) As long as the container is carefully sealed, the herring will stay fresh and delicious up to 2 weeks.

2. Remove from the refrigerator about 1 hour before serving.

Yield: 8 servings

TABOULÉ PROVENÇAL

Seasoned Couscous Salad

T he French seem to have adopted couscous as their own, as nations tend to do with all foods that they love. Couscous, the fine semolina grain that is part of all good North African and Middle Eastern cooking, appears in many forms in modern French bistro cooking. One of the most popular dishes—found in charcuteries, supermarkets, on café menus—is *salade de couscous,* or *taboulé.* While most of us are more familiar with the version made with bulgur—coarse, cracked whole wheat—the French version is generally made with the slightly more refined couscous, or semolina. This French version, seen often in Provence, also generally includes tomatoes. It's a refreshing summer salad that can be served as is, or as an accompaniment to a platter of raw vegetables or crudités, such as red bell peppers, strips of fresh fennel, carrots, cucumbers, and scallions.

*1 cup (about 160 g) medium-grain
    precooked couscous (or use bulgur)*
1 cup (25 cl) flat-leaf parsley leaves
*1 cup (25 cl) fresh mint leaves (or
    substitute ¼ cup dried crushed
    mint leaves)*
*4 medium tomatoes, peeled, cored,
    seeded, and chopped*
*10 thin scallions, white bulb cut into
    thin rounds*
*¼ cup (6 cl) freshly squeezed lemon
    juice*
¼ cup (6 cl) extra-virgin olive oil
Salt

1. Combine the couscous with 2 cups (50 cl) cold water. Let stand at room temperature until all of the liquid has been absorbed, about 30 min-utes. If any liquid remains after 30 minutes, place the couscous in a cheesecloth-lined sieve and drain off any excess.

2. In a food processor, chop the parsley and mint. Transfer to a small bowl. Add the remaining dressing in-gredients, except the salt, to the bowl and stir to blend. Season with salt to taste and set aside.

3. Place the couscous in a me-dium-size bowl; fluff with a fork to separate the grains. Stir in the dress-ing; taste for seasoning. Cover and refrigerate for at least 1 hour, but not more than 4 hours. Adjust the sea-soning before serving, adding addi-tional lemon juice or salt to taste.

Yield: 4 to 6 servings

GOUGÈRE FRANÇOISE POTEL

Françoise Potel's Cheese Puffs

F rançoise Potel is a lively and energetic Burgundian lady, who along with her intense and serious husband, Gérard, makes a lovely, voluptuous Volnay wine. Each time I've visited their lovely estate, she's offered warm-from-the-oven cheese puffs. They are great appetizers and go especially well with the red Burgundian wines.

½ teaspoon salt
¼ pound (4 ounces; 120 g) unsalted butter, chilled and cut into small pieces
1 cup minus 1½ tablespoons (130 g) unbleached all-purpose flour, sifted
4 large eggs
¾ cup (2 ounces: 60 g) freshly grated imported French or Swiss Gruyère cheese

1. Combine the salt, butter, and 1 cup (25 cl) of water in a medium-size saucepan. Bring to a boil over high heat, stirring all the while with a wooden spoon.

2. Quickly remove the pan from the heat and add all of the flour at once. Beat vigorously with a large wooden spoon to create a smooth dough. Reheat for 1 minute over medium heat, stirring all the time, to allow the dough to dry out just a bit.

3. Quickly transfer the dough to the bowl of an electric mixer. Add all of the eggs and half of the grated cheese and beat at medium speed until the eggs and cheese are thoroughly incorporated into the dough. The dough should still be warm.

4. Preheat the oven to 425°F (220°C).

5. Spoon the dough into a pastry bag fitted with a ½-inch (1.5 cm) tube. (Depending upon the size of your pastry bag, this may have to be done in 2 batches.) Squeeze into round 2-inch (5 cm) mounds, spacing them about 2 inches (5 cm) apart on 2 nonstick baking sheets. (If you do not have a pastry bag, carefully spoon the dough onto the baking sheets with a tablespoon.)

6. Sprinkle the tops with the remaining grated cheese. Bake until the puffs are an even golden brown, 20 to 25 minutes. (If the puffs are not baking evenly, allow 1 sheet to bake thoroughly, and remove it; allow the second sheet to bake until golden.)

Yield: About 40 cheese puffs

FILET DE BOEUF SUR PAIN GRILLÉ AUX TOMATES CONFITES JUVÉNILES

Juvéniles' Sandwich of Beef and Confit of Tomatoes

This is a wonderful, meaty sandwich to make when you have leftover beef and roasted tomatoes. Even if you don't have leftovers, make the sandwich with slices of roast beef from the market, fresh tomatoes, and a lovely salad of watercress dressed with mustardy dressing. This recipe could also be used with leftover cooked lamb, especially from the *Gigot à Sept Heures* (see Index), and for the tomatoes, use leftover, or freshly made, *Tomates à la Provençal* (see Index). The recipe comes from Juvéniles, the popular Paris wine bar run by Mark Williamson and Tim Johnston. The day I first sampled this sandwich, we drank a Bandol, Château Vannières.

1 tablespoon imported Dijon mustard
3 tablespoons crème fraîche (see Index)
or heavy cream
Salt and freshly ground black pepper
1 small bunch of watercress, washed,
dried, and stems removed
8 slices country or whole wheat bread
3 tablespoons (1½ ounces; 45 g) un-
salted butter
8 thin slices rare roasted beef
4 Tomates à la Provençale (see Index),
quartered, or 4 fresh tomatoes,
sliced

1. Combine the mustard, crème fraîche, and salt and pepper to taste in a small bowl and whisk to blend. Toss with the watercress leaves. Adjust the seasoning and set aside.

2. Toast the bread evenly on both sides. Spread 1 side of each slice with butter.

3. Layer the beef, dressed watercress, and tomatoes over 4 slices of the toast. Cover each with a second slice of toast. Serve.

Yield: 4 servings

La Tartine Chaude au Bleu des Causses et Jambon Cru Les Bacchantes

Les Bacchantes' Blue Cheese and Ham Sandwich

Les Bacchantes is a lively wine bar near Paris's Opéra and not far from the major department stores. I find it's a nice place to go for Saturday lunch. There's a good selection of sandwiches and salads, enormous platters of steaks and fries, omelets, and of course a great selection of wines, ranging from unknown reds from the Ardèche in southeastern France, to southwestern Madirans. I love this open-face sandwich, as hearty as it is warming, on a cold fall or winter day—so nice with a tossed salad of tomatoes and greens and a sip of red.

4 large slices country or whole wheat bread
½ cup (110 g) crumbled blue cheese, such as Bleu de Causses or Roquefort
4 thin slices unsmoked salt-cured ham, such as prosciutto

1. Preheat the broiler.
2. Grill or toast the bread evenly on both sides. Sprinkle with the cheese, then top the cheese with a slice of ham. Grill until the ham is warm and the cheese begins to melt, about 2 minutes.

Yield: 4 servings

PAN BAGNA

"Bathed" Provençal Sandwich

Pan bagna—literally bathed bread—is like a salade Niçoise on a bun. Basically, it's the kind of sandwich that can be made with whatever Provençal-style ingredients you have on hand. You could add cooked green beans, cucumber, green pepper, zucchini, black or green olives, lettuce, radish, hard-cooked egg or herbs. But I like a "less is more" sandwich. Whatever the combination, the sandwich should be moist and sort of messy to eat: There's nothing worse than a dry pan bagna!

1 large baguette or several large, thick-crusted hard rolls
6 garlic cloves, finely minced
¼ cup (6 cl) extra-virgin olive oil
1 can flat anchovy fillets (2 ounces; 57 g)
1 can (6½ ounces; 195 g) water-packed albacore tuna
2 tablespoons capers
1 medium onion, cut into thin rings
1 red bell pepper, cored, seeded, and cut into strips
2 medium tomatoes, cored and thinly sliced
½ cup (12.5 cl) Maggie's Roasted Red Peppers with their oil (see Index)

1. Slice the bread or rolls in half lengthwise. Combine the garlic and oil and, using a pastry brush, brush both the bottom and top portions with the garlic and oil mixture, pressing the mixture firmly into the bread.
2. Drain the anchovies and soak them in water to cover for several minutes. Drain again, and pat dry.
3. Combine the tuna, undrained, with the capers and spoon the mixture evenly over the bottom portion of the bread, pressing it firmly into the bread. Then, layer the tuna mixture with the onions, pepper, tomatoes, anchovies, and the roasted peppers in oil. (You want a very moist sandwich.)
4. Cover the sandwich with the top portion of bread. If using a baguette, cut the sandwich into four equal portions. Press down firmly on the bread. Do not be concerned if the crust cracks. Cover tightly and securely with plastic wrap, then weight the sandwiches down to flatten them even more. Refrigerate, with the weights (I press them between two heavy cutting boards) for several hours or overnight. Serve lightly chilled.

Yield: 4 servings

Les Soupes et Les Potages du Jour

Soups of the Day

I love to make soup, for there is something very homey and satisfying about a blend of fragrant ingredients simmering on the stove. The most classic bistro soup of all, of course, comes from the old market area in Paris, Les Halles, where workers traditionally dined on onion soup in the very early morning hours. Today, bistro soups are more likely to be main-course affairs, such as the Provençal fish soup known as bouillabaisse or the southwestern cabbage soup called *garbure*.

Sometimes I think as much as I love soup I love the assortment of various-colored dishes in which to serve soup—stout, round white porcelain bowls for onion soup, shallow ocher-colored bowls for bouillabaisse, and pretty flowery bowls for delicate, garden-fresh sorrel soup.

When making soup, always consider the type of crusty bread or rolls that will best serve as the accompaniment. Leek, potato, and bacon soup most certainly suggests a sturdy rye; Jacque Collet's Fennel and Saffron Bread goes with just about any of the fish-based soups; and a very dense multi-grain loaf would make a perfect partner for any of the vegetable-based soups.

SOUPE À L'OIGNON PIED DE COCHON

Pied de Cochon's Onion Soup

I s there any place in Paris that's better known for its onion soup than the 24-hour brasserie Pied de Cochon? Almost all of us who love Paris have at one time or another made the ritualistic late-night trip to Les Halles to indulge in this Parisian gastronomic pastime.

I find this version one of the lightest and most digestible onion soups I've tried. Perhaps it's because the onions are roasted first. Be sure to use good white sweet onions (yellow onions can turn bitter), and if this is likely to become a family favorite, it's worthwhile to invest in traditional round, stout, deep little onion soup bowls that sit on a small pedestal.

1 very large (1 pound; 500 g) white onion (such as Bermuda), thinly sliced
2 cups (50 cl) dry white wine, such as Muscadet or Mâcon-Villages
2 tablespoons (1 ounce; 30 g) unsalted butter
6 cups (1.5 l) unsalted chicken stock, preferably homemade
6 slices crusty baguette
2 cups (about 5 ounces; 160 g) freshly grated imported French or Swiss Gruyère cheese

1. Preheat the oven to 425°F (220°C).
2. Combine the onion, wine, and butter in a baking dish and braise, uncovered, until the onion is very soft and most of the liquid is absorbed, about 45 minutes. Increase the oven temperature to broil.

3. Meanwhile, bring the stock to a simmer in a large nonreactive saucepan.
4. Evenly distribute the cooked onions among 6 deep, round soup bowls. Pour in the simmering stock. Place a round of bread on top of each; evenly distribute the grated cheese. Place the soup bowls under the broiler and broil just until the cheese is melted and nicely gratinéed, 2 or 3 minutes. Serve immediately.

Yield: 6 servings

❝The onion is the truffle of the poor.❞

—R.J. COURTINE

LA BOURRIDE DE BAUDROIE RESTAURANT LOU MARQUÈS

Restaurant Lou Marquès' Monkfish Soup with Garlic Cream

M onkfish—known as *lotte,* or *baudroie* in Provence—is a popular and plentiful Mediterranean fish, and one that stands up well to flavorful soups such as this. With the addition of the garlic-rich mayonnaise known as aïoli, the soup is a meal all on its own, a dish I first sampled on the terrace of Lou Marquès, the restaurant of the Hôtel Jules César in Arles. The soup is best made with homemade fish stock, but if you don't have it on hand, substitute water for the soup liquid. With the soup, sample either a chilled white from Provence, such as a Cassis, or a Tavel or Bandol rosé. When serving this dish, I like to prepare the aïoli earlier in the day, so there is little last minute work.

1 pound (500 g) baking potatoes, such as russets, peeled and very thinly sliced
1 leek (white part only), trimmed, well rinsed, and cut into rounds
1 medium carrot, peeled and cut into rounds
1 garlic clove, finely minced
Grated zest (peel) of 2 oranges
1 fennel bulb, trimmed and thinly sliced crosswise
3 imported bay leaves
2 quarts (2 l) Fish Stock (see Index) or water
1 cup (25 cl) dry white wine, such as Cassis
2 pounds (1 kg) very fresh monkfish, membrane removed and cut cross-
wise into ½-inch (1.5 cm) slices
1 recipe Aïoli (recipe follows)
1 large egg yolk
¼ cup crème fraîche (6 cl) (see Index) or heavy cream
Salt and freshly ground black pepper
8 to 12 slices country bread, for garnish

1. Preheat the oven to warm (about 210°F; 100°C). Place a large soup tureen and 4 to 6 shallow soup bowls in the oven to warm.

2. In a large, heavy-bottomed, nonreactive saucepan, combine the potatoes, leek, carrot, garlic, orange

zest, fennel, bay leaves, stock, and wine. Cover and bring to a boil over high heat. Reduce the heat to medium-low and simmer until the vegetables are just tender, 12 to 15 minutes. Add the monkfish and cook, skimming frequently, until the fish is opaque throughout, about 5 minutes. Discard the bay leaves.

3. Meanwhile, in a medium-size bowl, combine ¾ cup (18 cl) of the aïoli with the egg yolk and crème fraîche; whisk to blend. Gradually stir ½ cup (12.5 cl) of the hot soup broth into the aïoli mixture. Over low heat, add the aïoli mixture to the soup. Cook, whisking to thicken slightly, for 1 or 2 minutes; do not let the soup boil. Season to taste with the salt and pepper.

4. Toast the bread.

5. To serve, ladle the soup into warmed bowls, making sure everyone gets some of the fish and an assortment of vegetables. Pass the remaining aïoli and toasted bread separately.

Yield: 6 servings.

AÏOLI

Garlic Mayonnaise

This is an authentic Provençal aïoli, which needs to be made from fresh, juicy garlic cloves. If you do not have a large mortar and pestle, you can crush the garlic and salt together to a paste with the flat side of a knife and make the aïoli with a whisk or an electric hand mixer. Don't use a food processor: The aïoli will be too much like glue.

6 large fresh garlic cloves
½ teaspoon salt
2 large egg yolks, at room temperature
1 cup (25 cl) extra-virgin olive oil

1. Peel and cut the garlic in half, then remove the green, sprout-like "germ" that runs lengthwise through the center of the garlic.

2. Pour boiling water into a large mortar to warm it; discard the water and dry the mortar. Place the garlic and salt in the mortar and mash together evenly with a pestle to form a paste.

3. Add 1 egg yolk. Stir, pressing slowly and evenly with the pestle, always in the same direction, to thoroughly blend the garlic and yolk. Add the second yolk and repeat until well blended.

4. Very slowly work in the oil, drop by drop, until the mixture thickens. Gradually, whisk in the remaining oil in a slow, thin stream until the sauce is thickened to a mayonnaise consistency.

Yield: About 1 cup (25 cl)

BOUILLABAISSE BACON

Bacon's Provençal Fish Soup

O f the various versions of bouillabaisse sampled along the Mediterranean coast of France, it's the fish soup from Restaurant Bacon, in Cap d'Antibes, that lives in my memory. I love it for its purity and simplicity of flavors, and the freshness of the fish served there.

A recipe for bouillabaisse is, necessarily, little more than a blueprint, for quantities and types of fish must vary—even as they do along the French coastline—according to their availability. Try to include at least three kinds of fish, so there is a contrast of flavors and textures. You may end up with some unconventional combinations, but I've tried this dish with swordfish, barracuda, cod, and halibut and it made for a great combination of mellow, deep flavors. With this dish, try the special Fennel and Saffron Bread from the Aix-en-Provence baker, Jacques Collet. The recipe follows.

5 to 6 pounds (2.5 to 3 kg) fish, choosing either monkfish or swordfish; a gelatinous fish, such as rockfish, halibut, or barracuda; and a delicate fish, such as flounder, whiting, sea bass, porgy, or red snapper. All whole fish should be filleted, all trimmings (heads, frames, tails) reserved.
Additional 1 pound (500 g) of trimmings, if available (optional)
½ cup (12.5 cl) extra-virgin olive oil
2 pounds (1 kg) fresh ripe tomatoes, cored and quartered
1 pound (500 kg) onions, quartered
6 fat fresh garlic cloves, crushed
2 fennel bulbs, trimmed and quartered
1 bunch fresh parsley, washed and dried
2 to 3 quarts (2 to 3 l) boiling water
Salt

¼ teaspoon saffron threads
6 to 8 small new red-skinned potatoes, scrubbed and peeled
Accompaniments:
  Aïoli (see page 20)
  Rouille (recipe follows)
  1 loaf French bread or Jacques Collet's Fennel and Saffron Bread (recipe follows), sliced and toasted

❝*If the bouillabaisse is somber, bourride is blonde, more vigorous, more meaty and abundant, with a robust perfume.***❞**
—LE GOURMAND VAGABOND
Promenades Gastronomiques, 1928

> **''A spot of marc?' the inn-keeper suggested. 'After aïoli, it's a must!'''**
>
> —GEORGES SIMENON
> *The Methods of Maigret*

1. Cut the larger fillets and steaks into 1-inch (2.5 cm) thick pieces. Even though the fishmonger has prepared the fish, check them over before beginning to cook the bouillabaisse. Be particularly careful to remove any remaining scales and any gills, which might turn the soup bitter. Rinse and pat dry all the fish and refrigerate until needed.

2. In a heavy nonreactive 12-quart (12 l) stockpot, heat the oil over medium-high heat until hot but not smoking. Add the tomatoes, onions, garlic, fennel, and parsley, and cook, uncovered, over medium-high heat, just until the mixture begins to soften, about 5 minutes.

3. Meanwhile, bring a large kettle of water to boil.

4. Once the vegetables are softened, add all of the fish trimmings. Add enough boiling water to just cover the ingredients. You want a rich, substantial soup, not a bland, watery one. Two to 3 quarts (2 to 3 l) of water should be sufficient. Add salt to taste, then cover, and allow to boil vigorously until the broth is orangy red and just moderately thick, about 45 minutes.

5. Line a colander with a double layer of dampened cheesecloth and strain the soup into a bowl. Discard the solids. You should have 2 to 3 quarts (2 to 3 l) of fish soup. (The fish soup can be made several hours ahead of time.)

6. Steam or boil the potatoes until tender. Set aside and keep warm.

7. Return the fish soup to the stockpot, add the saffron, and bring to a boil over high heat. Add the fish fillets and pieces to the soup—the firm-fleshed fish first, the tender-fleshed about 5 minutes later—and cook just until the fish are cooked through but still firm, a total of 10 minutes. Do not overcook the fish.

8. To serve, slice the potatoes and place them on the bottom of shallow, warmed soup bowls. Place 3 pieces of fish on top of the potatoes, pour the warm broth over all. Serve immediately, with aïoli, rouille, and toasted bread.

Yield: 6 to 8 servings

ROUILLE

Garlic, Saffron, and Red Pepper Mayonnaise

There are many versions of rouille, the rust-hued, garlic-rich mayonnaise that marries so well with the fish soups of Provence. This is a pure and simple recipe, really nothing more than a classic aïoli, or garlic mayonnaise, enriched with saffron and finely ground cayenne pepper.

6 large fresh garlic cloves
Salt
2 large egg yolks, at room temperature
1 cup (25 cl) extra-virgin olive oil
¼ teaspoon saffron threads
Finely ground cayenne pepper

1. Peel and cut the garlic in half, then remove the green, sprout-like "germ" that runs lengthwise through the center of the garlic.

2. Pour boiling water into a large mortar to warm it; discard the water and dry the mortar. Place the garlic in the mortar, add a pinch of salt, and mash evenly with a pestle to form a paste.

3. Add 1 egg yolk. Stir, pressing slowly and evenly with the pestle, always in the same direction, to thoroughly blend the garlic and yolk. Add the second yolk and repeat until well blended.

4. Very slowly work in the oil, drop by drop, until the mixture thickens. After you have added a few drops of oil, add the saffron and a pinch of cayenne. Gradually, whisk in the remaining oil in a slow, thin stream until the sauce is thickened to a mayonnaise consistency. Taste the rouille and add additional cayenne, if desired. Cover and refrigerate until ready to serve.

Yield: About 1¼ cup (31 cl)

PAIN DE FENOUIL ET SAFRAN JACQUES COLLET

Jacques Collet's Fennel and Saffron Bread

Jacques Collet is a young, energetic, and ambitious baker from Aix-en-Provence, where he runs several bread shops known as Boulangerie du Coin. His fragrant boutiques are filled with several dozen different creations, including compact molded breads bursting with oatmeal and barley, sunburst-shaped loaves packed with crushed sunflower seeds, long breads filled with fresh Provençal herbs and tiny black olives, as well as this saffron and fennel seed-flavored version designed as an accompaniment to the Mediterranean fish soup, bouillabaisse. The addition of hard durum wheat flour, or semolina, helps give the bread a hard, crispy, buttery flavor, perfect for dipping in the rich fish soup.

1¼ cups (31 cl) lukewarm water
1 tablespoon or 1 package active dry yeast
1 tablespoon sugar
2 to 2¼ cups (280 to 315 g) unbleached, all-purpose flour
2 teaspoons sea salt
1 tablespoon fennel seed, freshly ground
⅛ teaspoon ground saffron
1 cup (175 g) semolina (pasta) flour
Coarse cornmeal

1. In a large mixing bowl, combine the lukewarm water, yeast, sugar, and 1 cup (140 g) of the unbleached flour. Stir until thoroughly blended. Proof for about 5 minutes.

2. Once proofed and foamy, add the salt, fennel seed, and saffron, and stir to blend. Add the semolina flour, little by little, stirring to blend. Stir in up to 1¼ cups more unbleached flour, working the dough until it is too stiff to stir. Place the dough on a lightly floured work surface and begin kneading, adding additional unbleached flour if the dough is too sticky. Knead until the dough is smooth and satiny, about 10 minutes.

3. Place the dough in a bowl. Cover and let rise at room temperature until doubled in bulk, about 1 hour.

4. Sprinkle a baking sheet with coarse cornmeal. Punch down the dough. Shape the dough into a firm ball and set on the baking sheet. Cover with a cloth and let rise again until doubled in bulk, about 1 hour.

5. After about 40 minutes, preheat the oven to 375°F (190°C).

6. Bake the bread in the center of the oven until the crust is crisp and brown, about 40 minutes. Set on a rack to cool before slicing.

Yield: 1 loaf

A SUMMERY SUNDAY NOONTIME FEAST

The French believe any dish that includes aïoli ought to be served at lunch, giving you the rest of the day to digest the onslaught of garlic. Thus, plan this dish for a Sunday family feast. A chilled rosé and a bowl of fresh summer fruits for dessert is all you'll need to add.

BOUILLABAISSE BACON
Bacon's Provençal Fish Soup

♦

ROUILLE
Garlic, Saffron, and Red Pepper Mayonnaise

♦

AÏOLI
Garlic Mayonnaise

♦

PAIN AUX FENOUIL ET SAFRAN JACQUES COLLET
Jacques Collet's Fennel and Saffron Bread

SOUPE DE MOULES CHEZ BENOIT

Benoit's Mussel Soup

Every now and then I have an honest craving for mussels—I love the process of scrubbing them, then the aroma that wafts from the kitchen as the mussels begin to cook, opening their shells like giant, silvery-black blossoms. When a craving for soup comes at the same time, this is the dish that comes to mind.

Bistros never seem to offer enough soups, and this recipe, from Paris's beautiful bistro Benoit, is a soothing fall or wintertime dish. It's a very pretty, delicate, clearly elegant soup: I love the hint of smokiness that comes from the bacon, the bright green highlight of the beans, the soft texture offered by the leeks. Although the chefs of Benoit prepare this soup with fish stock, I substitute a light, homemade chicken stock when I don't have fish stock on hand.

2 pounds (1 kg) fresh mussels
½ cup (12.5 cl) dry white wine, such as Muscadet
½ cup (12.5 cl) crème fraîche (see Index) or heavy cream
2 tablespoons (1 ounce; 30 g) unsalted butter
1 large onion, minced
2 small carrots, peeled and minced
2 leeks (white part only), rinsed well and minced
3½ ounces (100 g) slab bacon, rind removed and minced
3½ ounces (100 g) side pork (fat-back), rind removed and minced
2 cups (50 cl) fish stock or light un-salted chicken stock, preferably homemade (see Index)
3 ounces (90 g) green beans, trimmed and cut on an angle into ½-inch (1.25 cm) lengths
Freshly ground black pepper

1. Thoroughly scrub the mussels and rinse with several changes of cold water. Beard the mussels. (Do not beard the mussels in advance, or they will die and spoil.)

2. Place the mussels, white wine, and crème fraîche in a large non-reactive skillet over medium-high heat. Cover and cook, shaking the pot, just until the mussels open, 3 to 4 minutes. Do not overcook, or the mussels will become tough. Remove from the heat and drain the mussels,

reserving the mussels and the cooking liquid separately. Discard any mussels that do not open. Strain the cooking liquid through several thicknesses of dampened cheesecloth; reserve.

3. Melt the butter in a large skillet over medium heat. Add the onion, carrots, leeks, bacon, and side pork. Stir until coated with the butter, and cook, stirring occasionally, until the onions begin to turn translucent, about 5 minutes. Add the fish stock and cook until the vegetables are very soft and flavors have had time to mingle, about 45 minutes.

4. Stir in the mussel cooking liquid, and cook until heated through, about 5 more minutes.

5. Blanch the green beans in a large pot of salted, boiling water, just until the beans are crisp-tender and bright green, about 4 minutes. Immediately drain the beans and rinse under cold running water until the beans are cooled throughout. This will help them retain their crispness and bright green color. Drain thoroughly and set aside.

6. Remove the mussel meats from the shells; discard the shells.

7. About 5 minutes before serving the soup, add the mussels, and cook just until they are heated through. Evenly divide the soup among 4 shallow soup bowls. Garnish each bowl with equal amounts of the green beans, shower with a touch of pepper. Serve immediately.

Yield: 4 servings

LA SOUPE DE POIS CASSÉS AUX HERBES

Herbed Split Pea Soup

T raditionally, soup was an important part of a bistro meal, but today it appears less often on the menu. Perhaps it is because we think of soup as too filling. Although I don't often order soup in restaurants, I love to make it at home, especially during the winter months.

Pea soup reminds me of the soup my mother made about once a year, around Easter, when she cooked up a big pot in order to use up the giant bone from the holiday ham. This version, a somewhat modern rendition of the old-fashioned pea soup, assumes that most of us don't have bones just sitting around waiting to be put to use. Use a good-quality ham, smoked or unsmoked, and don't skimp on the quality of the chicken stock.

1 pound (about 3 cups; 500 g) dried
  green split peas
2 quarts (2 l) unsalted chicken stock,
  preferably homemade (see Index)
8 ounces (250 g) smoked country ham
  or ham slices, cubed
4 garlic cloves, crushed
1 sprig of fresh parsley
2 imported bay leaves
½ teaspoon dried thyme
½ teaspoon dried marjoram
2 medium onions, halved
4 whole cloves
Salt

1. In a stockpot, combine the split peas, chicken stock, ham, garlic, and herbs. Stick a clove into each piece of onion and add to the soup. Bring to a roaring boil over high heat. Immediately reduce the heat to low, partially cover, and simmer until the peas have just about disintegrated and can be mashed against the side of the pot with a fork, about 2 hours.

2. Taste the soup and season to taste with salt and additional herbs, if desired. For a rustic soup, serve as is. For a more elegant soup, pass through a food mill or fine mesh sieve. Or purée in a food processor. Ladle the soup into warmed soup bowls and served immediately.

Yield: 8 to 10 servings

SOUPE À L'OSEILLE

Sorrel Soup from the Poitou

Potatoes and sorrel are a favorite combination: The bright, tart sorrel adds the flavor, the cooked potatoes the depth. On days when spa cuisine is in order, the eggs and cream can be reduced or deleted, and you might increase the sorrel by just a bit. This recipe from the Poitou, along the Atlantic Coast, is delicious hot or cold. Just don't hold the soup too long, or the potatoes will get soggy. For a chunky soup, serve as is, for a more elegant soup, purée it in the food processor.

8 ounces (250 g) fresh sorrel
Salt and freshly ground black pepper
1 pound (500 g) potatoes, peeled and
  cubed

2 large eggs
¾ cup (18.5 cl) crème fraîche (see
  Index) or heavy cream

1. Unless the sorrel is very young, it will need to be deribbed and stemmed. Wash and spin dry the sorrel, then pull off the stem, removing the firm center rib as you go.

2. Combine the sorrel and 1 teaspoon of water in a large nonreactive saucepan over low heat. Stir from time to time and allow the sorrel to wilt, cooking until it has given up most of its liquid.

3. Add 1½ quarts (1.5 l) of water and salt and pepper to taste. Bring to a boil. Add the potatoes and cook over low heat until the potatoes are cooked through, 15 to 20 minutes. (For a rustic soup, leave as is, for a more elegant soup, purée, in batches, in a food processor.)

4. Combine the eggs and crème fraîche in a warmed soup tureen; mix until well blended. Add a ladle of the potato and sorrel mixture and blend well. Pour in remaining potato and sorrel mixture, serve immediately.

Yield: 4 to 6 servings

LET'S BRING ON SPRINGTIME

◆

Spring makes me think of sorrel, and shallots, and golden pears. Try this with a white wine from the Loire valley or from Burgundy, a Vouvray or a Saint-Véran.

SOUPE À L'OSEILLE
Sorrel Soup from the Poitou

◆

POULET SAUTÉ AUX ÉCHALOTES
Chicken Sautéed with Shallots

◆

SALADE COLMARIENNE CHEZ JENNY
Chez Jenny's Sausage, Cheese, and Curly Endive Salad

◆

TARTE TATIN AUX POIRES
Caramelized Upside-Down Pear Tart

SOUPE CRESSON, POMMES DE TERRE

◆

Watercress and Potato Soup

I love this vegetable soup, one that can bring us spring thoughts year-round, since today watercress can pretty much be found in markets in all seasons. I also love the fact that, due to the starchy potatoes, this soup offers a creamy texture, without the addition of cream. (If you prefer a richer soup, however, there's nothing to stop you from swirling in a touch of butter and cream at the end!)

1 pound (500 g) watercress (about 2 bunches)
3 tablespoons (1½ ounces; 45 g) unsalted butter
1½ pounds (750 g) boiling potatoes, peeled, washed, and cut into ½-inch (1.25 cm) cubes
2 quarts (2 l) chicken stock, preferably homemade (see Index) or substitute water
Salt and freshly ground black pepper
Several sprigs of chervil or flat-leaf parsley, for garnish

1. Carefully pick over the watercress, trimming any woody stems and discarding any severely wilted sprigs. Using scissors or a large chef's knife, coarsely chop the watercress.

2. In a large stockpot over medium-high heat, melt the butter, then add the watercress. Cook for several minutes to thoroughly wilt the watercress.

3. Add the potatoes, stock, and salt to taste. Bring to boil over high heat. Reduce the heat, cover, and simmer until the potatoes are cooked through, 10 to 15 minutes. Adjust seasonings.

4. Serve immediately in warmed soup bowls. Garnish with the chervil.

Yield: 4 to 6 servings

SOUPE POIREAUX— POMMES DE TERRE ET LARD FUMÉ

Leek, Potato, and Bacon Soup

This is a thick, wonderfully fragrant, wintry soup that cries out for a roaring fire and lazy weekend afternoons. A crispy green salad, a platter of cheese, a few sips of wine and what more could anyone ask? This recipe comes from José Lampreia, a young and exciting chef whose restaurant, Maison Blanche, hardly fits the image of an old, crusty bistro. But his food is pure, and from the heart as well as the earth, so I've included this homey cold-weather soup.

5 pounds (2.5 kg) leeks
2 tablespoons olive oil
8 ounces (250 g) lean slab bacon, rind removed, trimmed of fat, and cubed
2 pounds (1 kg) firm boiling potatoes, peeled and cubed
Salt and freshly ground black pepper

TRUC

When buying leeks, look for those with roots and bit of dirt still attached. They'll stay fresher longer, if stored in a cool, dark place, well wrapped in plastic.

1. Trim off the toughest green portion of the leeks and discard. Rinse well, then dry, and slice both the white and the tender green part into thin rings.

2. In a large stockpot, heat the oil over medium-high heat until hot but not smoking. Add the bacon, reduce the heat, and brown thoroughly on all sides. Add the leeks and the potatoes and toss to coat with the bacon fat. Cook until the leeks are wilted and softened.

3. Add 2 quarts (2 l) of cold water and salt (2 teaspoons should properly season this soup). Cover and simmer for about 45 minutes. Turn off the heat and let the soup rest for at least 1 hour so the flavors can mingle. (The soup can, of course, be made ahead of time and be reheated later. It also freezes well.)

4. To serve, bring the soup back to a gentle simmer. Serve in warmed, shallow soup bowls with plenty of freshly ground black pepper.

Yield: 6 to 8 servings

POTAGE PARMENTIER

Leek and Potato Soup

I adore this sleek root vegetable soup, a superb blend of potatoes and leeks, laced with a touch of cream. Use fresh herbs, if at all possible. This is delicious both warm and cold.

3 large potatoes (about 1 pound; 500
    g), peeled and quartered
2 leeks (about 6 ounces; 180 g),
    trimmed, well rinsed, and cut into
    julienne
¾ cup (18.5 cl) crème fraîche (see
    Index) or heavy cream
Salt and freshly ground black pepper
3 tablespoons chopped fresh tarragon
    or chervil, for garnish

1. Combine the potatoes, leeks, and 1 quart (1 l) of water in a large saucepan. Bring to a boil over high heat. Season with salt and pepper. Reduce heat and simmer gently until vegetables are meltingly soft, 35 to 40 minutes.

2. Purée the soup in a blender or food processor or pass through a food mill. Return to the saucepan. Stir in the crème fraîche and cook over low heat just until heated through. Adjust the seasoning and serve, garnished with the fresh herb.

Yield: 6 to 8 servings

SOUPE AUX DEUX CÉLERIS

Double Celery Soup

I love this winter-spring dish, a light and feathery soup for those changeable days, when you're still in the mood for warming liquids, but heavy winter versions just won't do. Celery root—known as celeriac and in France, *céleri rave*—is a much underutilized root vegetable. It has a lemony tang and in this recipe it marries beautifully with branch celery and leeks. I created this dish one day in mid-April, when the Mistral was blowing and the rains had been falling for days. It's the kind of restorative soup the French call a *soupe de santé,* or a soup for the sick, sort of like our chicken soup. Serve it with some crisp crackers and a green salad.

1 medium celery root (about 1 pound; 500 g), peeled and diced
10 celery ribs, cubed
3 leeks (about 9 ounces; 270 g), trimmed, well rinsed and cut into thin rounds
Bouquet garni: 1 large sprig of thyme, 3 imported bay leaves, several sprigs of parsley, tied with a string
2 quarts (2 l) chicken stock, preferably homemade
Salt and freshly ground black pepper
A handful of chopped fresh herbs for garnish: including chervil, chives, flat-leaf parsley

In a large saucepan, combine the celery root, celery, leeks, and bouquet garni. Add the stock, and season gently with salt and pepper. Bring to a simmer over medium-high heat. Simmer until the vegetables are soft, about 25 minutes. Adjust the seasonings. Pour into warmed shallow soup bowls. Sprinkle with the chopped herbs and serve immediately.

Yield: 6 to 8 servings

GARBURE AUX CHOUX LES PYRÉNÉES

Les Pyrénées' Stew of White Beans, Cabbage, Ham, and Preserved Goose

Saint-Jean-Pied-de-Port in the Pays Basque is one of France's most charming villages. I don't think that anyone keeps track of things like this, but I would bet that it's also the most active small town (population 1,887) in France. In the summertime, between outdoor food markets, live animal auctions, and sporting events, cars line up on either edge of this lively little village. If you drive through town, you can't miss Les Pyrénées: It's bright, modernized, and unquestionably the smartest place in town to dine. I sampled this delightful soup on my first visit there one day early in autumn. Funny, *garbure* is such a heavy word, that it conjures up ideas of loathsome, fatty fare. Not at all. This is a rich but not heavy winter soup to enjoy in front of a warming fire. For those who cannot find goose confit, or preserved goose gizzards, I'd recommend substituting a good-quality smoked sausage, such as kielbasa, for it. The dish won't be authentically Basque, but it still will be delicious. A southwestern Madiran or a young Bordeaux goes well with this dish.

1½ cups (10 ounces; 300 g) dried
    white beans
3 ounces (90 g) Parma ham
8 garlic cloves, chopped
1 onion, finely chopped
4 carrots, peeled and cut into rounds
4 leeks, trimmed, well rinsed, and cut
    into thin rounds
Salt
½ green cabbage, quartered
1 pound (500 g) potatoes, peeled and
    cubed
1 piece goose confit, cut into bite-size
    pieces (see Note)
2 preserved goose gizzards, cut into
    bite-size pieces (see Note)

1. Rinse the beans and place them in a large saucepan. Add cold water to cover, and bring to a boil over high heat. Once boiling, remove the pan from the heat, leave the cover on, and let rest for 40 minutes. Drain the beans, discarding the cooking liquid.

2. In a large flameproof casserole, combine the beans, ham, and garlic. Add 2 quarts (2 l) of water and bring to a boil over high heat. Reduce

> **"** . . . *There were few people in the brasserie and when I sat down on the bench against the wall with the mirror in back and a table in front and the waiter asked if I wanted a beer I asked for a distingué, the big glass mug that held a liter, and potato salad.* . . .
>
> *The beer was very cold and wonderful to drink. The pommes à l'huile were firm and marinated and the olive oil delicious . . . When the pommes à l'huile were gone, I ordered another serving and a cervelas.* . . .
>
> *I mopped up all the oil and all the sauce with bread and drank the beer slowly until it began to lose its coldness and then I finished it and ordered a demi . . .* **"**
>
> —ERNEST HEMINGWAY
> AT BRASSERIE LIPP
> *A Moveable Feast*

the heat to medium-low and add the carrots and leeks. Season lightly with salt. Simmer, covered, for 1 hour.

3. Add the cabbage and potatoes and continue cooking until all of the vegetables are tender, about 15 minutes more. Add the goose confit and gizzards and simmer until the meats are warmed through, another 10 minutes.

4. Serve the soup immediately, in warmed, shallow bowls.

Yield: 4 to 6 servings

Note: Goose confit and preserved goose gizzards can be found in some food specialty shops. They can also be ordered by mail or by telephone from D'Artagnan, 399-419 Saint Paul's Avenue, Jersey City, New Jersey 07306. Telephone 1-800-D'ARTAGNAN.

POTAGE AUX LENTILLES AVEC SAUCISSES DE PORC

Lentil Soup with Pork Sausages

This is a dish for those who like their food well-seasoned and full-flavored. I love the hearty blend of lentils, a good dose of spices (in the form of cumin and cloves), and the meatiness of delicious smoked sausages. In France, I use the small smoked Montbéliard sausages from the Jura, but any top-quality smoked sausages will do. Also, make an effort to find the dark green *lentilles de Puy,* far superior to the pale greenish-brown traditional lentils.

4 ounces (125 g) smoked bacon,
   coarsely chopped
1 leek, well rinsed and finely minced
1 carrot, finely minced
1 onion, finely minced
1 celery rib, finely minced
1 teaspoon ground cumin
4 whole cloves
1 pound (500 g) imported green lentils
2 imported bay leaves
Salt and freshly ground black pepper
1 tablespoon (15 g) unsalted butter
4 small smoked pork sausages (about 1
   pound; 500 g)

1. In a large stockpot over medium-high heat, sauté the bacon until lightly browned. Add the minced vegetables, the cumin, and cloves, and sauté until all are nicely browned.

2. Add the lentils, bay leaves, and salt and pepper to taste. Stir in 2½ quarts (2.5 l) of water, and simmer, covered, until the lentils are cooked through, about 40 minutes.

3. Meanwhile, cook the sausages: Melt the butter in a large saucepan over medium-high heat. Add the sausages and brown on all sides, being careful not to pierce them. Add water to cover and heat just to a simmer. Immediately reduce the heat and cover, cooking until the sausages are thoroughly cooked through, about 30 minutes.

4. To serve, drain the sausages and slice into small rounds. Divide them evenly among 4 warmed soup bowls. Spoon the hot soup over all.

Yield: 6 to 8 servings

LES SALADES DU MARCHÉ

◆━━━◆

Market Basket Salads

No one knows how to construct a salad like the French. To begin with, there's such a rich assortment of salad greens—from the tiny dark green-leafed watercress to the slightly bitter curly endive, from lamb's lettuce to baby spinach—all of which serve as delightful backgrounds for the unlimited choice of ingredients that will be tossed alongside them. The salads in this chapter all have something in common: they're mostly complete salads that can readily stand on their own as main-course luncheon dishes. Many of them, such as the spinach and chicken liver salad, are bistro classics. Others, such as the salad of ham, walnuts, and duck gizzards, are modern-day dishes inspired by regional country fare. In gathering recipes for this book, I was always amazed at how certain ingredients just fell naturally together, making great marriages of flavors and textures. Roquefort, walnuts, and Belgian endive seem made for one another; as do white beans and smoked sausages; or potatoes, herring, and hard-cooked eggs. As always, note that recipes are simply blueprints for cooking, so feel free to add and subtract ingredients according to appetite, whim, and availability.

SALADE FRISÉE AUX LARDONS AUX LYONNAIS

Aux Lyonnais' Curly Endive Salad with Bacon and Sausage

T alk about a salad that makes a meal! When I make this at home, I'm always amazed at the thought that, when I sampled them in restaurants, I managed to make it to the main course.

Aux Lyonnais is a Paris bistro that's been around for a long time, serving up some of the most classic and old-fashioned fare. I sampled this salad one cool day in autumn, and it really hit the spot. The salad arrived in one of those huge white salad bowls, and the waitress slowly and gently tossed it at the table. That day I sampled the salad with a fine Beaujolais from Pierre Ferraud. Note that the equivalent to the French *frisée* is generally called curly endive or chicory.

1 pound (500 g) fresh country-style pork sausage, or about 4 individual fresh pork sausage links
2 tablespoons imported Dijon mustard
2 tablespoons best-quality red wine vinegar
Salt
½ cup (12.5 cl) peanut oil
6 cups (1.5 l) curly endive, rinsed, dried, and torn into manageable pieces
4 ounces (125 g) slab bacon, rind removed, cut into 1-inch (2.5 cm) cubes
2 large slices country or whole wheat bread, cut into 1-inch (2.5 cm) cubes

1. Place the sausage in a saucepan, cover with cold water, and bring just to a simmer over medium-high heat. Simmer gently—do not allow the water to boil—until the sausage is cooked through, 30 to 40 minutes. Drain and allow to cool slightly.

2. In a small bowl, whisk together the mustard, vinegar and salt to taste. Slowly pour in the oil and whisk until lightly blended. Set the dressing aside.

3. Place the salad greens in a large, shallow salad bowl. Remove the casings and cut the sausage into thin slices. Layer the sausage on top of the salad.

4. Place the bacon in a large skil-

let. Adding no additional fat, cook, stirring frequently, over medium-high heat just until the bacon begins to give off some fat, 4 or 5 minutes. Add the bread cubes and continue cooking, stirring from time to time, until the croutons and bacon are evenly browned and crisp, about 5 minutes more.

5. Spoon the bacon and croutons over the salad. Pour on the dressing and toss gently and thoroughly. Serve with additional slices of bread.

Yield: 4 servings

SALADE DE POIS CHICHES AUBERGE D'AILLANE

◆

Chick-Pea Salad from the Auberge D'Aillane

Chick-peas (garbanzo beans) are a highly underutilized bean, but one that marries so well with the oils, herbs, and flavors of Provence. I first sampled this dish, served as an appetizer, at the Auberge d'Aillane, a casual family restaurant on the outskirts of Aix-en-Provence. In the summer months, I love to keep the salad on hand as an appetizer, luncheon dish, or a side dish with grilled fish or meats. Serve this with a Côtes-de-Provence rosé, such as Commanderie de Peyrassol rosé.

1½ cups (8 ounces; 250 g) dried chick-peas
2 tablespoons best-quality red wine vinegar
5 garlic cloves, finely minced
2 tablespoons finely chopped mixed fresh herbs, such as rosemary, thyme, tarragon, and parsley
Salt
½ cup (12.5 cl) extra-virgin olive oil

Freshly ground black pepper
½ cup (about 3 ounces; 100 g) oil-cured black olives, preferably from Nyons, pitted
1 medium onion, finely minced

1. Twenty-four hours before preparing the salad, soak the chick-peas in enough cold water to cover. Cover and refrigerate.

2. The next day, drain the chickpeas and place in a medium-size saucepan. Cover with fresh cold water and bring to a boil over high heat. Reduce the heat to low, cover, and simmer until tender, about 2 hours. (Check the water level in the pot every half hour and add more, if needed.)

3. Meanwhile, prepare the vinaigrette: Combine the vinegar, garlic, herbs, and salt to taste. Mix. Slowly whisk in the oil; season to taste with pepper.

4. When the beans are cooked, drain well. While they are still warm, add the olives, onion, and the vinaigrette; toss. Season to taste and serve.

The salad can also be served cold, as a luncheon dish, a side dish, or an hors d'oeuvre. It will store well, covered and refrigerated, for about 1 week.

Yield: 8 to 10 servings

> **❝***Provençal cuisine is not, like that of Normandy or the Anjou, full of shading and nuance . . . It is lively, vehement. It is the military music of gastronomy.* **❞**
>
> —MAURICE GUÉGAN
> *Revue des Usagers de la Route,* 1928

SALADE À L'AIL CHEZ TANTE PAULETTE

Chez Tante Paulette's Salad with Garlic

The last time I walked into Chez Tante Paulette, a tiny bistro off a side street in Lyons, the air was permeated with the welcoming aroma of sizzling garlic. The fame of her chicken with garlic has now spread around the world, but on this trip, I was determined to gather the secrets of her incredible salad, an uncomplicated mix of greens, croutons, and cubed bacon, coated with a mustardy vinaigrette and sprinkled with freshly minced garlic.

When Marie-Louise Auteli—better known as Tante Paulette—ushered me into her kitchen, I took one look at what was going on on the stove, and knew I had what I was looking for. There in a thin black metal skillet, cubes of bacon and cubes of bread were sizzling away side-by-side. Of course! If you want croutons impregnated with the flavor of bacon, cook them together in the same pan!

2 tablespoons imported Dijon mustard
2 tablespoons best-quality red wine
    vinegar
Salt
½ cup (12.5 cl) peanut oil
6 cups (1.5 l) mixed salad greens,
    such as red chicory, butter lettuce,
    curly endive, escarole, and red oak-
    leaf lettuce, rinsed, dried, and torn
    into manageable pieces
4 ounces (120 g) slab bacon, rind re-
    moved, cut into 1-inch (2.5 cm)
    cubes
2 large slices country or whole wheat
    bread, cut into 1-inch (2.5 cm)
    cubes
2 fat garlic cloves, finely minced

1. Place the mustard in a small bowl. Whisk in the vinegar and salt to taste; mix well. Slowly pour in the oil and whisk until the mixture is lightly blended. (This is a very thick dressing, almost like a mayonnaise.) Set aside.

2. Place the salad greens in a large, shallow salad bowl.

3. Place the bacon in a large skillet. Adding no additional fat, cook, stirring frequently, over medium-high heat just until the bacon begins to give off some fat, 2 to 3 minutes. Add the bread cubes and continue cooking, stirring from time to time, until both bread and bacon are browned and crisp, about 5 minutes more.

4. Pour the bacon and croutons over the salad, sprinkle with the garlic, add the dressing, and toss thoroughly. Serve with additional slices of bread.

Yield: 4 servings

THANK YOU, AUNT PAULETTE

◆

Marie-Louise Auteli, better known as Tante Paulette, is one of my favorite lady chefs in all of France. I sampled this exact menu one day in August in her minuscule restaurant in Lyons, and it goes down as one of my most memorable bistro meals ever. Tante Paulette always serves Beaujolais, so I do too.

SALADE À L'AIL CHEZ TANTE PAULETTE
*Chez Tante Paulette's Salad
with Garlic*

◆

BOUILLABAISSE DE POULET CHEZ TANTE PAULETTE
*Chez Tante Paulette's Chicken Stew
with Fennel and Saffron*

◆

OMELETTE AUX POIRES CHEZ TANTE PAULETTE
*Chez Tante Paulette's Sweet
Pear Omelet*

SALADE DE MAGRET FUMÉ CRO-MAGNON

♦ ♦

Cro-Magnon's Smoked Duck Breast Salad

Cro-Magnon is a small, intimate family restaurant at the edge of Les Eyzies-de-Tayac in southwestern France. One warm spring evening we sampled a number of homey, regional dishes as we sat in the lovely oak-beamed dining room.

I began the meal with this salad, a celebration of all the best ingredients of the southwest: From the garden came the tiniest *frisée* (curly endive) and whole *pluches,* or sprigs, of fresh chervil. From the fields, plump kernels of golden corn. From the nut groves that line the roads throughout the Dordogne, flavorful walnuts. And from the barnyard came tender smoked duck breast. Another salad that could be served as a first course or a main course, with crusty bread and a bottle of wine. That evening, we sampled Jean Jouffreau's Cahors, from the Clos de Gamont. If smoked duck breast is unavailable, nothing should stop you from preparing this dish with top-quality smoked ham.

4 cups (1 l) very tender curly endive, rinsed, dried, and torn into manageable pieces

2 tablespoons best-quality sherry wine vinegar

½ cup (12.5 cl) fresh walnut oil or extra-virgin olive oil

Salt

½ cup cooked fresh corn or frozen kernels, thawed

4 thin slices smoked duck breast (or smoked ham), cut into thin strips (about 3 ounces; 100 g)

½ cup (60 g) fresh walnut halves

1. Place the salad greens in a large, shallow salad bowl.

2. In a nonreactive small saucepan over medium heat, warm the vinegar, oil, and salt to taste. Bring just to a simmer. Add the corn and warm it for just a minute or two.

TRUC

Salt does not dissolve in oil. Thus, when preparing a cold vinaigrette, always dissolve the salt in vinegar or lemon juice before whisking in the oil.

3. Pour the corn dressing over the greens; toss very gently but thoroughly.

4. Divide the greens among 4 large plates, spreading them out and pressing them down to lie flat. Arrange the duck slices like the spokes on a wheel on top of the greens. Sprinkle with the walnuts and serve.

Yield: 4 servings

SALADE NIÇOISE LA MÈRE BESSON

La Mère Besson's Salade Niçoise

S*alade niçoise,* the classic salad from Nice, has become such a generic, universally appealing dish, that one sees literally dozens of versions. Although the most traditional version doesn't include cooked ingredients—except for hard-cooked eggs—and officially no lettuce, this one, from La Mère Besson, a small family bistro in Cannes, is a personal favorite. The dressing has a pesto-like richness and marries well with the anchovies and vegetables. Any light Provençal wine can be served with this dish, such as a Tavel or Domaine de la Genestière.

3 garlic cloves, finely minced
½ cup (12.5 cl) basil leaves, cut into a chiffonade (thin strips) with a scissors
½ cup (12.5 cl) extra-virgin olive oil
Salt
1 green bell pepper
1 red bell pepper
2 celery ribs
1 can (2 ounces; 57 g) flat anchovy fillets in olive oil, drained
4 cups (1 l) loosely packed mixed greens, such as oakleaf lettuce, rocket, romaine, and curly endive

1 can (6½ ounces; 195 g) water-packed albacore tuna, drained and flaked
½ cup (about 2 ounces; 60 g) black olives, preferably from Nice

1. Prepare the dressing: Combine the garlic and basil in a small bowl and slowly stir in the oil. Season to taste with salt.

2. Core, seed, and dice the peppers. Dice the celery. Cut each an-

chovy fillet crosswise into 4 pieces.

3. Layer the salad ingredients in a large, shallow bowl in the following order: the greens, peppers, celery, tuna, olives, and anchovies.

4. Add the dressing, toss, and serve.

Yield: 4 to 6 servings

SALADE DE ROQUEFORT, NOIX, ET ENDIVES CHARDENOUX

Chardenoux's Salad of Roquefort, Walnuts, and Belgian Endive

T his is one of my favorite wintertime salads: crunchy Belgian endive, freshly cracked walnuts, and piquant Roquefort, all tossed in a lemony dressing of fragrant hazelnut oil. When I prepare this salad, I like to toss it in a huge glass salad bowl, leaving the Belgian endive leaves whole. It makes the salad a bit harder to eat—your guests will have to slice the salad greens themselves—but I love the way the nuts and cheese sort of get captured inside the leaves, making for a lovely burst of flavor when you come upon the trio in a single bite! While Roquefort is the traditional cheese used in this classic bistro salad, you might enjoy Fourme d'Ambert, a blue that I find is creamier and often more full-flavored. At the charming Paris bistro Chardenoux, they offer the classic version, with plenty of Roquefort and walnuts in olive oil dressing.

2 tablespoons freshly squeezed lemon juice
¼ teaspoon salt
¼ cup (6 cl) best-quality hazelnut oil or extra-virgin olive oil
2 pounds (1 kg) Belgian endive (about 6 endives)

1 cup (120 g) best-quality or organic walnut pieces
6 ounces (180 g) imported French Roquefort or Fourme d'Ambert cheese, crumbled

1. In a small bowl, combine the lemon juice and salt and stir to blend. Add the oil and stir to blend. Adjust the seasoning; set the dressing aside.

2. Separate the endive leaves; wash the endive in several changes of water and pat them dry. Place the whole leaves in a large salad bowl. Sprinkle on the walnuts and crumbled cheese.

3. Pour on the dressing and toss. Check for salt. Serve immediately.

Yield: 6 servings

COLD WEATHER FEASTS TO WARM THE SOUL

Winter is the time for Belgian endive, warming duck stews, cabbage, and pear desserts. With this, serve any favorite red. At Le Petit Marguery, we often drink the house Bourgueil, a delicately fruity red from the Loire.

SALADE DE ROQUEFORT, NOIX ET ENDIVES CHARDENOUX
Chardenoux's Salad of Roquefort, Walnuts, and Belgian Endive

♦

PETIT SALÉ DE CANARD LE PETIT MARGUERY
Le Petit Marguery's Salt-Cured Duck With Cabbage

♦

CLAFOUTIS AU POIRE
Pear Clafoutis

SALADE COLMARIENNE CHEZ JENNY

Chez Jenny's Sausage, Cheese, and Curly Endive Salad

In Alsace, nearly every bistro or *winstub* offers a salad that blends the local delicately smoked sausage—known as cervelas—with Comté cheese, from its southern French neighbor, the Jura. I first sampled this version at Chez Jenny, the lively, popular Parisian brasserie near Place de la République. It is a wonderfully refreshing winter salad, the sort that you can make a meal of at lunchtime, accompanied by crusty French bread and a sip of Alsatian white wine, such as Sylvaner or Gewürztraminer. The recipe takes its name from the Alsatian city of Colmar.

2 small tomatoes, peeled, cored, seeded, and chopped
1 small bunch of chives, finely minced
4 shallots, cut into thin rings
2 tablespoons best-quality white wine vinegar
½ cup (12.5 cl) peanut oil
Salt
8 ounces (250 g) precooked smoked pork sausages, such as knockwurst
8 ounces (250 g) imported French or Swiss Gruyère cheese, chilled
1 small head (about 4 cups, 1 l) curly endive, rinsed and dried
Freshly ground black pepper

1. Combine the tomatoes, chives, shallots, vinegar, oil, and salt to taste in a small bowl and stir to blend. Adjust the seasoning; set aside. (The dressing can be made an hour or so in advance to allow the flavors to blend and the shallots to soften.)

2. Remove and discard the casings from the sausages; cut into thick rounds. Place the slices in a medium-size bowl and toss with one-third of the dressing.

3. Cut the cheese while cold into thin sticks, the size of an average French fry. Place in a medium-size bowl and toss with one-third of the dressing. Set aside to come to room temperature.

4. Cut the curly endive into bite-size pieces. Toss with the remaining dressing.

5. Divide the curly endive among 4 large plates. Arrange some of the sausage in a circle on top of each portion of greens. Scatter the cheese over the sausage; season very generously with coarse freshly ground black pepper. Serve with plenty of crunchy country bread.

Yield: 4 to 6 servings

CHIPIRONS EN SALADE CHEZ PHILIPPE

Chez Philippe's Calamari Salad

Along the Atlantic coast in Bordeaux, big-city bistros such as Chez Philippe boast of the fruits of the sea, offering giant platters of oysters from nearby Arcachon, plus a very light and refreshing salad of calamari, or small squid known as *chipiron.* Lightly tossed in seasoned flour, sautéed ever so quickly in olive oil, and then tossed atop a bed of dressed greens, the tender squid are finally infused with a sharp touch of garlic and parsley before arriving at the table. With this, sample a young white, such as a dry white Graves.

¼ cup (6 cl) best-quality red wine vinegar
Salt and freshly ground black pepper
½ cup (12.5 cl) extra-virgin olive oil
4 garlic cloves
A small handful of fresh parsley
¼ cup (35 g) unbleached all-purpose flour
8 ounces (250 g) small squid, cleaned (see Index), mantles left whole
¼ cup (6 cl) olive oil
4 shallots, cut into thin rings
4 cups (1 l) mixed salad greens, including radicchio, curly endive, and escarole, washed, dried, and torn into bite-size pieces

1. In a small bowl, whisk together the vinegar and salt and pepper to taste. Then, whisk in the oil. Set the dressing aside.

2. Finely mince the garlic and parsley; set aside.

3. Season the flour with salt and pepper. Lightly dredge the squid in the flour, shaking off any excess.

4. In a large skillet, heat the oil over high heat until hot but not smoking. Add the shallots and the squid and cook over high heat, stirring gently and constantly, until tender, just 1 to 2 minutes. (Longer cooking will turn the tiny squid into rubberbands.) Remove from the heat to drain on paper towels. Season generously with salt and pepper; shower with the garlic and parsley.

5. Toss the greens with the dressing. Evenly divide the greens among 4 large plates. Place the squid on the greens and serve immediately.

Yield: 4 servings

SALADE DAUPHINOISE

Escarole, Ham, Cheese, and Walnut Salad

T his salad combines all of the best ingredients of the Dauphiné, the walnut-rich area of France, where walnuts, cheese, ham, and cream can be found in abundance. All one need do is step out into the garden, pick some fresh lettuce, and *voilà!* instant salad. I love the play of flavors and textures in this salad. The creamy dressing gives a nice boost to the hearty salad, which can be dry if not prepared with enough dressing.

2 teaspoons imported Dijon mustard
2 teaspoons freshly squeezed lemon
    juice
1 tablespoon best-quality red wine
    vinegar
2 tablespoons crème fraîche (see Index)
    or sour cream
3 tablespoons fresh walnut oil or
    extra-virgin olive oil
Salt and freshly ground black pepper
1 small head or bunch of salad greens
    (about 4 cups; 1 l) such as es-
    carole, curly endive, romaine,
    radicchio, or lamb's lettuce,
    washed and dried
½ cup (2 ounces; 60 g) walnut pieces
3 ounces (90 g) imported French or
    Swiss Gruyère cheese, cut into
    bite-size cubes
3 ounces (90 g) thickly sliced salt-
    cured unsmoked ham, such as
    prosciutto, cut into bite-size cubes
1 small bunch of chives, finely minced

1. Whisk together the mustard, lemon juice, and vinegar in a small bowl. Add the crème fraîche and oil and whisk until emulsified. Season with salt and pepper to taste; set the vinaigrette aside.

2. In a large bowl, combine the greens, nuts, cheese, ham, and chives. Pour the vinaigrette over the salad and toss until well-coated. Serve.

Yield: 4 servings

❝*Take one hard-boiled egg yolk per person. Mix with oil to make a paste. Add chervil, some tuna, ground anchovies, chopped pickles and chopped egg whites, salt and pepper. Add a good vinegar until it is liquid enough for a sauce. As soon as it is mixed I let fall from on high a pinch of paprika.* **❞**

—ALEXANDRE DUMAS

SALADE DE COQUES ET MOULES GABRIEL COULET

Gabriel Coulet's Clam and Mussel Salad

At the end of a long, successful tour of France's southwest, I spent a day with André and Pierre Laur, third-generation cheesemakers in the village of Roquefort. They took me to lunch at a wonderfully simple country restaurant with no name, so I decided that this refreshing salad should be dedicated to the "No Name Restaurant" and the Laurs' wonderful artisanal Roquefort cheese, known as Gabriel Coulet.

This is one of those "hands on" dishes that's fun to eat with a jovial crowd, for the chilled mussels and tiny clams, known as *coques,* are served in the shell. Be sure to have plenty of bread on hand—preferably a fresh baguette—to soak up the delicious sauce. That day, we drank a delicious local dry white wine, Picpoul de Pinet, but a Riesling would do just fine.

1 cup (25 cl) dry white wine, such as Picpoul de Pinet or Riesling
1½ pounds (750 g) mussels, thoroughly scrubbed in several changes of water and bearded just before cooking (see Note)
1½ pounds (750 g) small clams, degorged if necessary (see Note), then thoroughly scrubbed in several changes of water
4 shallots, finely minced
3 tablespoons best-quality sherry wine vinegar

1. In a 6-quart (6 l) Dutch oven, combine the wine, mussels, and clams. Bring to a boil over high heat. Cover and cook just until the mussels and clams open, about 5 minutes; do not overcook. Remove from the heat; arrange the mussels and clams in a shallow bowl, large enough to hold them comfortably. Discard any mussels or clams that do not open. Strain the liquid; reserve.

2. In a small saucepan, combine the strained cooking liquid and the shallots. Cook over high heat just until the shallots are soft, about 5 minutes. Add the vinegar and cook for 1 more minute. Pour the sauce over the mussels and clams and toss. Cover and chill for up to 4 hours. Serve chilled, with plenty of crusty

fresh bread and white wine.

Yield: 4 servings

Note: Do not beard the mussels in advance, or they will die and spoil.

> ### TROUBLE WITH SANDY CLAMS?
>
> Tiny clams, in particular, tend to be very sandy. To degorge them, or rid them of the sand, soak them for 1 to 2 hours in salt water, dissolving ½ cup (3½ ounces, or 117 g) coarse sea salt per quart (liter) of water.

PICODON À L'HUILE D'OLIVE

Goat Cheese in Olive Oil

I consider my cupboard bare if I don't have a jar of goat cheese in oil stashed somewhere about. For those days when I don't have time to get to the store, or when I simply forget about marketing, a little jar of Picodon marinating in oil is a godsend.

When selecting cheese to marinate in oil, look for one that is fairly firm and not too fresh, or it is likely to fall apart as it ages. The cheese usually keeps for 1 month (it keeps well both refrigerated and in the pantry), though I've been known to let it go longer. While in France, I use tiny Picodon, Crottin, and Cabécou goat cheese; in the United States, we recommend using a semisoft cheese such as Montrachet, usually sold in 11-ounce logs. Any semisoft domestic goat cheese can be used. I think that this is the best kind of cheese to use for making grilled goat cheese salads, for the cheese remains very tender. The oil can be reused to marinate cheese, if desired, or can be used to prepare a vinaigrette. Spread the cheese on toasted slices of crusty baguettes and serve atop a tossed green salad.

4 small semisoft goat cheese (Picodon, Crottin, or Cabécou), each weighing about 3 ounces (90 g)
1 teaspoon Herbes de Provence (see Index)
4 imported bay leaves
12 black peppercorns, slightly crushed
1 to 1½ cups (25 to 37.5 cl) extra-virgin olive oil

1. Cut each cheese horizontally in half (if using Montrachet, cut it into 1-inch; 2.5 cm, rounds). In a wide-mouth ½ pint (25 cl) jar, place the cheese, then the herbs, bay leaves, and peppercorns. Cover with oil. Close securely and store in a cool place for at least 1 week and up to 1 month. (The cheese can be stored in the refrigerator, but remember to bring the oil back to room temperature before serving.)

2. Remove the cheese from the jar and drain off the oil before serving.

Yield: 8 servings

SAUCISSON À L'HUILE D'OLIVE

◆————◆

Sausages Preserved in Olive Oil

I first learned about this ingenious method for storing and preserving sausage from the three Cousin brothers, owners of the fine Paris bistro, Le Petit Marguery. In the Cousin brothers' native region of Poitou, walnut trees were plentiful before World War I, when many of them were cut down for firewood and for making arms. Walnut oil was also plentiful—even more plentiful than the now ubiquitous sunflower oil—and was used for everyday cooking. Farm wives often would preserve slices of their homemade sausages in jars of walnut oil, then toss the slices into fresh-from-the-garden green salads. The Cousin brothers always keep a huge glass jar of sausages marinating in their kitchen, and I now follow suit.

I think I've tried just about every kind of sausage imaginable: I like to preserve fresh sausages for scattering over homemade pizzas and dried sausages for tossing in salads. Since good-quality walnut oil is difficult to find—and often prohibitively expensive—I suggest using good-quality olive oil instead. The sausage will keep indefinitely. I usually refrigerate it, and add more sausage as needed to keep the jar filled. The oil can, of course, be used to prepare salad dressings, so nothing goes to waste. The hot pepper flakes are optional, depending upon how you will use the sausages and oil.

1 pound (500 g) best-quality air-
dried sausages such as Abruzzi
dry Italian sausage
4 imported bay leaves
½ teaspoon hot pepper flakes (optional)
12 whole black peppercorns
1½ to 2 cups (37.5 to 50 cl) extra-
virgin olive oil

1. Slice each sausage into thin rounds. In a wide-mouth pint (50 cl) jar, layer the sausage with the bay leaves, hot pepper flakes, and peppercorns. Cover with oil. Close securely and store in a cool place for at least 1 week and up to 1 month. (The sausage can be stored in the refrigerator, but remember to bring the oil back to room temperature before serving.)

2. To serve, remove the sausages from the oil and drain. Toss with a green salad or scatter on pizza.

Yield: 1 pint (50 cl) preserved sausages

SALADE DE HADDOCK AUX EPINARDS L'AQUITAINE

◆━━━◆

L'Aquitaine's Smoked Haddock and Spinach Salad

T his is a wonderful marriage—crispy spinach, warm and delicately smoky haddock, and tiny new potatoes, bathed in a creamy mustard dressing. I like to call it a "build-it-on-the-fork salad," meaning, to get the full benefit of the fine mixture of flavors and textures, sample the spinach, the flaked haddock and the warm potatoes together all in one bite, building them up on the fork, then downing a forkful all at once. All you need add is a touch of cracked pepper at the end, for a great finale!

When you make this dish—shared with me by Christiane Massia of Paris's restaurant L'Aquitaine—take special care that all the ingredients are fresh and of top quality. Many different wines might be sampled with this salad, which could be a meal on its own: I love a rich, dry white such as a young Meursault, a California Chardonnay, an Alsatian Gewürztraminer, or a Chablis Grand Cru.

2 tablespoons freshly squeezed lemon juice
1 teaspoon imported Dijon mustard
⅓ cup (8 cl) peanut oil
2 tablespoons crème fraîche (see Index) or heavy cream
Salt and freshly ground black pepper
8 ounces (250 g) small new red-skinned potatoes, scrubbed
2 cups (50 cl) whole milk
1 pound (500 g) best-quality smoked haddock fillets
1 pound (500 g) tender young spinach leaves, washed, dried, and stemmed

1. In a small bowl whisk together the lemon juice, salt, and mustard. Slowly whisk in the oil, and then the crème fraîche. Season to taste. Set the dressing aside.

2. Cook the potatoes in plenty of salted water, cooking just until tender; do not overcook. Drain the potatoes. As soon as the potatoes are cool enough to handle, but while still warm, cut into thin, even slices. Place the potatoes in a bowl and toss with several tablespoons of the dressing. Set the potatoes aside to absorb the dressing.

3. Pour the milk into a shallow skillet and bring just to a simmer over medium-high heat. Add the smoked haddock, cover, reduce the heat, and simmer gently for about 10 minutes. Once cooked, the haddock can be

HADDOCK VÉRITABLE

In America haddock generally refers to the fresh white fish, while in France, haddock is always smoked haddock, also better known in France as *églefin frais fumé*—finnan haddie. In fact, so much "imposter" smoked fish (generally codfish, or *cabillaud*) is disguised as smoked haddock, recipes in French generally call for *haddock véritable,* the best of which is smoked very slowly at low temperature. Following French tradition, once bought, the haddock is poached in milk, to soften it and rid it of any excess salt.

kept warm in its cooking liquid for up to 15 minutes.

4. Stack several spinach leaves on top of one another, and, using a long chef's knife, cut the spinach into wide (1 inch; 2.5 cm) strips. Continue until all of the spinach is cut into a rustic chiffonnade. Arrange the spinach in a large, shallow salad bowl, spreading it out to layer the bottom of the bowl.

5. Remove the haddock from the skillet, drain, and remove the skin. The haddock should flake easily with a fork. Arrange the flaked haddock on top of the spinach. Add the potatoes. Toss with remaining dressing and shower generously with freshly ground black pepper. Serve on large flat plates, evenly dividing the haddock, spinach, and potatoes.

Yield: 4 to 6 servings

SALADE HARENGS— POMMES DE TERRE LA MEUNIÈRE

La Meunière's Herring and Potato Salad

La Meunière in Lyons is one of the last great bistros offering an authentic *saladier lyonnais*, that is, an incredible assortment of mixed salads and charcuterie, all served out of huge pottery bowls. The day I lunched there, the *saladier lyonnais* (as opposed to the assortment of charcuterie) consisted of nine different salads. The assortment included this delicious salad of marinated smoked herring mixed with chives, potatoes, and oil. That afternoon we drank a delicious cru Beaujolais, a Saint-Amour from Pierre Dupond.

8 ounces (250 g) small new red-
    skinned potatoes, scrubbed and
    peeled
Salt
4 canned fillets of smoked herring, or
    4 Harengs Marinés (see Index),
    quartered

3 tablespoons chopped fresh chives
¼ cup (6 cl) peanut oil, or the oil in
    which the herring has been cured

1. Place the potatoes in a saucepan, cover with water, add salt to

taste, and bring to a boil over high heat. Cook until nearly cooked through but still firm in the center, about 15 minutes. Drain. Quarter the potatoes.

2. In a large bowl, combine the warm potatoes, herring, and chives. Sprinkle with the oil, toss to blend, and serve.

Yield: 4 servings

HERRING TIP

I f your herrings are too salty, soak them for a good 3 hours in milk before proceeding with a recipe.

SALADE MESCLUN LA MÈRE BESSON

La Mère Besson's Mixed Summer Salad

One summer's evening as I sipped one of my favorite wines, the Bandol rouge from Domaine Tempier, a friend and I feasted on a lovely Provençal meal at La Mère Besson, one of the older, traditional bistros along the Côte d'Azur. Before digging into their meaty *estouffade de boeuf*—beef simmered in wine and herbs—I sampled this lovely salad. The star, of course, was the greens, a true mesclun, or mix of many kinds of bright greens, including arugula, lamb's lettuce, parsley, red chicory, escarole, and red oakleaf lettuce. When preparing this at home, be as adventuresome as possible, adding nasturtium blossoms, firm-leafed purslane, a few leaves of basil, summer savory, and hyssop.

1 tablespoon imported Dijon mustard
1 tablespoon best-quality red wine
    vinegar
Salt
½ cup (12.5 cl) extra-virgin olive oil
2 large eggs, at room temperature
3 tablespoons olive oil

2 cups (50 cl) bread cubes, cut into ½
    inch (1.25 cm) cubes
8 cups (2 l) mixed salad greens, rinsed
    and torn into manageable pieces
2 tomatoes, cored and diced
2 fat garlic cloves, finely minced

1. Place the mustard in a small bowl. Whisk in the vinegar and salt to taste; mix well. Slowly pour in the extra-virgin olive oil and whisk until the mixture is lightly blended. Set the dressing aside.

2. Place the eggs in a saucepan and cover generously with water. Cook, uncovered, over medium-high heat until the first large bubbles rise steadily from the bottom of the pan. Reduce the heat so the water continues to simmer gently but never boils. Simmer for 8 minutes. The cooked egg should have a firmly set yolk and white. Pour off the hot water and stop the cooking by running cold water over the eggs for a minute or two. When the eggs are cool, crack, peel, and coarsely chop them. Set aside at room temperature.

3. Make the croutons: Heat the 3 tablespoons of oil in a skillet over medium-high heat. When the oil is hot but not smoking, add the bread cubes and toss to coat. Sauté until the bread is browned on all sides, 3 to 4 minutes. Set aside.

4. Place the salad greens in a large, shallow salad bowl. Sprinkle on the tomatoes, eggs, garlic, and croutons. Add the dressing, and toss gently but thoroughly, until the greens are evenly coated. Serve.

Yield: 4 servings

Salade Lyonnaise La Meunière

◆────────◆

La Meunière's Salad of Escarole, Potatoes, Herring, and Eggs

L yons continues to amaze me. With each visit, my love and knowledge of bistro cooking seems to grow by leaps and bounds, and I am constantly astonished at how simple, everyday ingredients can be tossed together almost helter-skelter, and end up tasting so delicious! This is one of many variations on the classic *salade Lyonnaise*, one that almost always includes herring and potatoes in one manner or another.

This version comes from a small, old-fashioned bistro known as La Meunière, where the salad was uncommonly good and the dressing formed a very happy, natural marriage with the other ingredients. I asked the waiter what was in the dressing. "The owner's secret," he replied, glancing back at the kitchen. He cleared the table, looked me straight in the eye, and said, "There's a touch of herring in the dressing." Later, as I was in the process of preparing the salad at home, it occurred to me that he must use the oil in which the herring is cured. I followed my instinct and came up with a salad I think is a real winner.

2 large eggs, *at room temperature*
8 ounces (250 g) *small new red-skinned potatoes, scrubbed and peeled*
1 tablespoon *imported Dijon mustard*
1 tablespoon *best-quality red wine vinegar*
Salt
4 cups (1 l) *curly endive or escarole, rinsed, dried, and torn into manageable pieces*
4 Harengs Marinés *(see Index), cubed, oil reserved*
3 tablespoons *chopped fresh chives*
3 tablespoons *chopped fresh parsley*

1. Place the eggs in a saucepan and cover generously with water. Cook, uncovered, over medium-high heat until the first large bubbles rise steadily from the bottom of the pan. Reduce the heat so the water continues to simmer gently but never boils. Simmer for 8 minutes. The cooked egg should have a firmly set yolk and white. Pour off the hot water. Gently crack the eggs; stop the cooking by running cold water over the eggs for a minute or two. When the eggs are cool, peel them and set aside at room temperature.

2. Place the potatoes in a single layer in a saucepan. Add water to cover and salt to taste; bring to a boil over high heat. Cook until nearly cooked through but still firm in the center, about 15 minutes. Drain and let cool.

3. Place the mustard in a small bowl. Whisk in the vinegar and salt to taste and mix well. Slowly pour in 6 tablespoons (9.5 cl) of oil the herring marinated in, and whisk until the mixture is lightly blended. Set the dressing aside.

4. Place the salad greens in a large, shallow salad bowl. Sprinkle with the cubes of herring. Cut the potatoes into thin slices and layer them on top of the herring. Quarter the eggs and layer them on top of the potatoes. Sprinkle on the chives and parsley. Add the dressing and toss gently but thoroughly, until the greens are evenly coated. Serve with plenty of crusty country bread.

Yield: 4 servings

SALADE AUX LINGOTS ET SAUCISSE DE MORTEAU QUAI D'ORSAY

Quai d'Orsay's Salad of White Beans and Smoked Sausages

I'm crazy about composed salads, anything with a healthy bed of greens, on which you layer a mixture of full-flavored ingredients. After a mid-fall lunch at Paris's Quai d'Orsay, I adapted this version of the dish I sampled there that day. Greens are dressed with a very lemony dressing, warm white beans (known in France as *lingots*) are placed on top, and then warmed smoked sausage surrounds the beans. Sprinkle with pistachios and chives, and you have a blend of bright, electric flavors. Any good smoked sausage can be used here. In France the dish is made with saucisse de Morteau, from the Jura. With this, sample a young red, just slightly chilled, perhaps a Saumur-Champigny from the Loire.

Beans:
10 ounces (300 g) dried white beans
    (about 1½ cups)
2 tablespoons extra-virgin olive oil
2 imported bay leaves
Several sprigs of fresh thyme or several
    teaspoons dried
Salt

Dressing:
4 shallots, finely minced
⅓ cup (8 cl) lemon juice
⅔ cup (16 cl) extra-virgin olive oil
Salt

Sausage:
10 ounces (300 g) smoked pork sau-

sage, or several individual smoked
    sausage links
1 tablespoon olive oil
Several sprigs fresh thyme, or 1 table-
    spoon dried
1 imported bay leaf
1 onion, finely minced
2 garlic cloves
1 cup dry white wine

Salad:
2 cups (50 cl) young curly endive,
    rinsed, dried, and torn into man-
    ageable pieces
¼ cup (40 g) salted pistachio nuts
1 tablespoon minced fresh chives

1. Prepare the beans: Rinse the beans. Place in a large saucepan and add cold water to cover. Bring the water to a boil over high heat. Once boiling, remove the pan from the heat. Set aside, covered, for 40 minutes. Drain the beans, discarding the cooking liquid. Rinse the beans and cover again with cold water. Add the oil, bay leaves, and thyme and bring just to a simmer over medium heat. Cover and cook over medium heat until tender, about 1 hour. (Cooking time will vary according to the freshness of the beans. Older beans take longer to cook.) The beans should not be mushy, rather cooked through but firm. Add salt to taste.

2. While the beans are cooking, prepare the dressing: Whisk the shallots with the lemon juice and salt in a small bowl. Add the oil in a steady stream and whisk until blended. Season to taste.

3. Drain the beans thoroughly. Add half of the dressing to the beans; set aside and keep warm.

4. Prepare the sausage: Heat the oil in a large saucepan over medium-high heat. Add the sausage and brown on all sides, being careful not to pierce it. Add the thyme, bay leaf, onion, garlic, and wine, and bring just to a simmer. Cover and simmer gently, stirring occasionally, for 1 hour. Drain. Set aside and keep warm.

5. Assemble the salad: Place the greens in a large, shallow salad bowl. Pour on the remaining dressing and toss gently and thoroughly.

6. Divide the greens among 4 large plates, spreading the greens out and pressing them down to lie flat. Place several spoonfuls of the beans in the center. Remove the casings and cut the sausage into thin slices. Arrange them in a fan-like fashion around the edge of the beans. Sprinkle with the pistachios and chives and serve warm.

Yield: 4 servings

SALADE DU THÉÂTRE

Brasserie du Théâtre's Salad of Greens, Headcheese, Eggs, and Tomatoes

The Brasserie du Théâtre in Versailles is a lovely, lively bistro, serving all the famed traditional fare. I sampled this salad one afternoon in August, followed by a classic *gigot à la provençale,* delicious lamb, served with white beans and grilled tomatoes. I love combining greens with charcuterie, curly endive salad and chunks of *museau de boeuf,* or beef headcheese. Pork headcheese could also be substituted.

4 large eggs, at room temperature
2 tablespoons imported Dijon mustard
2 tablespoons best-quality red wine
    vinegar
Salt
½ cup (12.5 cl) peanut oil
6 cups (1.5 l) curly endive, rinsed,
    dried, and torn into manageable
    pieces
2 slices (about 6 ounces; 200 g) beef or
    pork headcheese
16 cherry tomatoes, rinsed and halved

1. Arrange the eggs in a single layer in a saucepan and cover generously with water. Cook, uncovered, over medium-high heat until the first large bubbles rise steadily from the bottom of the pan. Reduce the heat so the water continues to simmer gently but never boils. Simmer for 6 minutes. The cooked egg should have a firmly set white and a yolk that is still soft and dark yellow. Pour off the hot water and stop the cooking by running cold water over the eggs for a minute or two. When the eggs are cool, crack and peel them. Set aside at room temperature.

2. Place the mustard in a small bowl. Whisk in the vinegar and salt to taste; mix well. Slowly pour in the oil and whisk until the mixture is lightly blended. Set dressing aside.

3. Place the salad greens in a large, shallow salad bowl.

4. Cut the headcheese into bite-size cubes. Distribute over the greens, along with the tomatoes. Quarter the eggs; scatter them on top. Add the dressing and toss gently but thoroughly, until the greens are evenly coated. Serve with plenty of crusty country bread.

Yield: 4 servings

La Salade d'Epinards aux Foies de Volailles

Salad of Fresh Spinach and Sautéed Chicken Livers

This is a salad that's not particular to any special region of France, for you'll find it in bistros in Lyons as well as small family restaurants in the Charentes. I have to admit that for the longest time I had a distinct dislike for chicken livers, for in my early married days we ate them once or twice a week because they were inexpensive. I'm coming around again, especially when I know I can get chicken livers from fresh, farm-raised poultry.

*1 pound (500 g) spinach, rinsed,
   dried, and torn into manageable
   pieces*
12 fresh chicken livers, halved
Salt and freshly ground black pepper
*2 tablespoons (1 ounce; 30 g) unsalted
   butter*
*2 tablespoons best-quality red wine
   vinegar*
½ cup (12.5 cl) peanut oil

A SAVOYARD SUPPER

◆

This is the sort of menu you might find at a family dinner in the Savoy region of France. Chicken, potatoes, ham, walnuts, and apples and cream make up the bulk of the appealing country larder. With this, sample any young and fruity red, a Beaujolais, or a young Côtes du Rhône.

**LA SALADE D'ÉPINARDS AUX
FOIES DE VOLAILLE**
*Salad of Fresh Spinach and Sautéed
Chicken Livers*

◆

**FRICASSÉE DE POULET AUX
CHAMPIGNONS CHEZ ROSE**
*Chez Rose's Chicken Fricassee
With Mushrooms*

◆

**GRATIN DAUPHINOIS MADAME
LARACINE**
Madame Laracine's Potato Gratin

◆

**TARTE AUX POMMES
À LA CRÈME**
Golden Cream and Apple Tart

1. Arrange the spinach on 4 large salad plates.

2. Season the chicken livers with salt and pepper to taste. In a small skillet, melt the butter over medium-high heat. Add the chicken livers and sauté for just 2 or 3 minutes for rather pinkish livers, 5 to 7 minutes if you prefer your livers well done. They should remain moist and tender

and should just begin to give up their juices. While still on the heat, deglaze the chicken livers with the vinegar, stirring up any browned pieces that may have gotten stuck, then add the oil and stir until the mixture is warm and well blended.

3. Evenly arrange the warm chicken livers and the dressing on top of the spinach. Serve, allowing each guest to toss his own salad.

Yield: 4 servings

SALADE DE LENTILLES VERTES

◆

Green Lentil Salad

There are days in the winter that I truly crave lentils, the slightly earthy little seed grown in the mountainous Auvergne region of France. The best lentils come from the village of Le Puy, where the soil is particularly suited to growing what a friend once called "those delicious little French peas." Serve this with grilled sausages or as a salad all on its own, and pass the freshly baked country bread.

1 pound (500 g) imported French
    green lentils (about 2½ cups) (or
    substitute brown lentils)
1 medium onion, halved and stuck
    with 2 cloves
1 garlic clove, peeled
1 imported bay leaf
¼ cup (6 cl) best-quality red wine
    vinegar
2 tablespoons extra-virgin olive oil
Salt and freshly ground black pepper

TRUC

A French grandmother's tip for more flavorful lentils: Add a teaspoon of vinegar and a sugar cube to the cooking water.

1. Rinse the lentils and pick over carefully, discarding any pebbles you

may find. Place the lentils, onion, garlic, and bay leaf in a heavy medium-size saucepan; cover with cold water by 1 inch (2.5 cm). Cover and bring just to a boil over medium heat. Reduce the heat to low and simmer, covered, until the lentils are tender but still intact, 25 to 35 minutes. Check the lentils 2 or 3 times during cooking; during most of the cooking, water should be visible when you tilt the pan slightly. Add water as needed, but not more than ¼ cup (6 cl). By the end of the cooking time, the liquid should have been absorbed.

2. When the lentils are cooked, remove the pan from the heat; discard the onion, garlic, and bay leaf. Whisk together the vinegar, oil, and salt to taste in a small bowl. Pour over the warm lentils and toss to coat. Transfer the lentils to a serving bowl. Just before serving, season to taste with pepper and additional salt if necessary. Serve warm.

Yield: 6 to 8 servings

LA SALADE ET VINAIGRETTE DE TANTE YVONNE

Tante Yvonne's Tossed Green Salad with Vinaigrette

Yvonne Soliva, Tante Yvonne, is one of Provence's most lively characters, a motherly cook whose restaurant—Chez Tante Yvonne in Lambesc—more closely resembles a folklore museum. Her food is regional and from the heart. One evening she prepared a simple green salad with a marvelous dressing, one full of complex flavors and aromas, which she kindly shared with us.

2 heads soft-leaf or butterhead lettuce, such as Boston, Bibb, or buttercrunch, washed and dried
2 tablespoons freshly squeezed lemon juice
2 tablespoons best-quality sherry wine vinegar
1 teaspoon imported Dijon mustard

Salt and freshly ground black pepper
¾ cup (18 cl) extra-virgin olive oil

1. Break the lettuce leaves into bite-size pieces and place in a large bowl.

2. In a small bowl, combine the

lemon juice, vinegar, mustard, and salt to taste; whisk with a fork to blend. Add pepper to taste, and slowly whisk in the olive oil. Taste and adjust the seasoning, if necessary. Pour over the greens, toss gently and thoroughly, and serve.

Yield: 6 to 8 servings

SALADE QUERCYNOISE L'OULETTE

L'Oulette's Salad of Ham, Walnuts, and Duck Gizzards

L'Oulette is a Parisian bistro devoted to a very homey, yet modern, style of southwestern cooking. Chef Marcel Baudis serves this warming, copious salad as a first course. You can also make a meal of it, with some crusty homemade bread and a few sips of rough country wine, such as the Gaillac served at L'Oulette. I love the combination of meaty duck gizzards, or *gésiers confits,* walnuts and ham, a trio of ingredients native to France's southwest. Do make an effort to find truly fresh walnuts (organically grown, untreated ones if possible). And if you can't find fresh walnut oil, substitute top-quality olive oil. Preserved duck gizzards can be found in food specialty shops or ordered by phone or mail. In a pinch, sautéed chicken livers can be substituted or the gizzards can be left out altogether.

2 tablespoons freshly squeezed lemon juice
Salt and freshly ground black pepper
½ cup (12.5 cl) fresh walnut oil
4 cups (1 l) mixed salad greens, such as curly endive, arugula, lamb's lettuce, and radicchio, washed and dried
1 cup (3 ounces; 90 g) fresh walnuts

4 thick slices unsmoked ham, such as prosciutto, cut into bite-size cubes
4 preserved duck gizzards (see Note, page 34 for where to order) or raw chicken livers

1. In a small bowl whisk together the lemon juice and salt to

taste. Slowly whisk in the oil until well blended. Season with pepper to taste. Set the dressing aside.

2. In a large, shallow salad bowl, layer the greens, walnuts and ham.

3. Scrape the fat off the duck gizzards, reserving about 1 teaspoon in which to cook them. Cut each gizzard into 8 pieces. In a small skillet over medium-high heat, heat the reserved duck fat until it begins to sizzle. Add the gizzards and sauté until lightly browned and warmed through, 3 to 4 minutes. (If using chicken livers, melt 1 tablespoon of vegetable oil or butter in a small skillet over medium-high heat. Add the chicken livers and sauté for just 2 to 3 minutes for rather pinkish livers, 5 to 7 minutes if you prefer your livers well done.) Season to taste with salt and pepper. Drain.

4. Scatter the gizzards or livers on top of the salad and toss with the dressing. Serve.

Yield: 4 servings

ALL DRESSED UP, WITH SOMEPLACE TO GO

Select a dressing to suit the salad. There are, indeed, dressings that marry perfectly with certain greens. Some suggestions:

• For delicate greens, such as butter or Boston lettuce, toss with one part lemon juice, three parts cream.

• For beets, celeriac, or leftover cooked meats or poultry, toss with a dressing of 1 tablespoon imported mustard, 3 tablespoons cream, and the juice of half a lemon.

• For crunchy lettuce such as escarole, poach chicken livers in chicken stock for 2 minutes, crush with a fork, then prepare a vinaigrette with one part vinegar and three parts oil. Combine.

And once you've prepared your perfect dressing, be certain to really, really, coat the greens, turning the greens gently and carefully, over and over, until they are thoroughly coated. In French, the operation is known as "fatiguer la salade." Your job will be that much easier if you use an oversized shallow bowl.

LES PÂTES

Pastas

Pasta, but isn't that Italian? Yes and no. Pastas, fresh and dried, can traditionally be found in many regions of France, particularly in those along the Italian border and the Côte d'Azur. In Nice, small family restaurants classically serve portions of pasta with basil-flecked sauces, while a bit farther north in the Vaucluse, you'll find the local black truffles tossed with fresh egg pastas. In the Drôme, in northern Provence, ravioli is a local speciality, and many Parisian bistros have made this tiny goat-cheese-filled pasta a popular side dish. There's no question that pastas have become increasingly fashionable in Paris bistros: Fresh thin noodles tossed with tiny squid; pasta laced with ham, lemon, and black olives; and pasta with freshly steamed mussels are just a few examples. In all cases, these pasta recipes can serve as a first course or a main course—according to the appetite, season, or time of day.

PÂTES AUX CITRON, JAMBON, ET OLIVES NOIRES LE PROCOPE

◆ ◆

Le Procope's Pasta with Lemon, Ham, and Black Olives

I really get carried away with this dish. I never seem to make it the same way twice, always adding something here, subtracting something there, usually on the basis of what's at hand. The combination was inspired by a version (not very well executed, I must confess) I sampled one August night at Le Procope, the Paris brasserie that bills itself as the oldest café in the world. It's a vibrant marriage: lemon juice and flecks of lemon zest, thin pasta, olive oil, black olives, thin strips of cured ham. At the end, I like to shower the tossed pasta with tons of freshly snipped thyme and lots of coarsely ground black peppercorns. The first time I tested this recipe, I had just returned from a trip to the Loire Valley, and had a bottle of Vouvray sec chilling in the refrigerator. I knew even before I sampled the two together, that they'd be a marriage made in heaven. And they were!

¼ *cup (6 cl) freshly squeezed lemon juice*
Salt
½ *cup (12.5 cl) extra-virgin olive oil*
8 *slices salt-cured unsmoked ham, such as prosciutto (about 8 ounces; 250 g), cut into thin strips*
½ *cup (100 g) oil-cured black olives, preferably from Nyons, pitted*
2 *teaspoons freshly snipped thyme*
Grated zest of 2 lemons
Coarsely ground black pepper
1 *pound (500 g) thin pasta, such as angel hair or capellini*

A SALT TIP

When boiling water for pasta or blanching vegetables, I always forget whether or not I've salted the water. Now I always salt at the very end, measuring the amount of water at the beginning. Two tablespoons of salt for each 3 quarts (liters) of water makes for perfectly salted pasta or blanched vegetables.

1. Pour the lemon juice into a small bowl. Season lightly with salt. Add the oil and stir gently with a fork to blend. Set the dressing aside.

2. In a large, shallow serving bowl, combine the ham, olives, thyme, and lemon zest. Season with salt and pepper, and toss to blend.

3. Just before serving time, bring a large pot of water to a rolling boil. Salt the water, add the pasta, and cook just until tender. Drain. Add the pasta to the ingredients in the serving bowl. Pour on the dressing and toss gently.

4. To serve, place a portion of pasta on each dinner plate, being careful to evenly divide the ham and olives. Sprinkle each portion with coarsely ground black pepper and serve.

Yield: 6 to 8 servings

TAGLIATELLE AUX MOULES BRASSERIE LE COQ

Brasserie Le Coq's Fresh Pasta with Mussels

Although we tend to identify Italy as the origin of most pasta dishes, France is and has long been a nation of avid pasta eaters. It is rare to see a bistro or brasserie menu that does not include at least one pasta offering. This dish, which I sampled one sunny Saturday afternoon at Paris's Brasserie Le Coq on the Place de la Trocadéro, has become a household favorite. It's really a pasta salad, one that can be served luke-warm or at room temperature. This salad serves two as a satisfactory main course, or four as a first course.

3 tablespoons best-quality sherry wine vinegar
1 teaspoon Herbes de Provence (see Index)
2 tomatoes, peeled, cored, seeded, and chopped
2 shallots, cut into thin rings
¼ cup (6 cl) extra-virgin olive oil

Salt
8 ounces (250 g) fresh tagliatelle or fettuccine
2 pounds (1 kg) fresh mussels
3 large fresh garlic cloves
3 to 4 tablespoons finely minced fresh parsley

1. Combine the sherry vinegar, herbs, tomatoes, shallots, oil, and salt to taste in a small bowl. Stir to blend; set aside. The vinaigrette can be prepared several hours in advance.

2. Bring a large pot of water to a rolling boil. Add salt and the pasta and cook just until tender. Drain thoroughly. Transfer the pasta to a large, shallow serving bowl. Add the vinaigrette and toss to coat. Set aside.

3. Thoroughly scrub the mussels and rinse in several changes of water. Beard the mussels. (Do not beard the mussels in advance, or they will die and spoil.)

4. Place the cleaned mussels in a large shallow skillet and cover. (You need not add any liquid or seasonings; the mussels will give off liquid as they open.) Turn the heat to high and cook, covered, just until the mussels open, 2 or 3 minutes; do not overcook. Remove from the heat, discarding any mussels that didn't open. Set the mussels aside.

5. Strain the mussel cooking liquid through a fine sieve or several thicknesses of dampened cheesecloth. Add ½ cup (12.5 cl) of the liquid to the pasta and vinaigrette and toss. (Since the amount of liquid given off by mussels varies, add as much mussel liquid as necessary to make a proper sauce.)

6. Remove the mussels from the shells and add to the pasta. Allow the salad to marinate for about 20 minutes.

7. Just before serving, chop the garlic. Add the garlic and parsley to the pasta, and toss gently. Serve immediately.

Yield: 4 servings

MOULES AUX PÂTES À LA NIÇOISE

Mussels and Pasta with Anchovies, Capers, and Garlic

I've never seen this dish served in a bistro in Nice, but I found a version of it in a little mussel cookbook I bought on a trip to the Charentes, along the Atlantic Coast, where mussels are plentiful.

The first time I prepared it, I thought I had purchased fresh chervil. Wrong, it was fresh and pungent cilantro, not an herb used in abundance in the south of France. The mistake turned out to be a great one, for the dish was a big hit.

Since then, I've varied it each time I prepare it, using handfuls of other fresh herbs from my garden. With it, serve a wine that can stand up to all this power, such as a chilled rosé de Provence.

2 pounds (1 kg) fresh mussels
1 cup (25 cl) dry white wine, such as
    Riesling
4 shallots, minced
10 medium tomatoes (about 2 pounds;
    1 kg), peeled, cored, seeded, and
    chopped
1 pound (500 g) fresh tagliatelle
1 can (2 ounces; 57 g) flat anchovy
    fillets in olive oil, drained, patted
    dry, and coarsely chopped
1 tablespoon drained capers
4 fat garlic cloves, finely minced
A handful of fresh herbs, preferably a
    mix of basil, parsley, and tarra-
    gon, or all cilantro

1. Thoroughly scrub the mussels and rinse with several changes of water. Beard the mussels. (Do not beard the mussels in advance, or they will spoil and die.)

2. Combine the wine and mussels in a nonreactive large, deep skillet and bring the wine to a boil over high heat. Cover and cook just until the mussels open, about 5 minutes. Do not overcook. Remove from the heat, strain, and reserve the liquid. Discard any mussels that do not open. Leave the cooked mussels in their shells.

3. Combine the strained cooking liquid and the shallots in a nonreactive small saucepan. Cook over high heat just until the shallots are soft, about 5 minutes.

4. Stir in the tomatoes and cook until soft, about 20 minutes. The mixture should be fairly soupy.

5. Bring a large pot of water to a boil. Salt the water and add the pasta and cook just until tender.

6. While the pasta cooks, stir the chopped anchovies and the capers into the tomato and shallot mixture. Add the mussels and toss to coat with the sauce. At the last minute, sprinkle the garlic and herbs over the sauce.

7. To serve, drain the pasta and divide it among 4 to 6 warmed, shallow soup bowls. Spoon the sauce and mussel mixture over the pasta, allowing each diner to toss the sauce himself.

Yield: 4 to 6 servings

SAUTÉ DE CHIPIRONS AUX PÂTES FRAÎCHES

Squid in Tomato Sauce with Fresh Pasta

One wintry February day my husband and I sort of stumbled upon a Parisian bistro with a name I love: Jean-Claude et Ses Amis, or Jean-Claude and his friends. We wandered in and had a marvelous time, sitting elbow-to-elbow with the businessmen and shopkeepers who frequent this lively bistro just off the fashionable Avenue George V. I sampled this rather spicy, piquant dish that combines tender squid, a well-seasoned tomato sauce, and tender ribbons of fresh pasta. Three days later, I prepared a variation using Mediterranean-fresh squid, my own well-seasoned tomato sauce, and fresh fettuccine. I don't like to boast, but the homemade version was even better! With this dish, serve a robust red, such as Vacqueyras, from the Provençal town of the same name.

1 pound (500 g) fresh squid
4 shallots, finely minced
4 large fresh garlic cloves, finely
    minced
1 teaspoon Herbes de Provence (see
    Index)
¼ teaspoon hot pepper flakes (optional)
Salt
12 ounces (375 g) fresh tagliatelle or
    fettuccine
2½ cups (62.5 cl) Basic Tomato Sauce
    (see Index)
¼ cup (6 cl) extra-virgin olive oil

1. Cut the squid mantle crosswise into very thin rings. Chop the tentacles. Set aside.
2. In a small bowl, combine the shallots, garlic, herbs, and hot pepper flakes; toss gently. Set aside.
3. Bring a large pot of water to a rolling boil. Add the salt and pasta

CLEANING SQUID

To clean squid, first cut off the tentacles just above the eyes. Then squeeze out and discard the hard little beak just inside the tentacles at the point where they join the head. Use your fingers to pull out the guts and the cuttlebone, or quill, from the body. Don't worry about removing the grayish skin, which is edible. Rinse thoroughly in cold water and drain well.

and cook just until tender. Drain. Return the pasta to the pan. Add the tomato sauce and toss thoroughly. Keep warm over very low heat.

4. Heat the oil in a large skillet over high heat until hot but not smoking. Add the garlic and shallot mixture and sauté until the shallots begin to turn translucent, 1 to 2 min-

utes. Add the squid and sauté until the squid turns white, just 2 to 3 minutes. Do not overcook or the squid will get rubbery.

5. To serve, arrange the pasta on a large platter. Spoon the squid on top, leaving the liquid it gives off in the pan. Serve immediately.

Yield: 4 servings

TAGLIATELLE SAUCE CATANESE

Fresh Pasta with Tomato, Eggplant, and Pepper Sauce

I think that the cultures of the Mediterranean must have at least 365 variations on the tomato, eggplant, and red pepper triumvirate, enough to sample one version each day of the year. This dish comes from a tiny family bistro in the center of old Nice, a combination pasta-shop and restaurant known as Tosello. One winter evening, having spent the day strolling through the maze of narrow streets in search of local street food, my friend Maggie and I were in the mood for a simple plate of pasta. I fell in love with this dish, and it's now a part of my regular pasta repertoire. If, by the slightest chance, you have any left over, it's delicious the next day as a cold salad. With it drink a sturdy red, such as a Côtes-du-Rhône.

4 tablespoons extra-virgin olive oil
10 medium tomatoes (about 2 pounds; 1 kg), peeled, cored, seeded, and coarsely chopped
1 large (about 1 pound; 500 g) eggplant, unpeeled, cut into bite-size cubes

4 large red bell peppers, cored, seeded, and cut into bite-size cubes
½ teaspoon hot red pepper flakes (optional)
Salt and freshly ground black pepper
1 pound (500 g) fresh tagliatelle

1. Heat 2 tablespoons of the oil in large, deep-sided skillet over medium-high heat. Add the tomatoes and cook for about 10 minutes, stirring from time to time.

2. Meanwhile, in another large skillet heat the remaining 2 tablespoons oil over medium-high heat until hot but not smoking. Add the eggplant, and cook for several minutes, stirring, to brown on all sides.

3. Add the eggplant and then the bell peppers to the tomatoes. Stir. Season with the hot pepper flakes and salt and pepper to taste. Cover and simmer gently for about 1 hour.

4. Just before serving time, bring a large pot of water to a rolling boil. Salt the water, add the pasta, and cook just until tender. Drain.

5. To serve, divide the pasta evenly among 4 to 6 dinner plates. Spoon the sauce over the pasta, allowing each diner to toss the sauce when served.

Yield: 4 to 6 servings

TRUC

If your recipe cards are always flying around the kitchen as you cook, secure the recipe between the tines of a fork, then place the fork tine-side up in a tall glass.

PÂTES AU PISTOU VIEUX NICE

Pasta with Creamy Pesto from Old Nice

I first sampled this dish one January evening in the old town of Nice, in the small family bistro Tosello. The Tosello family makes all sorts of superb fresh pasta, and that evening, this dish really hit the spot. It's a version of pesto, substituting cream for the usual olive oil.

*2 cups (50 cl) loosely packed fresh
  basil leaves*
*1 cup (25 cl) crème fraîche (see Index)
  or heavy cream*
1 pound (500 g) fresh tagliatelle or

* fettuccine*
*1 cup (3.5 ounces; 100 g) freshly
  grated imported Parmesan cheese*

1. In a food processor, chop the basil. Add the crème fraîche and process to blend. Place the creamy basil sauce in a large bowl in which you will serve the pasta.

2. Bring a large pot of water to a rolling boil. Add the salt and pasta and cook just until tender. Drain.

3. Just before serving, stir the Parmesan into the sauce and blend thoroughly. Add the pasta to the bowl, toss, and serve.

Yield: 4 servings

LES PÂTES FRAÎCHES AUX TRUFFES DE VAUCLUSE

Fresh Pasta with Black Truffles and Cream

Chef Guy Jullien is a man of passions, a man who displays an unabashed love for his heady local wines and fragrant black truffles. At the small country restaurant he runs with his wife, Tina, the fruits of the soil of his native Provence are treated with a rare and wholesome respect.

This traditional preparation of fresh pasta and black truffles is a dish born of simplicity and filled with gutsy intensity. With the pasta, he served a rare white Châteauneuf from Château de Beaucastel, a 1986 Roussanne Vieille Vigne, a small production wine made up of some of the older vines on the estate. Although one commonly thinks of red wine with black truffles, Monsieur Jullien feels that with almost all truffle preparations—from foie gras to omelets, even with truffle salads—white wine is best. And he's right. The intense aroma of fresh truffles, the cream, the flowery fullness of white Châteauneuf served as a perfect palate opener. For this, and all his truffle dishes, the truffles are never cooked, but only gently warmed, so their flavor and fragrance are shown to their best advantage. Fresh truffles, of course are best, but good-quality preserved truffles can also be used.

Salt
1 pound (500 g) fresh fettuccine
1 cup (25 cl) crème fraîche (see Index)
  or heavy cream
4 ounces (120 g) black truffles, gently
  rinsed and patted dry (see Note)

1. Bring a large pot of water to a rolling boil. Add the salt and pasta and cook just until tender. Drain.

2. Meanwhile, in a small saucepan, warm the crème fraîche over low heat and bring it just to a gentle simmer.

3. About 1 minute before draining the pasta, break or chop the truffles into large chunks. (For example, a truffle the size of a marble should be broken or chopped into eighths.) Add the truffles to the cream and warm the truffles but do not cook them.

4. Toss the drained pasta with the truffles and cream. Arrange on 4 warmed dinner plates; serve immediately.

Yield: 4 servings

Note: If using fresh truffles, carefully brush them clean with a small, firm brush. If using preserved truffles in a jar (preferable to those in a tin, because you can see what you are getting), simply drain them and use as is.

"Gourmandise unites ancient Greek elegance, ancient Roman luxury, and French delicatesse."

—BRILLAT-SAVARIN

PISTOU LA MERENDA

La Merenda's Pasta with Pesto

Green on green, I love it! Whenever I lunch at La Merenda, a small family restaurant near Nice's lush *Cours Saleya* market, I order this dish. I know that the pesto is made with the fruity local olive oil from Alziari, and I derive great pleasure in watching Madame Guisti lovingly, carefully toss the pasta in her huge white salad bowl. I always order the same meal here: deep-fried zucchini blossoms to start, this pasta for a main course, fresh raspberries for dessert. Some rituals are just too good to change! With it sample a sun-filled red, such as a Côtes-du-Provence.

Salt
1 pound (500 g) fresh spinach pasta, preferably fettuccine
Pistou (recipe follows), double the recipe

1. Bring a large pot of water to a rolling boil. Salt the water. Add the pasta and cook until just tender. Drain. Place the pasta in a large, shallow bowl.

2. Add the pistou to the pasta and toss gently and thoroughly until the pasta is evenly coated with the sauce.

Yield: 4 servings

PISTOU

Basil and Garlic Sauce

Pistou is a cliché that does not deserve to be one. Singing of summer and the sun, this rich sauce, also familiar as the Italian pesto, finds its way into pastas, soups, and even as a spread for toasted country bread. When basil is plentiful, prepare the recipe without the pine nuts or Parmesan and freeze it for later use. Once thawed, place the pistou in a food processor, add the pine nuts, and process until smooth. Then stir in the freshly grated Parmesan.

2 cups (50 cl) loosely packed fresh basil leaves
½ cup (12.5 cl) extra-virgin olive oil
2 tablespoons fresh pine nuts
3 large garlic cloves, halved
Salt
½ cup (2 ounces; 50 g) freshly grated Parmesan cheese

1. Place the basil, oil, nuts, garlic and salt in a food processor. Process to a fine purée.

2. Scrape the mixture into a medium-size bowl. Stir in the cheese. Season with salt to taste.

Yield: 1 cup (25 cl)

> **❝**The first conditions of a pleasant meal depend, essentially, upon the proper choice of guests.**❞**
>
> —HENRI BÉRAU

LA MACARONADE

Macaroni Gratin

To prepare an authentic *macaronade,* you must first prepare a meat stew, either an *estouffade* or a *daube,* the traditional beef stews of the south of France. Once the noodles have been cooked, you moisten them with the wine-rich broth, layer them with freshly grated Parmesan cheese, and allow the gratin to brown lightly in the oven.

Salt
1 pound (500 g) elbow macaroni
1 cup (25 cl) liquid reserved from a
    beef stew
1 cup (3.5 ounces; 100 g) freshly
    grated imported Parmesan cheese

1. Preheat the broiler
2. Bring a large pot of water to a rolling boil. Salt the water and add the pasta and cook until tender. Drain.

   3. Spoon half of the noodles into a 2-quart (2 l) gratin dish. Moisten with the stew liquid. Sprinkle with half of the cheese. Add the remaining noodles, liquid, and cheese. Place under the broiler and broil just until the cheese is browned and sizzling.

Yield: 4 servings

RAVIOLES À LA CRÈME DU LAURIER ET DE LA SAUGE

Ravioli with Cream, Bay Leaf, and Sage

Along with a big platter of red peppers sautéed with chunks of spicy sausage, this is one of my favorite Provençal preparations for a crowd. Our village has a superb fresh pasta shop, run by a charming couple who came from Milan years ago. They make excellent cheese-filled ravioli, which I buy in quantity, cook up, and then serve, bathed in a blend of bay leaf-infused cream, sprinkled, at the very last minute, with snips of fresh sage from the garden. The dish, inspired by one I sampled several years ago at a bistro in old Nice, easily can be doubled or tripled, depending upon the number of guests you are serving.

1 cup (25 cl) heavy cream
6 imported bay leaves
Salt
1 pound (500 g) fresh cheese-filled
    ravioli
Large handful of fresh sage, rinsed
    and patted dry
Freshly ground black pepper

1. In a large, shallow skillet that will hold all of the pasta later on, combine the cream and bay leaves. Bring to a boil over high heat. Reduce the heat to very low and simmer gently for 3 or 4 minutes, to infuse the cream with the flavor of bay. Remove and discard the bay leaves.

2. Meanwhile, bring a large pot of water to a boil. Salt the water and add the ravioli and cook until just tender. Drain.

3. Add the ravioli to the cream mixture and toss to coat with the cream.

4. Evenly divide the pasta among 4 shallow, warmed serving bowls. Spoon the sauce over the pasta. With scissors, snip the sage and sprinkle it on top of each serving. Sprinkle generously with the pepper and serve immediately.

Yield: 4 servings

A SUMMERTIME FEAST FOR FOUR TO FORTY

I've served this exact menu dozens of times in Provence, and it's always a hit. It's a collection of recipes that can all be doubled or tripled as necessary, and none takes any last-minute work. I generally serve a Côtes du Rhône, such as a Cru de Coudoúlet from Château Beaucastel, or a Gigondas from Georges Faraud.

RAVIOLES À LA CREME DU LAURIER ET DE LA SAUGE
Ravioli with Cream, Bay Leaf, and Sage

◆

LES POIVRONS ROUGES DE MAGGIE
Maggie's Roasted Red Peppers

◆

GIGOT RÔTI AU GRATIN DE MONSIEUR HENNY
Roast Lamb with Monsieur Henny's Potato, Onion, and Tomato Gratin

◆

TARTE AMANDINE LE PETIT MARGUERY
Le Petit Marguery's Fruit and Almond Tart

LES LÉGUMES DE SAISON

Seasonal Vegetables

As a bona fide vegetable lover and one-time vegetarian, I am constantly on the lookout for new ways to prepare vegetables. Many of the following recipes, it comes as no surprise, take root in Provence, for that's where the bulk of France's fresh vegetables are grown. Plump red tomatoes are sprinkled with garlic, parsley, and bread crumbs for the fragrant Provençal Roast Tomatoes. For the ever-favorite ratatouille, winemaker Françoise Rigord goes to her vegetable garden for eggplant, zucchini, tomatoes, and peppers. Of all the recipes, though, my personal favorite comes from my friend Maggie Shapiro, who first sampled a dish of roasted red peppers at a neighborhood Paris bistro, then recreated it at home to make it her own. Since then we've both embellished the dish, boosting the quantity of hot peppers, and showing a rather wholesome enthusiasm for garlic. But that, after all, is what bistro food is all about—personalizing simple dishes, changing them to fit the mood and the palate.

Terrine de Poireaux aux Lamelles de Truffes Michel Trama

Michel Trama's Leek Terrine with Truffles

Several years ago, on my first visit to Michel and Maryse Trama's romantic little restaurant in the southwestern countryside, I sampled this marvelously simple, yet luxurious vegetable terrine. I've made it often since, for it is quick, easy, and impressive, especially when you are generous with the truffles. But if truffles don't seem appropriate, I delete them and enjoy the terrine, just the same. Once you've tasted this dish—really a classy variation on the bistro favorite, leeks in vinaigrette—you'll understand why the French call leeks "the poor man's asparagus."

12 leeks (about 4 pounds; 2 kg)
Salt and freshly ground black pepper
2 large black truffles (optional; see
    Note), gently rinsed and patted
    dry
¼ cup (6 cl) freshly squeezed lemon
    juice
1 cup (12.5 cl) extra-virgin olive oil
¼ cup (6 cl) boiling water

1. Trim off the white root base of the leeks, cutting as close to the base as possible, to keep the leeks neatly intact after cooking. Trim the leeks from the dark green end, to fit the length of the terrine. Carefully clean the leeks, rinsing them first in cold running water and then in a bowl of cold water until no grit appears. Cook the leeks in a large quantity of salted, boiling water (about 1 teaspoon salt for each quart of water) until tender, about 10 minutes. Gently remove each leek from the water, trying to keep the vegetable intact. Carefully refresh under cold water until thoroughly cooled. Drain well. (I like to wrap the leeks in a thick bath towel to absorb the excess liquid.)

2. Line a rectangular terrine, baking dish or loaf pan measuring about 12 × 4 inches (25.5 cm × 9 cm) with aluminum foil, leaving enough extra foil to wrap over the top of the terrine. Carefully arrange the leeks in a layer, with the white

root portions facing the same end. Press down to try to drain out any excess liquid. Arrange the second layer, with the white portions facing the opposite end. Continue in this manner until the terrine is filled to the top. There should be a minimum of 4 layers.

3. Cover with aluminum foil, pressing down firmly on the leeks. Weigh down the terrine and cover with more foil. Refrigerate for at least 12 hours.

4. Just before serving, cut the truffles into paper-thin slices, reserving any shavings for the vinaigrette. In a small bowl, combine the lemon juice, truffle shavings, and salt and pepper to taste. Whisk in the oil. Whisk in the boiling water.

5. Carefully unmold the terrine onto a long, rectangular serving dish. With a very sharp knife, carefully trim off the ends to neaten up the terrine. Cut into thick slices, and sauce with the vinaigrette, decorating with the truffles.

Yield: 8 servings

Note: If using fresh truffles, carefully brush them clean with a small, firm brush. If using preserved truffles in a jar (preferable to those in a tin, because you can see what you are getting), simply drain them and use as is.

PERFUMED OILS

Marinate a fresh or a preserved truffle in a small jar of extra-virgin olive oil for 3 or 4 days in the refrigerator. The truffle can still be used in cooking, and you'll have the advantage of the truffle-flavored oil for cooking or for salads.

TIAN DE LÉGUMES

Layered Vegetable Gratin

François Perraud, chef at the Domaine de l'Enclos in Gordes, in Provence, serves this traditional layered vegetable terrine, locally known as a *tian,* with grilled beef in a grainy mustard sauce. I could—and do—make a meal out of the *tian* alone, for it features all of the best flavors of Provence, including tomatoes, zucchini, eggplant, and thyme. It's a cinch to make, and I find that it tastes even better the next day, if you should happen to have some left over!

2 small onions, each weighing about 4
ounces (125 g)
2 small eggplants, each weighing
about 10 ounces (300 g)
4 small zucchini, each weighing about
4 ounces (125 g)
5 small tomatoes, each weighing about
3 ounces (90 g)
1 garlic clove, peeled
2 teaspoons fresh thyme
Salt
¼ cup (6 cl) extra-virgin olive oil

1. Preheat the oven to 350°F
(175°C).

2. Wash the vegetables, and peel
the onion. Cut vegetables into thin
rounds.

3. Generously rub the bottom
of a shallow 5-cup (1.25 l) gratin dish
with the garlic. Sprinkle with some
of the thyme. Add the sliced onion
in a single layer. Sprinkle with salt to
taste and more of the thyme. Drizzle
on some of the olive oil. Continue
layering in this manner with the
eggplant, zucchini, and tomatoes,
sprinkling each layer with salt,
thyme, and oil. Cover securely with
aluminum foil. Bake until the vegetables are very soft and tender, about
1 hour. Serve immediately.

Yield: 4 servings

A BISTRO BUFFET WITH AN AMERICAN ACCENT (BRING A DISH TO PASS)

When I was growing up, people always brought a dish to pass, usually
a vegetable dish or a salad. Try this
assortment of vegetable dishes with
your favorite chicken.

GRATIN D'OIGNONS À LA FÉLIX BENOÎT
Félix Benoît's Onion Gratin

RATATOUILLE FRANÇOISE RIGORD
Françoise Rigord's Mixed Provençal Vegetables

TIAN DE LÉGUMES
Layered Vegetable Gratin

TOMATES À LA PROVENÇALE
Provençal Roast Tomatoes

POMMES À L'HUILE
Warm Potato Salad with Herbed Vinaigrette

POULET MISTRAL
Mistral's Chicken with Garlic

QUATRE-QUARTS AUX POIRES
Pear Pound Cake

OSEILLE FONDUE

Wilted Sorrel Sauce

This is a basic recipe, meaning you can use the sauce as is, as a vegetable, as a base for soups, for omelets, or mixed with spinach. On its own, I love it as an omelet filling. As you'll note, the sorrel isn't really cooked, it's wilted or melted, or as the French say *fondue*.

8 ounces (250 g) fresh sorrel
1 tablespoon (½ ounce; 15 g) unsalted
     butter
1 tablespoon crème fraîche (see Index)
     or heavy cream
Salt and freshly ground black pepper

1. Unless the sorrel is very young, it will need to be ribbed and stemmed. Wash and spin dry the sorrel. Cut off the stem and remove the firm center rib.

2. Combine the sorrel and the butter in a nonreactive large saucepan over low heat. Stir from time to time as the sorrel begins to wilt. When it has given up most of its liquid, stir in the crème fraîche and continue cooking just until all of the leaves have wilted and turned from bright green to dark green. Season with salt and pepper to taste. Serve immediately.

Yield: 4 servings

GRATIN D'OIGNONS À LA FÉLIX BENOÎT

Félix Benoît's Onion Gratin

Félix Benoît is a food writer and journalist from Lyons, the city many consider the capital of bistro cuisine. Over the years, not only has he tracked down all of the best bistros to be found in Lyons and its surroundings, but as a good historian, he has also recorded the recipes from these homey, family-style eating spots. Therefore, it seems fitting that this incredible onion gratin has been named in his honor.

Do find the freshest sweet onions possible (the delicious ones from Vidalia, Georgia, are perfect), and don't skimp on either the freshly ground pepper or the freshly grated nutmeg. The last time I prepared this, I used almost an entire nutmeg! I love the way your mouth tingles after a few bites of these deliciously seasoned onions. (Remember, it's the nutmeg that really flavors this dish, so please don't skimp!) This gratin would go nicely with a simple roast, or serve as a vegetarian dish, accompanied by a simple green salad.

2 pounds (1 kg) large sweet white
    onions
3 tablespoons crème fraîche (see Index)
    or heavy cream
Freshly grated nutmeg
Salt and freshly ground black pepper

1. Preheat the oven to 375°F (190°C).

2. Peel the onions. Place them in a large pot of boiling, salted water and cook, uncovered, until fairly soft, but not falling apart, about 20 minutes.

3. Drain the onions, and, when they are cool enough to handle, slice each onion into 3 or 4 even rounds. Don't worry if some of the slices fall apart and the onions separate. In a large bowl, toss the onions with the crème fraîche; season very generously with the nutmeg, salt, and pepper.

4. Spoon the onions into a medium gratin dish or a 10½-inch (27 cm) round glass or porcelain baking dish. Bake until the onions are soft and golden, about 30 minutes. Serve immediately.

Yield: 8 servings

TRUC

To prevent whole onions from breaking apart as they cook, peel them, make an incision in the form of a cross at the root end, then proceed with the recipe.

TOMATES FARCIES CHEZ LA VIEILLE

Chez La Vieille's Stuffed Tomatoes

During the summer and early fall, *tomates farcies,* or stuffed tomatoes, are often part of the copious first-course selections that are passed from table to table at Adrienne Biasin's cozy Paris bistro, Chez la Vieille. Adrienne varies the stuffing according to what she has on hand, like any natural cook who prepares the same dish often. If she has made *pot-au-feu,* or boiled beef, the day before, she may chop up some of the flavorful meat and add it to the savory sausage and ham stuffing. I like her tip for adding rice to the bottom of the baking dish: The rice absorbs the liquid and cooks to tooth tenderness as the tomatoes bake away, making for a flavorful sauce to spoon over the tomatoes.

In other seasons, Adrienne wraps boiled cabbage leaves around the stuffing, and bakes little cabbage rolls in the same manner. This dish can be served warm or cold as a first course, or can make a nice luncheon dish all on its own, accompanied by a tossed salad and grilled country bread.

4 tablespoons (2 ounces; 60 g) un-salted butter
¼ cup (50 g) long-grain rice
4 large tomatoes, 6 medium, or 8 small tomatoes (about 2 pounds; 1 kg)
3 shallots, finely minced
2 garlic cloves, finely minced
6 ounces (190 g) sliced boiled ham
6 ounces (190 g) bulk pork sausage
1 large egg
A small handful of fresh herbs, prefer-ably a blend of chives, flat-leaf parsley, and thyme
Salt and freshly ground black pepper

1. Preheat the oven to 425°F (220°C).

2. Using 1 tablespoon of the butter, coat a straight-sided 10½-inch (27 cm) round glass or porcelain baking dish. Sprinkle the rice on the bottom of the dish.

3. Cut a slice off the stem end of each tomato and reserve each top. Scoop out the pulp and seeds and reserve.

4. Melt 1 tablespoon of the butter in a small skillet. Add the shallots and garlic and cook over medium-low heat until golden, about 5 minutes. Reserve.

5. Place the ham in a food processor and coarsely chop. Add the sausage, egg, herbs, the shallot and garlic mixture, and the reserved tomato pulp and seeds, and process until the ingredients are thoroughly blended. Season very lightly with salt and pepper.

6. Stuff the tomatoes with the mixture, heaping it until all of the stuffing mixture is used. Replace the tomato tops, and arrange the stuffed tomatoes on top of the rice in the prepared baking dish. Dot with the remaining 2 tablespoons of butter. Bake until nicely browned, about 35 minutes.

Yield: 4 to 8 servings

TOMATES À LA PROVENÇALE

Provençal Roast Tomatoes

I first tasted these tomatoes at our local pizzeria in Provence, La Pizzeria de Vieux Vaison. There the dish is roasted in a giant, wood-fired bread oven, where the tomatoes become just slightly charred and begin to take on that sweet, caramel flavor. A friend tried these one wintry day in the north, and replied: "These were delicious, even with horrid out-of-season tomatoes." Eight cloves of garlic may seem like a lot, but believe me, you'll thank me once you sample these.

8 firm, ripe, round tomatoes (about 2 pounds, 1 kg), cored and halved crosswise
Salt and freshly ground black pepper
8 garlic cloves
¾ cup (100 g) fresh bread crumbs
A handful of fresh flat-leaf parsley, finely minced
3 tablespoons extra-virgin olive oil

1. Preheat the oven to 400°F (205°C).

2. Arrange the tomatoes, cut sides up, in a large baking dish. (Unless the tomatoes are exceptionally watery, do not seed or drain them: The tomatoes will hold their shape better and the natural juices will mingle nicely with the garlic and herbs.) Season generously with salt and pep-

per. Slice the garlic into thin chips and sprinkle over the tomatoes. Combine the bread crumbs and parsley, and scatter the mixture over the tomatoes. Drizzle on the oil.

3. Bake, uncovered, until the tomatoes are soft, browned, and sizzling, about 1 hour. Serve immediately.

Yield: 8 servings

LES POIVRONS ROUGES DE MAGGIE

Maggie's Roasted Red Peppers

I'm not sure why, but I always feel just a bit more secure when there's a jar of what I call "Maggie's Peppers"—a blend of sweet red peppers, hot peppers, garlic, and olive oil, cooked to a melting tenderness—sitting on the top shelf of my refrigerator. I've found so many uses for these sweet, pungent peppers that I sometimes wonder what I did before my friend Maggie Shapiro made them for me one Saturday in the spring.

I find these peppers are delicious served hot (they're super over grilled tuna), and they're an essential ingredient in Pan Bagna, that hearty Provençal sandwich that's been called *salade niçoise* on a bun (see Index). They're also delicious, all on their own, as a chilled condiment, or can be tossed into warm pasta. I can't always find hot peppers in the market, so I often substitute hot pepper flakes. The hot peppers, of course, can be added to taste. The natural oils from the pepper mingle with the olive oil to make for a lovely, beautiful preserve. The peppers can be stored, well sealed and covered with liquid, for several weeks.

5 ounces (150 g) small, mildly hot green chiles (such as serrano), or 2 to 3 ounces (60 to 90 g) hot green chiles, cut into thick strips (or substitute 1 teaspoon hot red pepper flakes)

6 large red bell peppers (about 3 pounds; 1.5 kg), cored, seeded, and cut into thick strips

2 heads of garlic, minced

¼ cup (6 cl) extra-virgin olive oil

1. Preheat the oven to 400°F (205°C).

2. Seed the chiles and slice them into thin strips, removing the white ribs on the inside. (When preparing chiles, be sure to wear rubber gloves to protect your hands.)

3. Layer the chiles, bell peppers, garlic, and olive oil in a very large, shallow baking dish. Cover with aluminum foil. Bake until the peppers are quite soft, 45 minutes to 1 hour. Uncover and continue baking until the peppers are just slightly charred and very soft, about 45 more minutes.

4. Serve hot as a side dish, or store, covered, in a large jar and serve chilled, as a condiment.

Yield: 6 to 8 servings

RATATOUILLE FRANÇOISE RIGORD

Françoise Rigord's
Mixed Provençal Vegetables

Ratatouille is a classic bistro dish, found as often in Paris as in its home base of Provence. This recipe comes not from a bistro but from a winemaker, Françoise Rigord, who lives in the vine- and olive-rich segment of Provence due east of Aix-en-Provence.

In the fall, as harvesters are gathering the grapes that go into their delicate, floral rosé de Provence and their perfumed, elegant red Côtes-de-Provence, Madame Rigord offers up a mouth-watering menu of Mediterranean specialties. There will be, of course, her own ratatouille (with the vegetables cooked separately, so they maintain their own distinct flavors and identities), plus a grand aïoli, garlicky mayonnaise served with boiled, salted cod along with snails gathered from the vineyard throughout the period of the grape harvest. There might be lamb from their pastures, to be roasted whole, and no butter will be served, ever, only extra-virgin olive oil pressed from the Rigord's own olives. What's to drink? "It all depends upon who is picking," laughs the outgoing Madame Rigord. "I think red kills the taste of aïoli, I always suggest a rosé. But, inevitably, the core of pickers go for the red. And generally, they win."

6 tablespoons extra-virgin olive oil
5 medium onions (about 1 pound;
    500 g), coarsely chopped
Bouquet garni: 12 parsley stems, 8
    peppercorns, ½ teaspoon thyme,
    ¼ teaspoon fennel seed, and 1 im-
    ported bay leaf tied in a double
    thickness of cheesecloth
3 large red bell peppers (about 1
    pound, 500 g), cored, seeded, and
    cubed
2 to 3 small eggplant (about 1 pound;
    500 g), cubed
2 to 3 medium zucchini (about 1
    pound; 500 g), cubed
5 medium tomatoes (about 1 pound;
    500 g), cored and cut into eighths
Salt
1 lemon, halved
A handful of fresh parsley, finely
    minced

1. In a large, heavy, nonreactive skillet, heat 2 tablespoons of the oil over medium-low heat. Add the onions and bouquet garni and stir to coat with the oil. Cook, covered, stirring occasionally, until the onions are tender, and light golden, 20 minutes. Do not allow them to burn.

2. Add the bell peppers, stirring gently to mix, and continue to cook until the mixture is very soft, about 30 more minutes.

3. In another heavy nonreactive skillet, heat 2 tablespoons of oil over medium-low heat. Add the eggplant and stir to coat with the oil. Cook, covered, until soft, stirring from time to time to keep the eggplant from sticking to the pan, about 20 minutes.

4. In another heavy nonreactive skillet, heat the remaining 2 tablespoons of oil over medium-low heat. Add the zucchini and stir to coat with the oil. Cook, covered, until soft, stirring from time to time to prevent sticking, about 20 minutes.

5. While the eggplant and zucchini cook, add the tomatoes to the onion and pepper mixture. Cook, covered, over low heat, for another 15 minutes.

6. Gently spoon all of the vegetables into a colander set over a nonreactive saucepan or skillet that will collect the liquid. Spoon the vegetables into a large bowl. Place the pan of liquid over high heat and reduce

until thick and syrupy, 5 to 10 minutes. Pour over the vegetables and stir to blend. Season with salt to taste. Cover and refrigerate for 24 hours.

7. To serve, remove the ratatouille from the refrigerator about 15 minutes before serving. Adjust the seasoning. Squeeze the lemon juice over the top and sprinkle with the minced parsley. Serve.

Yield: 12 to 16 servings

GRATIN DE COURGETTES ET TOMATES

Tomato and Zucchini Gratin

This is really two recipes in one: a vegetable side dish to serve with a roast leg of lamb, simple roast chicken, or grilled fish; and a vegetable main course, embellished with a sprinkling of freshly grated Parmesan cheese. I love it either way. Unlike gratins made with potatoes, which take a good hour or so to cook, this one is ready in about 20 minutes. With it, serve a Bandol from the Mediterranean, such as Domaine Tempier.

1 garlic clove, halved
1 pound (500 g) zucchini (about 2 medium), ends trimmed, thinly sliced
8 small firm tomatoes (about 2 pounds; 1 kg), cored and thinly sliced
2 tablespoons extra-virgin olive oil
1 teaspoon fresh thyme
1 cup (3.5 ounces; 100 g) freshly grated imported Parmesan cheese (optional)

1. Preheat the oven to 450°F (230°C).

2. Rub the bottom of a large oval porcelain gratin dish about 14 × 9 × 2 inches (40.5 × 25.5 × 5 cm) with the garlic. Alternating slices of zucchini and tomato, arrange the vegetables in a single layer over the bottom of the gratin. Sprinkle with the thyme and the oil.

2. Bake, uncovered, until meltingly soft, about 20 minutes.

3. If serving as a side dish, place

under the broiler just until lightly browned. If serving as a main course, sprinkle with the Parmesan and broil until the cheese is bubbly and browned. Serve immediately.

Yield: 4 servings

CRÊPES AUX COURGETTES LA MÈRE POULARD

La Mère Poulard's Zucchini Crêpes

I first sampled these delightful crêpes at La Mère Poulard, the famous omelet restaurant at Mont-Saint-Michel in Normandy. There, they were served as a light side dish to accompany the *poulet au vinaigre,* or chicken in vinegar. Since then, I've found they're a welcome and unusual side dish—delicate, golden, and nonaggressive—and so they seem right with just about any dish. They're also fine on their own, accompanied by a tossed green salad.

2 medium zucchini (each about 8 ounces; 250 g)
1 large egg
2 tablespoons heavy cream
1 tablespoon all-purpose flour
2 garlic cloves, finely minced
About 2 tablespoons corn or peanut oil
About 2 tablespoons (1 ounce; 30 g) unsalted butter

1. Rinse the zucchini and trim off the ends. Shred the zucchini in a food processor or on a hand grater. In a stainless-steel strainer, arrange the shreds in layers, salting between layers. Place the strainer over a bowl to catch the liquid, and, pressing out the liquid from time to time, set aside for 30 minutes. With your hands, squeeze out any excess water.

2. In a medium-size bowl, whisk the egg with a fork. Add the cream, flour, and minced garlic and whisk to blend. Add the zucchini and toss with a fork in the egg mixture. The mixture should just coat the zucchini.

3. Heat 1 tablespoon of the oil and 1 tablespoon of the butter in a 12-inch (30.5 cm) nonstick crêpe pan over medium-high heat. When the fats are hot but not smoking, spoon

a heaping tablespoon of the zucchini mixture into the pan. Press the mixture down flat with the bottom of the spoon and smooth out the edges to form an even, 3-inch (7.5 cm) circle. Continue with 3 more spoonfuls to form additional crêpes. Cook until golden brown, 3 to 4 minutes. Using a large spatula, turn the crêpes, press down again, and cook the other side until browned, 2 to 3 more minutes. Adjust the heat as necessary. Repeat with the remaining batter, adding more butter and oil as necessary. Serve immediately.

Yield: 8 to 10 small crêpes

FENOUIL À LA GRECQUE

Fennel Braised in Broth and Wine

I f there is one thing I love about bistros, it's the unlimited assortment of first-course salads. There's such beauty in the simplicity and generosity in giant white bowls brimming with delicious plump mushrooms in herbs and oil, sweet ratatouille, sliced ripe tomatoes, or *fenouil à la grecque*. Unfortunately, it's getting harder and harder to find this sort of bistro, for such a complex assortment demands a great deal of labor. I like to make this dish in great quantities: It's delicious hot as well as cold.

6 *small fennel bulbs*
1 *cup (25 cl) chicken stock, preferably homemade*
½ *cup (12.5 cl) extra-virgin olive oil*
1 *cup (25 cl) dry white wine, such as French Riesling*

Wash the fennel and remove any darkened portions. Halve the bulbs if large. Place the fennel in a large, deep nonreactive skillet, add the stock, oil, and wine. Bring to a simmer over medium heat. Cover and simmer gently, turning the fennel from time to time, until tender, about 45 minutes. Serve warm or cold.

Yield: 6 servings

CHOUX ROUGES BRAISÉS

◆

Braised Red Cabbage

I love cabbage in any form, especially fine strips of red cabbage, braised for hours with sliced apples, onions, cloves, a touch of red wine vinegar, and a healthy dose of hearty red wine. This vegetable side dish goes especially well with a simple roast duck, roast *pintade* (guinea hen), or any sort of pork. I also like it on its own, cold the next day as a luncheon salad.

2 tablespoons (1 ounce; 30 g) unsalted
    butter or lard
2 medium onions, thinly sliced
1 red cabbage (about 2 pounds; 1 kg),
    shredded
½ teaspoon salt
½ teaspoon sugar
4 apples, peeled, cored, and thinly sliced
4 whole cloves
1 medium onion, quartered
½ cup (12.5 cl) best-quality red wine
    vinegar
1 bottle (75 cl) dry red wine

1. Melt the butter in a nonreactive skillet over medium-high heat. When hot but not smoking add the sliced onions and cook until translucent. Add the cabbage, salt, sugar, and apples, and stir to evenly distribute the ingredients. Stick 1 whole clove in each of the onion quarters. Add the onion quarters, the vinegar, and the wine to the skillet. Cover and braise over very low heat, stirring from time to time, until the flavors mingle, the cabbage is very soft, and much of the liquid has been absorbed, about 2 hours. Adjust the seasonings.

2. Serve warm, with roast poultry or pork.

Yield: 8 to 10 servings

TRUC

Never blanch or cook red cabbage in boiling water, or all the bright red color will end up in the cooking water. If you don't braise the cabbage, as in this recipe, use it raw, grated, or sliced for salads.

LES POMMES DE TERRE

◆———————◆

Potatoes

I doubt that there's a bistro in France that does not have at least one potato dish on its menu. Gratins in a dozen disguises, potatoes that are sautéed, steamed, or boiled, potatoes laced with garlic and walnut oil, or grated and turned into rich golden pancakes—I'd be hard pressed to name my favorite among the recipes offered, except to say that I have wonderful visions of sitting in the sunshine of Provence, a giant ocher bowl of water at hand, peeling away for the next family feast!

Potatoes, of course, are one of the world's most magnificent, versatile, and inexpensive staples. After years of gathering guests around the table, I've realized that potatoes are a sure-fire winner, for almost no one dislikes them. So, whenever I entertain I always try to weave in at least one potato dish. The following preparations are part of my everyday repertoire.

GRATIN DAUPHINOIS MADAME CARTET

Madame Cartet's Potato Gratin

There are some recipes one can never have too many of in one's repertoire. And potato gratin is one of them. This is one of the easiest potato gratins I know, cooking in just under one hour, a simple but full-flavored blend of potatoes, fresh cream, garlic, and freshly grated Gruyère cheese. Twice each day, Thérèse Nouaille, of Paris's tiny neighborhood bistro Cartet, prepares this gratin for her steady customers: Make it yourself and you'll understand why they keep coming back!

1 garlic clove
2 pounds (1 kg) baking potatoes, such
    as russets, peeled and very thinly
    sliced
1 cup (about 3 ounces; 80 g) freshly
    grated French or Swiss Gruyère
    cheese
1 cup (25 cl) crème fraîche (see Index)
    or heavy cream
Salt

1. Preheat the oven to 350°F (175°C).
2. Thoroughly rub a shallow, 6-cup (1.5 l) porcelain gratin dish with the garlic. Layer half of the potatoes in the dish. Sprinkle with half of the cheese and then half of the crème fraîche. Sprinkle with salt. Add another layer, using the rest of the ingredients.
3. Bake, uncovered, until the gratin is crisp and golden on top, from 50 to 60 minutes. Serve immediately.

Yield: 4 to 6 servings

> **❝In 1793 potatoes were considered so indispensable that a decree of the French Republic ordered a census to be taken of luxury gardens, so that they could be devoted to the cultivation of this vegetable. As a result, the principal avenue in the Jardin des Tuileries and the flower beds were turned over to potato cultivation. This is why potatoes were for a long time given the additional name of 'royal oranges'.❞**
>
> —ALEXANDRE DUMAS
> *Dumas on Food*

GRATIN DAUPHINOIS MADAME LARACINE

Madame Laracine's Potato Gratin

Wherever I travel in France, I always ask cooks for tips on preparing potato gratins. In the Savoy region, many cooks mentioned the double-cooking method, in which you first cook the potatoes in milk and water, or simply in whole milk, discard the cooking liquid, and then bake the potatoes in a blend of cream and Gruyère cheese. It makes for a rich, satisfying gratin.

It's always dangerous to label anything the best, but in my memory, Madame Laracine—chef-proprietor of a small family *ferme-auberge* in the village of Ordonnaz—made a most stunning gratin, prepared with home-grown potatoes, milk and cream from her own cows, and cheese from a nearby dairy.

3 pounds (1.5 kg) baking potatoes,
   such as russets, peeled and very
   thinly sliced
2 cups (50 cl) whole milk
3 garlic cloves, minced
¾ teaspoon salt
3 imported bay leaves
Freshly ground nutmeg
Freshly ground black pepper
1 cup (25 cl) crème fraîche (see Index)
   or heavy cream
2 cups (about 5 ounces; 160 g) freshly
   grated imported French or Swiss
   Gruyère cheese

1. Preheat the oven to 375°F (190°C).

2. Place the potatoes in a large saucepan and cover with the milk and

2 cups (50 cl) of water. Add the garlic, salt, and bay leaves. Bring to a boil over medium-high heat, stirring occasionally so that the potatoes do not stick to the bottom of the pan. Reduce the heat to medium and cook, stirring from time to time, until the potatoes are tender but not falling apart, about 10 minutes.

3. Using a slotted spoon, transfer half of the potatoes to a large, 14 × 9 × 2 inch (35.5 × 23 × 5 cm) gratin dish. Sprinkle with the nutmeg, pepper, half the crème fraîche, and half the cheese. Cover with the remaining potatoes, and sprinkle again with nutmeg, pepper, and the remaining crème fraîche and cheese.

4. Bake the gratin until crisp and golden on top, about 1 hour. Serve immediately.

Yield: 6 to 8 servings

POMMES DE TERRE COMTOISES

◆

Potato Gratin with Cheese and Smoked Ham

Potatoes, ham, and cheese are the mainstays of the diet in the mountain-filled region of the Jura, home of some of the finest cow's milk cheese and some of the loveliest smoked meats in France. This gratin could easily be served as a main course. It goes well with a chilled red, such as Arbois from the Jura, or a good Beaujolais.

5 medium-thick slices smoked ham
  (about 4 ounces; 125 g)
4 tablespoons (2 ounces; 60 g) unsalted butter
2 pounds (1 kg) baking potatoes, such as russets, peeled and very thinly sliced
3 cups (about 8 ounces; 240 g) freshly grated imported French or Swiss Gruyère cheese
Freshly grated nutmeg
Salt and freshly ground black pepper

1. Preheat the oven to 375°F (190°C).

2. Trim all of the fat from the ham. Cut each slice into 1-inch (2.5-cm) wide strips.

3. Use 1 tablespoon of the butter to coat the inside of an oval porcelain baking dish about 14 × 9 × 2 inches (35.5 × 23 × 5 cm). Arrange half of the potatoes in an even layer in the dish.

4. Arrange half of the ham strips evenly over the potatoes. Distribute

half of the cheese over the ham. Season with nutmeg, salt, and pepper to taste. Arrange the remaining potatoes, ham, and cheese in even layers in the dish. Sprinkle on more nutmeg, salt, and pepper. Cut the remaining 3 tablespoons of butter into bits; dot the top evenly with butter.

5. Bake, uncovered, until the gratin is golden, about 50 minutes; do not overcook or the gratin will be dry and the ham rubbery. Serve immediately.

Yield: 6 servings

GRATIN DU JABRON

◆————◆

Individual Potato Gratin

I call this my quick gratin, for some of the work in preparing this dish can be done in advance, and the rest can be done at the last moment. The recipe, named for the Jabron river in the Drôme, comes not from a bistro, but from a wonderful restaurant in Provence, La Bonne Etape, run by the outgoing Gleize family. The restaurant may be an elegant one, but that doesn't stop them from offering bistro-style fare from time to time. What's nice about individual gratins is that they allow everyone to have an even portion of the best part of the gratin, the upper crust!

1 pound (500 g) baking potatoes, such as russets, peeled
Salt
5 tablespoons (2½ ounces; 75 g) unsalted butter
3 large garlic cloves, finely minced
Freshly ground black pepper
½ cup (2 ounces; 40 g) freshly grated imported French or Swiss Gruyère cheese
¼ cup (6 cl) crème fraîche (see Index) or heavy cream

1. Place the potatoes in a single layer in a saucepan. Cover with water; add salt to taste. Bring to a boil over high heat and cook until nearly cooked through but still firm in the center, about 15 minutes. Drain and let cool. Cut into thin slices. (This step can be done several hours in advance.)

2. Preheat the broiler.

3. Melt the butter in a large skillet over medium-high heat. When hot, add the potatoes and garlic and sauté, shaking the pan from time to time, until nicely browned, about 10 minutes.

4. With a spoon, transfer the potatoes in a single layer to 4 individual 6-inch (15 cm) round gratin dishes. Sprinkle with salt and pepper to taste. Sprinkle with cheese; dot with the crème fraîche. Broil until brown and bubbly, about 2 minutes.

Yield: 4 servings

GRATIN DE POMMES DE TERRE ET DE CÉLERI-RAVE

Potato and Celery Root Gratin

E ven in France, where a great deal of *céleri rave* (also known as celeriac) is consumed, cooks are not very creative with their use of this earthy root vegetable. It appears generally as *céleri rémoulade,* a crisp and creamy salad of grated celery root. Here, it's combined with potatoes to make a winning vegetable gratin.

4 baking potatoes, such as russets,
    peeled
Salt
1 celery root
2 tablespoons freshly squeezed lemon
    juice
2 tablespoons peanut oil
4 large tomatoes (about 1 pound; 500
    kg), peeled, cored, seeded, and
    chopped
1 garlic clove, minced
Freshly ground black pepper
¾ cup (18.5 cl) crème fraîche (see
    Index) or heavy cream
2 cups (about 5 ounces; 160 g) freshly
    grated French or Swiss Gruyère
    cheese

1. Preheat the oven to 400°F (205°C).

2. Place the potatoes in a single layer in a saucepan. Cover with water, add salt to taste, and bring to a boil over high heat. Cook until nearly cooked through but still firm in the center, about 15 minutes. Drain. When cool, cut into thin slices; set aside.

3. Meanwhile, peel the celery root; cut into thin rounds. Bring a large pot of water to a rolling boil. Add the lemon juice and celery root and cook until tender, about 10 minutes. Drain, reserving ¼ cup (6 cl) of the cooking liquid for the gratin.

4. In a large skillet, heat the oil over medium-high heat until hot but not smoking. Add the tomatoes and garlic; season with salt and pepper. Simmer for 5 minutes. Add the crème fraîche and the reserved celery

root cooking water; stir to blend. Remove from the heat.

5. Butter a large gratin dish. Layer the sliced potatoes in the dish. Sprinkle with half the cheese. Arrange the celery root in a layer. Season with salt and pepper. Spoon the tomato sauce over all. Sprinkle on the remaining cheese.

6. Bake, uncovered, until golden brown, about 40 minutes. Serve immediately.

Yield: 6 servings

A NEWCOMER

Originally, gratins were made with herbs, with swiss chard, or with cardoons, the thistly vegetable from Lyons and Provence. It was only in the 18th century that gratins were made with potatoes.

GRATIN GRAND-MÈRE

Grandma's Potato, Red Pepper, and Zucchini Gratin

This simple vegetable gratin comes from the Auberge de la Madone, a small family *auberge* hidden high in the mountains above Nice. One summer evening, sitting on the terrace beneath an ancient olive tree laden with olives, I was served this gratin as an accompaniment to a deliciously moist sautéed rabbit. They call it *gratin grand-mère,* perhaps because it has a soft, homey, yet original touch.

1 garlic clove, peeled and halved
4 tablespoons extra-virgin olive oil
2 pounds (1 kg) baking potatoes, such as russets, peeled and very thinly sliced
2 teaspoons fresh thyme
2 teaspoons salt
2 red bell peppers, cored, seeded, and cut into thin rings
4 small zucchini (each about 4 ounces; 125 g), very thinly sliced

1. Preheat the oven to 350°F (175°C).

2. Generously rub the bottom of a shallow 5-cup (1.25 l) gratin dish with the garlic. Grease lightly with about 1 teaspoon of the olive oil.

3. Layer half of the potatoes in the bottom of the dish, overlapping the slices as necessary. Season lightly with the thyme and salt; drizzle with 1 tablespoon of the olive oil. Add a layer of half of the red peppers and then half of the zucchini. Season again with salt and thyme; drizzle 1 tablespoon of the oil over the vegetables. Repeat the layering and seasoning. Drizzle any remaining olive oil over the top.

4. Cover securely with aluminum foil. Bake until the vegetables are very soft and tender, about 1 hour. Serve immediately.

Yield: 4 servings

TRUC

Chef José Lampreia of Paris's Maison Blanche offers a suggestion for elegant, individual gratins: Prepare any gratin in individual nonstick ramekins or cake molds. Butter them lightly first, then bake. The presentation is prettier, and there's more crust—the best part—to go around!

GRATIN AUVERGNAT

◆   ◆

Blue Cheese Potato Gratin

The rugged, sparsely populated Auvergne region in the center of France is known for its marvelous variety of blue-veined cheeses, including Bleu d'Auvergne (known as "the cow's milk Roquefort"), the dense and full-flavored Fourme d'Ambert (also made from cow's milk), and the lighter cow's milk Bleu des Causses. When I entertain, I love to serve a mixed platter of varied blue cheeses, including, of course, the famed Roquefort sheep's milk cheese from the Languedoc. With the leftover bits of cheese, I make this simple potato gratin. The dish is flavorful enough to stand on its own, served with a salad of curly endive showered with bacon.

If you don't have a single gratin dish large enough to hold the potatoes in two thin layers, divide the ingredients between two smaller shallow baking dishes. With this, the ideal wine would be the red berry-like Chanturgue, a local Auvergnat wine rarely seen outside the region. A fruity Beaujolais or Côtes-du-Rhône would also be excellent.

1 quart (1 l) whole milk
½ cup (110 g) crumbled blue cheese,
    at room temperature
½ cup (12.5 cl) crème fraîche (see
    Index) or heavy cream
4 tablespoons (2 ounces; 60 g) un-
    salted butter
3 pounds (1.5 kg) baking potatoes,
    such as russets, peeled and sliced
    very thin
Freshly grated nutmeg
Salt and freshly ground black pepper

1. Preheat the oven to 375°F (190°C).

2. In a saucepan, scald the milk; set aside.

3. In a food processor blend the blue cheese and the crème fraîche.

4. Use some of the butter to heavily coat a large oval gratin dish, about 14 × 9 × 2 inches (35.5 × 23 × 5 cm). Layer half of the potatoes in the dish. Season very generously with nutmeg, salt, and pepper. Dot the potatoes with half of the blue cheese mixture. Layer with the remaining potatoes, and season again with nutmeg, salt, and pepper. Dot the top with the remaining cheese mixture and butter. Pour the milk over the potatoes.

5. Bake until the gratin is crisp and golden on top, about 1½ hours. Serve immediately.

Yield: 6 to 8 servings

POMMES DE TERRE COIFFÉES AU MUNSTER FONDU

◆———————◆

Boiled New Potatoes with a Gratin of Munster

This is a hearty fall and winter dish that cries out for a warming fire and plenty of chilled white wine. It's a traditional Alsatian specialty, served in local farmhouses, bistros, and even in the vineyards, where, during harvest time, a typical snack might include hot, boiled potatoes served with slices of rich, local Munster cheese. In this version, the potatoes are boiled ahead of time in their skins—or *robes de chambre,* their bath robes—then they are sliced and layered in a gratin dish, covered with strips of Munster, sprinkled with cumin, and placed under the broiler until crispy and brown. I love this as a Saturday lunch, served with a good tart salad of fresh sorrel.

1½ pounds (750 g) small new potatoes, in their skins
1 tablespoon (½ ounce; 15 g) unsalted
butter
6 ounces (180 g) imported French
Munster cheese (or substitute Ma-
roilles or Véritable Chaumes)
2 teaspoons cumin seed

1. Cook the potatoes in plenty
of salted water just until tender,
about 20 minutes; do not overcook.
Meanwhile, butter a porcelain baking
dish (about 14 × 9 × 2 inches or
35.5 × 23 × 5 cm).

2. Drain the potatoes. As soon
as they are cool enough to handle,
but while still warm, cut into thin,
even slices. Layer the slices in 1 or 2
layers in the buttered gratin dish.

3. Preheat the broiler.

4. Coarsely grate the cheese (remove the rind if you are using Vér-

> **The gratin savoyard is the masterpiece of the local cuisine. It does not include milk, like the gratin dauphinois, but between each layer of potatoes, one adds a layer of wild cèpe mushrooms, which heightens this dish to the seventh heaven of the most sublime of fla-vors.**
>
> —MAURICE GUÉGAN,
> CHRONIQUE GASTRONOMIQUE
> *Revue des Usagers de la Route, 1928*

itable Chaumes). Sprinkle the cheese
over the potatoes. Sprinkle on the
cumin seed. Place under the broiler
until the cheese melts and is crispy
and brown, 2 to 3 minutes. Serve
immediately.

Yield: 4 to 6 servings

POMMES À L'HUILE

◆

Warm Potato Salad with Herbed Vinaigrette

This salad always makes me think of my first trip to France and my first bistro meal in Lyons. I grew up on all sorts of potato salads— my mother was famous for the salads she would prepare for our backyard picnics. But it took the French to teach me one secret of a great potato salad: Dress it while it's warm, so the potatoes can absorb all of the flavor and richness of the dressing. Also, if you shower the salad with shallots, parsley, and chives at the very last minute, it will have a crispy bite.

1½ *pounds (750 g) small new red-*
skinned potatoes, scrubbed but not
peeled
½ *cup (12.5 cl) plus 2 tablespoons*
virgin olive oil
3 *tablespoons best-quality white wine*
vinegar
2 *tablespoons dry white wine*
Salt and freshly ground black pepper
2 *shallots, finely minced*
Chopped fresh parsley
Snipped fresh chives

1. Steam the potatoes, covered, in a vegetable steamer over simmering water just until tender, about 20 minutes.

2. Meanwhile, whisk together ½ cup (12.5 cl) of the oil, 2 tablespoons of the vinegar, the wine, and 1 teaspoon of salt in a small bowl.

3. Drain the potatoes; let cool briefly, and then peel. Cut into ½-inch (1.5-cm) slices. Combine the potatoes with the oil and vinegar mixture; toss gently. Set aside to allow the potatoes to absorb the dressing, about 20 to 30 minutes.

4. Meanwhile, in a small bowl, make the final dressing. Whisk together the remaining 2 tablespoons olive oil, the remaining 1 tablespoon vinegar, the parsley, shallots, and chives, to taste in a small bowl until thoroughly blended.

5. Just before serving, toss the potatoes gently with the herbed dressing. Season to taste and serve.

Yield: 4 servings

❝After a few weeks I became acquainted in the 'quartier'. I found a prix-fixe restaurant in a quiet side street less than a hundred yards and more than a hundred years from Place Pigalle. The restaurant had a tiled floor, sprinkled with sawdust. There were small tables for four, covered with large sheets of white paper. When a guest had finished his meal, the waiter would write the 'addition' on the paper, roll the paper with the bread crumbs together, and take it away. The next guest was given a fresh sheet of paper.**❞**

—JOSEPH WECHSBERG
Blue Trout and Black Truffles

POMMES DE TERRE SOLOGNOTES

Potato Gratin from the Sologne

Once you've discovered the pleasures of herb-infused milk, you'll find all sorts of ways to use it—as a base for soups, for sauces, and in this delightful potato gratin, which comes from the Sologne region of the Loire. Of course the fresher the herbs, the better. Serve this light gratin with a roast, or alone, with a tossed salad.

2 cups (50 cl) milk
½ cup (12.5 cl) minced fresh herbs,
    including tarragon, thyme, pars-
    ley, and chives
2 imported bay leaves
5 whole black peppercorns
2 pounds (1 kg) baking potatoes, such
    as russets, peeled and thinly sliced
Salt and freshly ground black pepper
1 garlic clove, halved
½ cup (12.5 cl) crème fraîche (see
    Index) or heavy cream
1 teaspoon fresh thyme or ½ teaspoon
    dried
1 cup (about 3 ounces; 80 g) freshly
    grated imported French or Swiss
    Gruyère cheese

1. Preheat the oven to 375°F (190°C).

2. Combine the milk, the mixed fresh herbs, bay leaves, and peppercorns in a large saucepan. Cover and scald over medium-high heat. Remove from the heat and let steep, covered, for 10 minutes. Strain the milk into a large saucepan discarding the herbs and peppercorns.

3. Add the potatoes to the strained milk. Cover and cook until the potatoes are tender, about 15 minutes. Season with salt and pepper to taste; set aside.

4. Rub the inside of an oval porcelain gratin dish (about 14 × 9 × 2 inches or 35.5 × 23 × 5 cm) with the garlic. Spoon the potato mixture into the dish. Dot with the crème fraîche and sprinkle with the thyme.

5. Bake until the gratin is golden, about 45 minutes. Remove the gratin dish from the oven, and sprinkle with the grated cheese. Return to the oven and bake until the top is very crisp and golden, about 15 more minutes. Serve immediately.

Yield: 6 to 8 servings

Gâteau de Pommes de Terre L'Ami Louis

L'Ami Louis's Potato Cake

This is the late Antoine Magnin's famous potato cake, the rich mound of golden potatoes that comes steaming out of the kitchen, to accompany the meaty steaks, delicious roast chicken, or warming duck confit. At the famed Paris bistro L'Ami Louis, the potatoes are pan-fried in goose fat in a giant black steel pan, then baked in a small tin-lined copper sauté pan. At home, I have found that if you use a nonstick pan to bake the potatoes, you will end up with a nice crisp cake that will unmold easily. Do not bake the potatoes in a ceramic or porcelain baking dish, or they will turn mushy. Also, do not try to double the recipe in a single cake. For a crowd, try baking two separate potato cakes.

3 tablespoons poultry fat or unsalted butter
2 pounds (1 kg) baking potatoes, such as russets, peeled and very thinly sliced
Salt
1 tablespoon (½ ounce; 15 g) unsalted butter
3 garlic cloves, coarsely chopped
3 tablespoons coarsely minced fresh parsley

1. Preheat the oven to 400°F (205°C).
2. Melt the poultry fat in a large saucepan over medium-high heat. Add the potatoes and season with salt. Sauté, partially covered, tossing the potatoes from time to time until most of the potatoes are partially

> **"**Years before, when Albertine had been strong enough to work in the fields, they used to lift the potatoes together. Whilst working they would recite all the ways in which potatoes could be eaten: potatoes in their jackets, potatoes with cheese in the oven, potato salad, potatoes with pork fat, mashed potatoes with milk, potatoes cooked without water in the black iron saucepan, potatoes with leeks in the soup—and best of all, potato fritters with cabbage salad.**"**
>
> —JOHN BERGER
> *Once in Europa*

browned on both sides, about 25 minutes. Reduce the heat, if necessary, to avoid burning the potatoes.

3. Using a large, slotted spatula, transfer the browned potato slices to a 9-inch (22.5 cm) round, nonstick, oven-proof skillet. Press the potatoes firmly and evenly into the pan. Bake, uncovered, until the potatoes are crisp and golden, about 20 minutes.

4. Place the skillet over medium-high heat and rub the butter around the edges of the pan, letting it melt down into the inside rim of the pan. Place a large plate on top of the pan and invert both skillet and plate to unmold the potato cake. (Whether the potatoes unmold into a firm cake or a looser cake will depend upon the firmness and freshness of the potatoes used.).

5. Scatter garlic and parsley on top of the cake. Serve immediately.

Yield: 4 to 6 servings

DINNER WITH L'AMI LOUIS

Here's a typical winter menu from one of Paris' famed bistros, L'Ami Louis. It's about as authentic and satisfying fare as you will find. With it serve a simple dessert, such as pears in red wine.

COQUILLES SAINT JACQUES À LA PROVENÇALE L'AMI LOUIS
L'Ami Louis' Scallops with Garlic, Tomatoes, Basil, and Thyme

GÂTEAU DE POMMES DE TERRE L'AMI LOUIS
L'Ami Louis' Potato Cake

L'AIL CONFIT
Garlic Confit

POULET RÔTI L'AMI LOUIS
L'Ami Louis' Roast Chicken

POMMES BOULANGÈRE

The Baker's Wife's Potatoes

The first time I prepared this delicate potato, onion, and leek gratin—one seasoned with wine and chicken stock in place of the traditional cream and/or cheese—I baked it in our wood-fired bread oven. The aromas swept through the courtyard and into the living room, where we were cozily installed in front of the fire. All the better if you have a nice leg of lamb or guinea hen to roast alongside.

*2 tablespoons (1 ounce; 30 g) unsalted
  butter*
2 small onions, finely minced
*3 to 4 medium leeks, white portion
  only (about 8 ounces; 250 g), well
  rinsed, dried, and finely minced*
*2 pounds (1 kg) baking potatoes, such
  as russets, peeled and very thinly
  sliced*
*1 cup (25 cl) chicken stock, preferably
  homemade (see Index)*
1 cup (25 cl) dry white wine
*2 teaspoons fresh thyme or 1 teaspoon
  dried*
Salt and freshly ground black pepper

1. Preheat the oven to 375°F (190°C)

2. Melt the butter in a large, nonreactive skillet. Add the onions and leeks and cook, covered, over low heat, until they are soft, about 10 minutes.

3. Add the potatoes and mix well. Add the stock, wine, thyme, and salt and pepper to taste. Continue to cook, covered, over medium heat, for 15 minutes.

4. Spoon the ingredients into a shallow 8-cup (2 l) gratin dish. Bake until the potatoes are soft and golden on top and most of the liquid has been absorbed, 50 to 60 minutes.

Yield: 8 to 10 servings

POMMES DE TERRE À L'AIL ET À L'HUILE DE NOIX

Potatoes Sautéed with Garlic and Walnut Oil

There are days when sautéed potatoes and a green salad make a most welcoming supper. But what sautéed potatoes! The house smells delicious with the fragrance of the rich walnut oil blending with garlic, and just a whiff of nutmeg. It's a marvelous combination—one from the kitchens of the Charentes, along the Atlantic Coast—a simple dish to make with ingredients on hand. If you can't find fresh walnut oil, substitute the best extra-virgin olive oil you can find. If you happen to have very fresh, very thin-skinned red potatoes, you may want to leave the skins on the potatoes. They're prettier this way, and you'll get even more flavor out of the dish.

2 pounds (1 kg) small, firm, smooth-
 skinned potatoes
¼ cup (6 cl) best-quality walnut oil
Freshly grated nutmeg
Salt and freshly ground black pepper
4 garlic cloves, finely minced
1 small bunch of parsley, minced
1 small bunch of chives, minced

1. Peel and thinly slice the potatoes. Wrap them in a thick towel
to absorb any liquid.

2. In a large skillet (preferably
cast-iron or nonstick), heat the oil
until hot but not smoking over medium-high heat. Add the potatoes
and sauté, shaking the pan to toss
from time to time, until the potatoes
are thoroughly cooked and browned
on both sides, about 20 minutes. Season with nutmeg, salt, and pepper to
taste as the potatoes are being tossed.

3. To serve, sprinkle on the
garlic, parsley, and chives, and toss
to blend.

Yield: 4 servings

GALETTE LYONNAISE

♦

Lyonnaise Potato Galette

T he bistros of Lyons are a potato lover's paradise. This version, typical
of the simple potato and onion mixtures typically served with roast
meats or steak, is quick and easy to prepare. I think of this dish as
"smashed" potatoes, for that's just what they are!

2 pounds (1 kg) baking potatoes, such
 as russets
2 medium onions
6 tablespoons (3 ounces; 90 g) unsalted butter
Freshly grated nutmeg
Salt and freshly ground black pepper

1. Peel the potatoes. Boil or
steam them until tender and mash-
able. Drain. Let the potatoes rest for

a few minutes. Coarsely mash with a
fork, leaving a few irregular chunks.

2. Preheat the broiler.

3. Halve the onions lengthwise;
cut each half into thin half-moon
rounds.

4. In a large skillet, melt 2 tablespoons (30 g) of the butter over
medium-high heat. Add the onions
and sauté until soft and golden, about
10 minutes.

5. Add 2 tablespoons (30 g)

more of butter and melt. Add the potatoes, season generously with nutmeg, salt, and pepper, and cook, tossing the mixture about 2 or 3 more minutes.

6. Transfer the mixture to a gratin dish. Smooth with the back of a large spoon, then dot with the remaining 2 tablespoons butter. Brown lightly under the broiler. Serve immediately.

Yield: 6 to 8 servings

QUARTIERS DE POMMES DE TERRE SAUTÉS DANS LEUR PEAU

Potato Quarters Sautéed in Their Skins

Simplicity is bliss, and this streamlined, rustic potato dish is blissfully simple. Most of the work can be done in advance, leaving the final sauté for the few moments before you're ready to gather family or guests around the table. For this dish, choose potatoes with smooth skin, selecting them for their beauty as well as taste. I love this as an accompaniment to a golden roast chicken and a beautifully dressed green salad.

1 pound (500 g) small, firm, smooth-skinned potatoes
2 tablespoons (1 ounce; 30 g) unsalted butter
Salt and freshly ground black pepper
2 tablespoons finely minced parsley

1. Scrub the potatoes well, but do not peel them. Steam until cooked through, about 20 minutes. Allow to cool. (This step can be done several hours in advance.)

2. Just before serving the potatoes, cut them in quarters (if they are particularly small, halve them). Melt the butter in large sauté pan over medium-high heat. When the butter begins to sizzle, add the potatoes, and shuffling the pan vigorously back and forth across the burner, sauté them until golden brown on all sides, about 5 minutes. Place the potatoes in a large serving bowl and season them liberally with salt and pepper. Sprinkle on parsley, toss gently, and serve.
Yield: 4 to 6 servings

POMMES PAILLASSON

Straw Potatoes

This golden potato cake is fun and easy to make, and a dish I find a perfect accompaniment to a simple roast chicken. Use a large nonstick skillet and you won't have any trouble flipping it over! A *paillasson,* by the way, is a French straw mat, which this cake resembles.

4 medium baking potatoes, such as russets (about 1 pound; 500 g), peeled
6 to 8 tablespoons (3 to 4 ounces; 90 to 120 g) unsalted butter
Salt and freshly ground black pepper

1. Using the shredding disk of a food processor or the coarsest side of a hand grater, shred or coarsely grate the potatoes. Rinse the shredded potatoes in a colander under cold running water. Squeeze the potatoes by handfuls to press out as much water as possible. Repeat rinsing and squeezing. Spread out the potatoes in a single layer on a large absorbent kitchen towel. Roll up the potatoes in the towel and twist to extract any remaining liquid. If not properly dried, the potatoes will remain soggy when cooked. (Do not do this ahead of time or the potatoes will color.)

2. Melt 2 tablespoons (1 ounce; 30 g) of the butter over medium-high heat in a large nonstick skillet with a tight-fitting lid. When the foam subsides, turn the well-dried potatoes into the skillet and press down firmly with a spoon or spatula to form a single even layer. Season lightly with salt and pepper. Cut 2 tablespoons of the butter into small pieces; tuck them in around the edges of the pan to prevent sticking.

3. Cook, covered, over low to medium-low heat until the bottom is golden and crusty, 15 to 20 minutes. As the edges begin to brown, shake the pan or slide a spatula under the edges to loosen the potatoes. Remove the pan from the heat.

4. Prepare to turn out the potato cake: Either invert the skillet onto a large flat plate, or carefully dry the inside of the lid and invert the skillet onto the lid.

5. Return the skillet to medium-low heat. Add 2 to 4 tablespoons (1 to 2 ounces; 30 to 60 g) of the butter (use the lesser amount if the potatoes seem well browned and crisp, the larger amount if they are less well done). When the foam subsides, gently slide the potato cake back into the pan, browned side up. Cook, uncovered, until well browned, 8 to 10 minutes. Invert onto a warmed platter. Season with additional salt and pepper. Serve immediately.

Yield: 4 servings

Les Oeufs, les Fromages, les Terrines, et les Tartes

Eggs, Cheese, Terrines, and Tarts

Main stars in the litany of simple bistro dishes include the variety of meaty terrines and pâtés that often sit at the entrance to small family restaurants. The terrines, in particular, serve as inexpensive fare that can be made ahead and served throughout the day. Of the following first-course dishes, I adore the rabbit and hazelnut terrine, for it represents the very fragrant, earthy sort of food I love, food with very complex but straightforward flavors. While in traditional bistros one might be served three or four slices of terrine, modern-day bistros tend to follow a lighter approach, offering thin slices with a tossed green salad alongside. With these, one can serve tiny tart cucumber pickles, or the beautiful sweet and sour dried figs.

The Savory Swiss Chard Tart—found in bistros as well as charcuteries throughout Nice—is one of my favorite summertime dishes, to serve as a palate-teasing appetizer or as a main-course luncheon dish accompanied by a tossed green salad.

OEUFS EN MEURETTE

Poached Eggs with Red Wine Sauce

This is one of my favorite Sunday night suppers. It's a great dish to have in your repertoire when the cupboard is rather bare, that is, limited to eggs, wine, bread, and a few staple vegetables. It can be served as a first course or main course, depending on your appetite.

Traditionally, the wine sauce is blended with a rich dark brown sauce, but I prefer this purer, simpler version, with its deep red wine color. I also like adding fresh herbs to the sauce as the wine reduces, giving the sauce a bit more personality in the end. Be sure to use a good sturdy red wine.

1 carrot, peeled and cubed
2 shallots, minced
2 imported bay leaves
2 garlic cloves, minced
1 sprig of fresh rosemary or tarragon
2 cups (500 ml) full-bodied red wine, such as a Côtes-du-Rhône, Cahors, or Madiran
8 slices French bread or any good homemade bread, cut into ½-inch (1.5 cm) thick slices, crusts removed, cut into even 3-inch (7.5 cm) rounds with a biscuit cutter
2 garlic cloves, peeled and halved
1 tablespoon (½ ounce; 15 g) unsalted butter, softened
1 tablespoon all-purpose flour
2 tablespoons distilled vinegar
8 extra-large eggs, at room temperature
Salt and freshly ground black pepper

1. In a medium-size nonreactive saucepan, combine the carrot, shallots, bay leaves, minced garlic, rosemary, and wine over high heat. Boil until reduced by half, about 10 minutes. Strain the wine; discard the vegetables and herbs. (This step may be done well in advance and the wine refrigerated.)

2. Preheat the broiler.

3. Toast the bread on both sides until golden brown. Remove from the oven and immediately rub on both sides with a cut garlic clove.

4. Complete the red wine sauce: On a plate, mash the butter and flour together to form a well-blended paste (*beurre manié*). In a small nonreactive saucepan, bring the reduced wine to a simmer. Carefully whisk in the butter and flour paste, a little at a time, until the sauce is lightly thickened and glossy. Remove from the heat and keep warm.

5. In 2 shallow 10-inch (25.5 cm) pans, bring 3 inches (7.5 cm) of water and 1 tablespoon of vinegar to a boil. Turn off the heat and imme-

diately break 4 eggs directly into the water in each pan, carefully opening the shells close to the water's surface, so the eggs slip into the water in one piece. Immediately cover the pans with tight-fitting lids to retain the heat. Do not disturb the pans. Allow the eggs to cook for 3 minutes before lifting the lids. The eggs are ready when the whites are opaque and the yolks are covered with a thin, translucent layer of white.

6. While the eggs cook, place 2 toasts (croutons) on each of 4 warmed plates. Using a flat, slotted spoon, carefully lift the eggs from the water and place on top of the croutons. Spoon the wine sauce all around, season with salt and pepper to taste, and serve immediately, with additional toasted bread, if desired.

Yield: 4 servings

> **"***La Meurette . . . it's a sauce. It consists of placing in a casserole red vin de pays, carrots, garlic, leeks, salt, pepper, and . . . a cube of sugar. As soon as it boils, turn down the heat and let it 'frissoner' for a quarter of an hour.***
>
> ***Pass this sauce through a fine-mesh sieve and pour it over fish that you have flamed with a glass of eau-de-vie de marc.***"
> —MAURICE GUÉGAN, CHRONIQUE GASTRONOMIQUE
> *Revue des Usagers de la Route,* 1928

LE CACHAT

◆

Herbed Goat Cheese Spread

Cachat is a wonderfully earthy, strong cheese spread found all over Provence. It's sold in cheese shops and can often be found on the cheese trays of the more rustic local bistros. But most people make their own, since *cachat* is traditionally made with leftover bits of cheese, to which you can add the cottage-cheese-like *fromage blanc,* a touch of Roquefort, herbs, and a good dose of eau-de-vie.

This isn't really a recipe, but rather a blueprint. The cheese spread should be served at room temperature, out of a small crock, for spreading on toasted homemade bread. When it's time to make another batch, use the original *cachat* as a "starter," adding to taste.

6 *small firm goat cheeses (Picodon, Pé-*
lardon, Crottin), about 1 pound
(500 g) total
⅔ pound (330 g) cottage cheese
1 tablespoon extra-virgin olive oil
Several sprigs of thyme and summer
savory
Eau-de-vie or brandy

In a food processor, combine the goat cheese, cottage cheese, oil, and herbs. Process to blend well. Scrape the mixture into a small earthenware crock, pressing to flatten. Cover with a thin film of eau-de-vie. Store in a cool place, stirring every few days. The mixture will keep almost indefinitely. Whenever there is a piece of leftover goat cheese, it can be added, along with additional ingredients, to make a strong, spreadable cheese.

Yield: About 2 cups (50 cl)

TERRINE AUX HERBES DE PROVENCE MADAME CARTET

Madame Cartet's Provençal Herb Terrine

The highly-seasoned, full-flavored meat terrines have always been a favorite first course at Madame Cartet's tiny bistro off Paris's Place de la République. When I watched chef Raymond Nouaille prepare this recipe in the restaurant's kitchen, I was at first surprised by the quantity of herbs and spices he tossed in with the meat mixture. But one taste, and you understand. The lively herbs of Provence—thyme, marjoram, oregano, and summer savory—add intensity and depth, turning what could be ordinary meat loaf into what the French call a *régale*.

Although the ingredients list is long, it's a very quick terrine to prepare. I'd strongly advise grinding all your own herbs; the little bit of extra work will pay off in flavor in the end! If you don't have a meat grinder, ask your butcher to grind the meat for you. With the terrine, serve a crisp white, such as a Loire Valley Savennières, or a young fruity red, such as Beaujolais.

*2½ pounds (1.25 kg) pork neck meat
or picnic shoulder, coarsely ground*
*1½ pounds (750 g) fresh pork liver,
coarsely ground*
12 shallots
6 garlic cloves
*⅔ cup (16 cl) dry white wine, such as
French Riesling*
3 tablespoons port
3 tablespoons Cognac
2 tablespoons plus 2 teaspoons sea salt
*1 heaping tablespoon freshly ground
black pepper*
2 heaping tablespoons dried thyme
1 heaping tablespoon dried oregano
*1 heaping tablespoon dried summer
savory*
2 heaping tablespoons dried marjoram
¼ teaspoon freshly ground cinnamon
¼ teaspoon freshly ground allspice
¼ teaspoon freshly ground cloves
¼ teaspoon freshly ground nutmeg
*1 slice fatback or barding fat, 8 ×
10 inches (20.5 × 25.5 cm),
thinly sliced*
*1 piece caul fat, 10 × 12 inches
(25.5 cm × 30.5 cm), or substitute 4 or 5 very thin strips of
mild bacon*

IN HONOR OF MADAME CARTET

This menu is a tribute to Madame Cartet, who first opened a minuscule bistro in the 1930s that soon became known for its copious fare. Three of the recipes from this menu are still served almost daily in the Paris restaurant near the Place de la République. The fourth is a poultry dish I love, one that balances well with the rest of the meal.

TERRINE AUX HERBES DE PROVENCE MADAME CARTET
*Madame Cartet's Provençal
Herb Terrine*

PINTADE DE LA DRÔME AUX OLIVES DE NYONS
*Guinea Hen From the Drôme With
Black Olives From Nyons*

GRATIN DAUPHINOIS MADAME CARTET
Madame Cartet's Potato Gratin

TARTE AU CITRON MADAME CARTET
Madame Cartet's Lemon Tart

1. Preheat the oven to 375°F (190°C).

2. Grind the pork and pork liver together in a meat grinder, or ask your butcher to do this. Place the ground pork and liver in a large bowl.

3. Put the shallots and garlic through the grinder next, or chop them in a food processor.

4. Add the shallots and garlic to the ground meat mixture and mix with your hands. Add the wine, Port, Cognac, salt, pepper, herbs, and spices; mix again.

5. Line the bottom, but not the sides, of a 10-cup (2.5 l) rectangular mold or terrine with the fatback or barding fat. Spoon the meat mixture

into the mold, pressing it flat with your fingers. Place a piece of caul fat, or several thin strips of mild bacon, over the top of the terrine, tucking in the ends.

6. Place the terrine in a deep roasting pan and add hot, but not boiling, water to reach two-thirds of the way up the sides of the terrine. Bake, adding additional water, if necessary, to maintain the water level, for 2 to 2½ hours. (If the terrine browns on top, cover it loosely with aluminum foil.) To test for doneness, insert a metal skewer into the center of the terrine, and leave it there for about 30 seconds. If the skewer is hot to the touch, the terrine is done.

7. Remove the terrine from the water bath. Place a plate with a weight on top of it on top of the terrine. Some juices may spill over, but resist the temptation to discard this excess liquid, which will, in the end, serve to flavor the terrine and keep it moist as it ripens. The weights will help the terrine firm up as it cools, making it more dense and easier to cut. Refrigerate, removing the weights when the terrine is thoroughly cooled. Allow to ripen for at least 1 day and up to 3 days before serving. The terrine will stay fresh for up to 1 week.

8. To serve, remove the terrine from the refrigerator about 30 minutes before serving, so the cold does not mask the flavors. Cut the terrine into thick slices and serve with plenty of cornichons, slices of French bread, and butter.

Yield: 12 to 16 servings

TERRINE DE LAPIN AUX NOISETTES

Rabbit and Hazelnut Terrine

My microwave oven has become an essential appliance in my kitchen. I use it almost daily for one thing or another and especially love the way it saves time and effort in preparing bistro-style terrines. One day in fall, at our house in Provence, I put together this earthy country terrine that simply sings of the fields and woods of Provence: rabbit, juniper, hazelnuts, and figs. The only complicated part of the recipe is boning the rabbit. It's an easier task than it seems (I now manage to do it in about 10 minutes, using a good sharp knife), and if you can convince your butcher to do it for you, this terrine is child's play. After you have prepared the terrine, chop up the rabbit carcass and use it to prepare a flavorful stock (just as you would chicken stock) in your microwave.

The terrine may be sampled the day it is made but will be better a day or two later. Refrigerate, covered, up to 30 minutes before serving.

1 fresh rabbit, weighing about 2 pounds (1 kg), boned (ask your butcher to do this for you), fat, liver, and kidneys reserved
1 teaspoon juniper berries, coarsely ground
3 shallots, finely minced
1 tablespoon Herbes de Provence (see Index)
1 pound (500 g) bulk pork sausage
1 egg
2 tablespoons gin
2 tablespoons olive oil
Salt
½ cup (65 g) shelled whole hazelnuts
4 imported bay leaves
3 slices bacon
Sweet and Sour Dried Figs (recipe follows)

1. Cube the boned rabbit pieces. In a food processor, mince the juniper berries and shallots. Add the rabbit meat, reserved fat, liver, kidneys, and Herbes de Provence. Process until coarsely ground.

2. Scrape the rabbit mixture into a large bowl. Add the sausage, egg, gin, olive oil, and salt to taste. Using your hands, thoroughly blend the ingredients.

3. Spoon half of the meat mixture into a 1-quart (1 l) oval or rectangular porcelain terrine, pressing it down firmly with your hands. Sprinkle half of the hazelnuts over the mixture. Fill the terrine with the remaining meat mixture. Sprinkle with the remaining hazelnuts, gently pressing them into the meat. Place the bay leaves on top and cover with the bacon, tucking the ends down into the sides of the terrine. Cover with the terrine's lid, or tightly with plastic wrap.

4. Place the terrine on the turntable of a microwave oven. (If your oven does not have a turntable, sim-

ply rotate the terrine a one-quarter turn 4 times during the cooking.) Cook the terrine at medium power for 35 minutes. Remove from the oven. To test for doneness, insert a metal skewer into the center of the terrine, and leave it there for about 30 seconds. Remove the skewer. If the skewer is hot to the touch, the terrine is done.

5. Remove and discard the bacon and bay leaves. Cut a piece of cardboard to the size of the terrine and wrap it in plastic. Place the cardboard on top of the terrine and weigh it down with a few cans. Set aside to cool to room temperature. Wrap the terrine tightly with plastic wrap or with its own cover. Refrigerate for 2 days.

6. To serve, allow the terrine to rest at room temperature for 30 min-

utes. Cut into thin slices and serve on small plates, accompanied by Sweet and Sour Dried Figs.

Yield: 8 servings

FIGUES SÈCHES AU VINAIGRE

Sweet and Sour Dried Figs

One day while doing my Sunday marketing in the village of Isle-sur-la-Sorgue in Provence, I purchased a tiny jar of homemade preserved dried figs, displayed next to the cash register at the local butcher shop. They were so delicious, I set about to prepare my own sweet and sour fruit "pickles," simple fare that can be prepared any time of year. I've tried, with equal success, pickled dried apricots, pears, and prunes. They are excellent with all meat terrines or with sliced sausages. Eat them the way you would any cucumber pickle. They take only a few seconds to prepare and can be refrigerated indefinitely, as long as they are covered with the spiced vinegar.

TERRINE OR PÂTÉ?

In common usage in French, there is little difference between a terrine and a pâté, both of which are generally a mix of ground meats, poultry, fish or shellfish, or vegetables, cooked, covered, in an oven in a *bain-marie* and served either hot or cold. The word "terrine" is also used to describe the dish in which a terrine is cooked, often a fairly deep dish with straight sides, usually of glazed earthenware or porcelain.

Strictly speaking, a pâté is a dish consisting of a pastry shell filled with meat, fish, or vegetables, baked in the oven and served hot or cold.

---

1 pound (500 g) dried figs (or substitute dried apricots, pears, or prunes)
1¼ cups (31 cl) best-quality red wine vinegar
3 tablespoons sugar
8 whole cloves
½ teaspoon freshly ground cinnamon

Pack the dried fruits in a sterilized jar. Pour in enough vinegar to cover, then add the sugar and spices. Cover tightly, shake to blend the ingredients, and refrigerate. The pickle can actually be sampled within 24 hours, but will benefit from at least a week's mellowing.

Yield: 1 pint (50 cl) pickled figs

TRUC

To keep meat terrines fresh for more than a few days, pour off all of the cooking juices and replace them with melted pork fat. Cover securely and refrigerate. The terrines will remain fresh for up to one month.

LA TERRINE DE QUEUE DE BOEUF

Oxtail Terrine

As a child, the soup I loved most was the rich oxtail soup my mother would make once or twice each winter. I still have a great fondness for this earthy, gelatinous meat, a "poor man's" cut that takes some time and attention, but rewards you in the end with flavor and texture. Serve it in slices, pass the cornichons, pickled onions, and horseradish and an unpretentious red, perhaps a Chiroubles, Beaujolais cru.

3 pounds (1.5 kg) oxtail, cut into 4-inch (10 cm) pieces
1 tablespoon coarse (kosher) salt
8 carrots, cut into ¾-inch (2 cm) slices
2 leeks, white portion only, cleaned and coarsely chopped
2 celery ribs, coarsely chopped
1 onion, coarsely chopped
2 garlic cloves, minced
1 bouquet garni: 12 parsley stems, 8

peppercorns, ¼ teaspoon thyme, ¼ teaspoon fennel seed, and 1 imported bay leaf tied in a double thickness of cheesecloth
2 tablespoons drained capers
Salt and freshly ground black pepper
1 bunch of fresh chives, chopped

1. Two days before you plan to serve the terrine: Tie the oxtail in a large bundle with household string. Place the oxtail pieces in a large enameled casserole or Dutch oven and cover completely with cold water. Bring just to a simmer over medium heat. Simmer, skimming very carefully to remove all of the impurities or grease, a good 20 minutes. When the impurities have turned to foam, skim again, and move the pot halfway off the heat so that the foam rises on one side only, making it easier to skim. Continue cooking for another 20 minutes.

2. Season the liquid lightly with coarse salt (about 1 tablespoon). Add the vegetables, garlic, and bouquet garni. Return to a simmer, skim again and simmer until the meat is falling off the bone, for 3 to 4 hours. Refrigerate overnight to allow the fat to solidify.

3. The next day, carefully spoon off and discard all of the fat from the top of the mixture. Remove the pieces of oxtail from the pot. Use a fork to remove the meat from the bones, discarding the fat.

4. Remove and discard the bouquet garni. Return the shredded meat to the pot. Add the capers and bring just to a boil to melt the gelatinous liquid. Check the seasoning and add salt and pepper to taste, remembering that this will be consumed chilled, so you might want to boost the seasoning a bit. Transfer the meat and vegetables to a 2-quart (2 l) terrine, pressing down on the meat to make a compact terrine. Cover just to the top with the bouillon. Cover and refrigerate for 24 hours.

5. To serve, remove the terrine from the refrigerator about 5 minutes before serving. Cut into thin slices, sprinkle with chives, and serve with cornichons, pickled onions, and horseradish.

Yield: 12 to 16 servings

PISSALADIÈRE

◆

Onion, Anchovy, and Black Olive Tart

Nearly every bakery and pastry shop in Provence—as well as a good number of bistros and pizzerias—sell *pissaladière,* this substantial dish of thick bread dough sprinkled with onions, anchovies, and black olives. It's sold by the slice, for eating out of hand or for taking home to warm in the oven. It makes a perfect luncheon dish, with a simple green tossed salad and a few sips of Côtes-de-Provence rouge.

2 tablespoons extra-virgin olive oil
5 medium onions (about 1 pound;
    500 g), sliced into thin rounds
2 large garlic cloves, thinly sliced
1 large sprig of fresh thyme
2 large tomatoes, peeled, cored, seeded,
    and chopped
8 ounces (250 g) Basic Bread Dough
    (see Index)
8 flat anchovy fillets, rinsed and
    drained
12 oil-cured olives, preferably from
    Nyons, pitted and halved

1. In a large skillet, heat the oil over medium-low heat. Add the onions, garlic, and thyme, and toss to coat with the oil. Cover and cook, stirring occasionally, until the onions turn a light golden color, about 20 minutes.

2. Stir in the tomatoes, raise the heat to high, and cook until their liquid has evaporated and the mixture is thick, about 5 minutes. Discard the thyme sprig.

3. On a lightly floured surface, roll out the dough into an 11 × 14-inch (28 × 35.5 cm) rectangle. Transfer the dough to a baking sheet. Cover and let rest for 15 minutes.

4. Preheat the oven to 450°F (230°C).

5. Spread the onion-tomato sauce evenly over the bread dough, going right out to the edges. Arrange the anchovies in a spoke-like pattern on top and sprinkle the olives on top. Let stand for 15 minutes.

6. Bake the *pissaladière* until the crust is crisp, 15 to 20 minutes. Slice and serve warm or at room temperature.

Yield: 6 to 8 servings

❝*La Pissaladera is nothing more than a little Pissala. It's a tart, with a base of white onions napped with anchovy fillets and black olives. This hors d'oeuvre is like a game of checkers, only the checkers are edible.***❞**
—MAURICE GUÉGAN, CHRONIQUE GASTRONOMIQUE
Revue des Usagers de la Route, 1928

FLAMICHE AUX POIREAUX

Leek Tart

North of Paris, in villages around the cities of Amiens and Lille, this *flamiche,* a dense, full-flavored vegetable tart filled with a blend of leeks, cheese, eggs, and ham, can be found in every pastry shop and bistro. Funny, it's almost a cliché, like quiche lorraine. It needn't be: Try it once and you'll be a convert forever. This tart, which is a perfect brunch dish or ideal for a Sunday-night dinner, deserves a regal wine, such as a Trimbach Riesling.

1 recipe Pâte Brisée (see Index), prepared through Step 1
12 small leeks (about 3 pounds; 1.5 kg)
4 tablespoons (2 ounces; 60 grams) unsalted butter
1 teaspoon salt
Freshly ground black pepper
2 large eggs
¼ cup (6 cl) crème fraîche (see Index) or heavy cream
4 slices (about 3 ounces; 100 g) ham, such as Parma ham, coarsely chopped
1 cup (about 3 ounces; 80 g) freshly grated imported Gruyère cheese

1. Prepare the pastry shell: Roll out the dough to line a 10½-inch (27 cm) tart pan. Carefully transfer the dough to the pan. Chill for 30 minutes, or until firm.

2. Preheat the oven to 425°F (220°C).

3. Prepare the filling: Trim the leeks at the root. Cut off and discard the fibrous, dark green portion. Split the leeks lengthwise for easier cleaning, and rinse well in cold water until

> **❝**I feel now that gastronomic perfection can be reached in these combinations: one person dining alone, usually upon a couch or a hillside; two people of no matter what sex or age, dining in a good restaurant; six people, of no matter what sex or age, dining in a good home. **❞**
>
> —M.F.K. FISHER

no grit appears. Coarsely chop the leeks.

4. Melt the butter in a medium-size saucepan over low heat. Add the leeks, salt, and pepper to taste and cook, covered, until the leeks are very soft but not browned, about 20 minutes. If the leeks have given up an excessive amount of liquid, drain them in a colander.

5. Combine the eggs and crème fraîche in a medium-size bowl and mix until thoroughly blended. Add the leeks and mix again. Reserve ¼ cup (6 cl) each of the ham and the cheese to sprinkle on top of the tart. Mix the rest into the leek mixture.

6. Pour the leek mixture into the prepared pastry shell. Sprinkle with the reserved ham, and then the cheese. Season generously with freshly ground black pepper.

7. Bake until nicely browned, 40 to 45 minutes. Serve warm or at room temperature.

Yield: 6 to 8 servings

> **❝***The Prix-Fixe was a good place to round out one's education. I learned that it was all right to read L'Instransigéant while you ate the hors d'oeuvre, but not afterward. The hors d'oeuvre—thon à huile, oeuf dur mayonnaise, or a slice of pâté Maison served on a lonely salad leaf—could be handled with the right hand while the left hand held the paper. After the hors d'oeuvre, you could place the paper under your seat and were supposed to converse with the neighbors at your table about local problems of the arrondissement. Listening to the quiet voices, you wouldn't have known that there existed Paris, or France, or Europe, or the rest of the world.* **❞**
>
> —JOSEPH WECHSBERG
> *Blue Trout & Black Truffles*

TOURTE AUX BLETTES

Savory Swiss Chard Tart

P rovence offers a number of superb savory tarts, ranging from the rustic *pissaladière*—thick bread dough topped with sautéed onions, anchovies, and black olives—to the unusual *tourte aux blettes*—a fragrant vegetable tart topped with swiss chard (the French call it *bette* or *blette*), eggs, Parmesan cheese, and sometimes even pine nuts, raisins, or black olives. This version is more of a savory dish, while I also offer its sweet counterpart in the dessert chapter. I love the superb, flaky base, a dough enriched with the local olive oil, rather than the more traditional butter or eggs. With this, you'll enjoy any crisp, young white wine.

Pastry:
1 cup (140 g) unbleached all-purpose
*   flour*
¼ teaspoon salt
¼ cup (6 cl) extra-virgin olive oil

Filling:
1 pound (500 g) swiss chard leaves
*   (or substitute spinach)*
Salt and freshly ground black pepper
3 large eggs
1 cup (3.5 ounces; 100 g) freshly
*   grated imported Parmesan cheese*

1. Preheat the oven to 400°F (205°C)

2. Prepare the pastry: Combine the flour and ¼ teaspoon salt in a medium-size bowl. Stir in ¼ cup (6 cl) water and then the oil, mixing until thoroughly blended. Knead briefly. The dough will be very moist, much like a cookie dough. Press the dough into a 10½-inch (27 cm) loose-bottomed metal tart tin.

3. Prepare the filling: Wash and dry the green leafy portion of the chard, discarding the center white stem. Break up the leaves and coarsely chop them, in several batches, in a food processor.

4. Place the chard in a large, shallow skillet and season with salt

PERFECT EGGS

When cooking eggs in water—whether you're looking for a very soft cooked egg with a liquid yolk or one that is perfectly hard-cooked with firmly set whites and yolks—follow these tips: If refrigerated, allow eggs to warm to room temperature. Place them in a saucepan in a single layer, cover them generously with cold water, then cook over medium-high heat just until several large bubbles begin to rise from the bottom of the pan. Reduce heat to a very gentle simmer and begin counting your cooking time.

• **4-minute egg:** Soft-cooked, with a liquid yolk and only partly set white. Great warm placed whole atop a bed of greens.

• **6-minute egg:** Soft-cooked, but with a soft-centered yolk and a firmly set white. Easy to handle, serve warm, whole or halved.

• **8-minute egg:** Hard-cooked, with firm yolk and white. The yolk will be two-toned, with a firm exterior, tender center. To halve or quarter, slice or chop.

• **10-minute egg:** Hard-cooked, with an evenly firm and even-colored, pale-yellow yolk, and a firm-set white. For serving cold, halved or quartered, sliced, or chopped.

and pepper to taste. Over low heat, wilt the chard and cook until most of the liquid has evaporated.

5. Combine the eggs and the cheese in a medium-size bowl; mix until thoroughly blended. Stir in the chard and mix well. Pour the vege-table mixture into the prepared pastry shell.

6. Bake until the crust is golden and the chard mixture is firm and browned, about 40 minutes. Serve at room temperature.

Yield: 8 servings

LES POISSONS ET LES FRUITS DE MER

Fish and Shellfish

Without question, the number and variety of fish and shell-fish recipes here reflect a positive modern bistro trend: more fish, more shellfish, simply prepared.

This chapter represents a mix of classic and modern bistro offerings: Among the classics, you'll find the Lille Festival's Steamed Mussels; Madame Cartet's Purée of Salt Cod, Garlic, and Cream; and Oysters with Spicy Sausages from The Happy Oyster restaurant. Other recipes reflect more contemporary interpretations, such as the grilled porgy from Willi's Wine Bar, and Chardenoux's Salmon Cooked with Its Skin. When it comes to fish and shellfish, there is one rule that always bears repeating: Get acquainted with a reliable fishmonger, and always go marketing with a variety of recipes in mind so that you can shop for freshness—not simply availability.

GRATIN DE MORUE

Salt Cod Gratin

This is one of my favorite fish dishes in the world. The fish markets of Provence are always filled with displays of *morue*—or dried cod— for preparing salads, purées (such as the famed *brandade*) and rich codfish gratins. This gratin is delicious in any season, served as a main course and accompanied by a crisp green salad, fresh bread, and a chilled Tavel rosé, such as Domaine de la Genestière.

1 pound (500 g) boneless, skinless salt cod
2 cups (50 cl) milk
2 teaspoons chopped fresh thyme
3 imported bay leaves
1 pound (500 g) baking potatoes such as russets, peeled and thinly sliced
2 large egg yolks
½ cup (12.5 cl) crème fraîche (see Index) or heavy cream
Salt and freshly ground black pepper
1 garlic clove, halved
3 tablespoons (1½ ounces; 45 g) unsalted butter

1. One to 2 days before preparing the gratin, depending upon the saltiness of the fish, place the salt cod in plenty of cold water and soak, covered, in the refrigerator. Change the water 3 to 4 times during the soaking period to remove excess salt. Drain and rinse the fish.

2. Place the cod in a large saucepan. Add cold water to cover and bring to a simmer over medium heat.

Immediately remove the pan from the heat, cover, and let stand for 15 minutes. Drain well. Scrape off any fatty skin and remove any bones. Tear the fish into bite-size pieces.

3. In a large saucepan, combine the milk, thyme, and bay leaves. Bring to a simmer over medium heat. Remove from the heat, cover, and let stand for 15 minutes.

4. Preheat the oven to 350°F (175°C).

5. Add the potatoes to the seasoned milk. Simmer, covered, over medium heat until the potatoes are tender, about 20 minutes.

6. In a small bowl, whisk together the egg yolks and crème fraîche. Remove the potato mixture from the heat and stir in the egg and cream mixture. Season with salt and pepper to taste.

7. Rub the cut sides of the garlic over a medium gratin or baking dish. Rub the gratin dish with 1 tablespoon of the butter. Spoon half of the potato mixture into the dish. Add the cod and top it with the remaining

potato mixture. Dot with the remaining 2 tablespoons butter. Bake the gratin until the top is golden brown, about 45 minutes. Serve hot. **Yield:** 6 to 8 servings

AÏOLI MONSTRE

Grand Aïoli (Salt Cod and Vegetables)

I like to think of the grand aïoli as a simple excuse to eat garlic. Aïoli gives its name to both the pungent garlic mayonnaise as well as the Provençal dish in which the mayonnaise serves as the star of a grand, processional meal. My favorite aïoli is served on Friday afternoons at Le Bistro de Paradou in Le Paradou, not far from Les Baux de Provence. There, the stone mortar filled with fragrant aïoli is placed in the center of the table, alongside a platter that includes hard-cooked eggs, boiled potatoes, salt cod, and local land snails known as *petit gris.* There is no limit to the amount of cooked or raw vegetables one can include in an aïoli, which in Provence is often called an *aïoli monstre,* or grand aïoli. Since aïoli includes so many ingredients, and takes a bit of time to prepare, it's the sort of dish that works best for a crowd. With this, serve either a Côtes-de-Provence white or rosé.

2 pounds (1 kg) salt cod
1 pound (500 g) medium beets
2 pounds (1 kg) small potatoes,
    scrubbed
1 pound (500 g) medium carrots,
    peeled
1 head of cauliflower, cut into florets
1 pound (500 g) thin green beans
8 hard-cooked eggs, in their shells
Aïoli (See Index), recipe tripled

1. One or 2 days before preparing the aïoli, depending upon the saltiness of the fish, place the salt cod in a large bowl of cold water and soak, covered, in the refrigerator. Change the water 3 to 4 times during the soaking period to remove excess salt. Drain and rinse the fish.

2. Place the cod in a large saucepan. Add fresh cold water to cover and bring just to a simmer over medium heat. Immediately remove the

pan from the heat. Cover and let stand for at least 15 minutes. Drain well. Scrape off any fatty skin and remove any bones. Tear the fish into large pieces.

3. Steam or boil the vegetables separately, about 40 minutes for the beets, 20 minutes each for the potatoes and carrots, 7 minutes for the cauliflower, and 4 to 6 minutes for the beans. Let cool. Peel the beets. Halve or quarter the beets and halve the carrots lengthwise. Arrange the vegetables on a large heated platter, along with the cod and unpeeled eggs. Pass the aïoli separately.

Yield: 12 to 16 servings

MORUE À LA PROVENÇALE LE CAMÉLÉON

Le Caméléon's Codfish With Herbed Tomato Sauce

I first sampled this dish, not in Provence, but in a small family bistro in Paris, Le Caméléon, run by the friendly Raymond and Jacqueline Faucher. I have a friend who dined there once a week for months, and never ordered anything else! I can see why. This is one of those very simple dishes—most of which can be done in advance—that somehow ends up tasting even better than the sum of its parts. At Le Caméléon, they serve the dish with boiled potatoes and a giant bowl of golden aïoli, a rich, garlicky mayonnaise.

1 pound (500 g) salt cod
2 tablespoons extra-virgin olive oil
4 medium onions (about 1 pound;
    500 g), coarsely chopped
5 garlic cloves, chopped
3 pounds (1.5 kg) ripe tomatoes,
    quartered, or 2 large (28 ounce;
    794 g) cans imported plum toma-
    toes
4 imported bay leaves
A handful of fresh herbs, preferably a
    mixture of basil, chervil, tarragon,
    thyme, and flat-leaf parsley,
    minced
½ teaspoon hot red pepper flakes (op-
    tional)
Salt
2 teaspoons fresh thyme or 1 teaspoon
    dried
2 tablespoons finely minced fresh chives
1 cup (25 cl) Aïoli (optional) (see
    Index)
1 pound (500 g) steamed Red Bliss
    potatoes (optional)

1. One day before preparing the gratin, soak the salt cod in plenty of cold water, changing the water 3 or 4 times during the soaking period, to remove excess salt.

2. In a large nonreactive skillet, heat the oil over medium heat. Add the onions and about 3 of the garlic cloves and cook, stirring frequently, until soft but not brown. Increase the heat to medium-high and add the to-matoes, 1 bay leaf, minced herbs, and salt to taste. Cook over medium heat, stirring frequently, until thick, 30 to 45 minutes. Check the seasonings. This will make a thick and rustic sauce. If you prefer a more refined sauce, pass it through a food mill or fine-mesh sieve. (The tomato sauce can be made ahead of time, and re-frigerated for several days or frozen for several weeks.)

3. Drain the cod. Place it in a small skillet and add fresh water to cover. Add the thyme, the remaining 3 bay leaves, and the remaining 2 garlic cloves. Bring just to a simmer over medium heat. Immediately re-move the pan from the heat. Cover and let stand for 15 minutes. Drain. Scrape off any fatty skin and remove any bones. Cut or tear the codfish into bite-size pieces.

4. Meanwhile, bring the tomato sauce to a simmer in a nonreactive large skillet. Add the cod and stir to blend thoroughly. Divide the fish and sauce equally among 4 warmed din-ner plates. Sprinkle with the chives and serve with the steamed or boiled small red potatoes and aïoli, for spreading on the potatoes.

Yield: 4 to 6 servings

TRUC

A tip for conserving leftover peeled garlic: Toss it in a bit of olive oil, cover securely, and refrigerate until you need it next. It will flavor the oil nicely, too.

LA BRANDADE DE MORUE DE MADAME CARTET

Madame Cartet's Purée of Salt Cod, Garlic, and Cream

In my files, I have a piece of blue-lined paper on which Madame Cartet, longtime owner of the popular Paris bistro that bears her name, carefully penned her recipe for *brandade de morue,* that rich gratin of codfish, garlic, cream, and oil. I sampled this the very first time I ate at Madame Cartet's, sometime in the spring of 1980. All over France, you still see *brandade* as a Friday special, the day on which fish was traditionally eaten. The potatoes are, as the French say, *facultatif,* or optional, depending upon how rich or how light you prefer your *brandade.* With a dish such as this, a little goes a long way! The *brandade* can be served as a first course—with a light main course to follow—or as a main luncheon dish. I enjoy this with a chilled rosé de Provence.

*1 pound (500 g) boneless, skinless salt
    cod
2 to 3 boiling potatoes, peeled (op-
    tional)
Salt
¾ cup (18.5 cl) crème fraîche (see
    Index) or heavy cream
½ cup (12.5 cl) extra-virgin olive oil
5 to 6 large garlic cloves, finely minced
Freshly ground black pepper
6 slices toasted white bread, rubbed
    with garlic and cut into triangles*

1. One to 2 days before preparing the gratin, depending upon the
saltiness of the fish, place the salt cod
in plenty of cold water and soak, covered, in the refrigerator. Change the
water 3 to 4 times during the soaking
period to remove excess salt. Drain
and rinse the fish.

2. Place the cod in a large saucepan. Add cold water to cover and
bring to a simmer over medium heat.
Immediately remove the pan from
the heat, cover, and let stand for 15
minutes. Drain well. When cool
enough to handle, scrape off any fatty
skin and remove any bones. Tear the
fish into bite-size pieces.

3. If you will be adding potatoes
to the *brandade,* cook the potatoes:

Place the potatoes in a single layer in a saucepan. Cover with water, add salt to taste, and bring to a boil over high heat. Cook until soft, 20 to 25 minutes. Drain. Let cool; mash gently with a fork.

4. Scald the crème fraîche in a medium-size saucepan over medium-high heat. At the same time, in a small saucepan over medium heat, heat the olive oil, until hot but not smoking.

5. Place the salt cod and garlic in a food processor and pulse to just mix. (If using potatoes, add them at this time as well.) Add the hot oil in a thin stream, pulsing the machine on and off, so the cod is not over-worked. When the oil is fully incorporated and the mixture is fairly smooth, slowly add the crème fraîche, pulsing on and off to avoid overmixing, until fluffy and smooth.

6. Taste the *brandade* and season to taste with freshly ground black pepper. Transfer to a bowl and serve with triangles of garlic toast.

Yield: 6 to 8 servings

HADDOCK AU CHOU FRISÉ CHEZ LA VIEILLE

Chez La Vieille's Smoked Haddock With Savoy Cabbage

This is a beautiful and warming dish, one that combines golden, smoky, flaky haddock and tender Savoy cabbage, all sauced with a smooth lemon-butter sauce. The recipe was shared with me by Adrienne Biasin, of Paris's Chez La Vieille. She advises cooking the cabbage twice to give it a more delicate flavor, and soaks the haddock in milk, to soften it. With it, drink a Bandol rosé or a rosé de Provence.

2 pounds (1 kg) smoked haddock fillets
4 cups (1 l) milk
1 Savoy cabbage
Salt
12 tablespoons (6 ounces; 180 g) un-salted butter

3 tablespoons freshly squeezed lemon juice
Freshly ground black pepper
3 tablespoons finely minced fresh parsley

1. Several hours before you plan to serve the haddock, soak the haddock: Place the fillets in a very shallow skillet, and cover with about 2 cups (50 cl) of water and 2 cups (50 cl) of the milk. Soak for about 1 hour.

2. Prepare the cabbage: Bring a large pot of salted water to a boil. Trim the cabbage, quarter it, and remove the thick center rib. Cut each quarter in half. After the water returns to a boil, cook the cabbage for 10 minutes.

3. Meanwhile, bring a second pot of salted water to a boil. Drain the cabbage and boil again for 10 minutes more. Drain well. Set aside and keep warm.

4. Meanwhile, prepare the haddock: Drain the haddock, discarding the soaking liquid. Return the fish to the skillet and cover with the remaining 2 cups (50 cl) milk. If necessary, add enough water to cover. Bring just to a simmer over medium heat. Simmer gently for 10 minutes; do not allow the liquid to boil.

5. Melt 6 tablespoons (3 ounces; 90 g) of the butter in a large, shallow saucepan over medium heat. Add the cabbage and cook gently, stirring just to coat with the butter. Remove to a warmed platter.

6. Carefully drain the haddock fillets; remove the skin. Place the fish on top of the cabbage. Keep warm.

7. In a small saucepan, melt the remaining 6 tablespoons (3 ounces; 90 g) butter over medium heat. Cook the butter just until pale brown. Remove from the heat, stir in the lemon juice, and season with salt and pepper to taste. Spoon the sauce over the haddock, sprinkle on the parsley, and serve immediately.

Yield: 6 servings

THON GRILLÉ SAUCE VIERGE

Grilled Tuna with Herbed Tomato, Garlic, Oil, and Lemon Sauce

Throughout France, the fish markets are filled with giant fresh red tuna, or *thon rouge,* which is wonderful for slicing into thick steaks and grilling or broiling rare. This sauce—known as *sauce vierge*—is a marvelous accompaniment, one that sings with the flavors and aromas of the south. This is a variation of the deliciously fresh grilled tuna I was first served at the waterside fisherman's bistro Arrantzaleak in the fishing port of Saint-Jean-de-Luz, in the Pays Basque. Serve this dish with a good red Côtes-du-Rhone, such as Château de Fonsalette.

Sauce:
3 tomatoes, peeled, cored, seeded, and
    chopped
½ cup (12.5 cl) extra-virgin olive oil
3 tablespoons freshly squeezed lemon
    juice
3 garlic cloves, minced
Salt
Large handful of fresh herbs, prefera-
    bly a blend of chervil, chives, tar-
    ragon, and parsley

Tuna:
1 pound (500 g) fresh tuna steak,
    sliced 3 inches (7.5 cm) thick
1 tablespoon extra-virgin olive oil

1. Prepare the sauce: Combine the tomatoes, olive oil, lemon juice, and garlic in a bowl; stir to blend. Season with salt to taste; set aside for 1 to 2 hours to allow the flavors to blend. Just before cooking the tuna, add the herbs and stir to blend.

2. Preheat the broiler, prepare a grill for grilling, or heat a dry cast-iron skillet over high heat.

3. Brush the tuna with the olive oil. Cook the tuna for just 1 minute on each side; the tuna will be very rosy and rare on the inside and charred on the outside.

4. Remove the tuna to a large preheated platter and top with half of the sauce. Then, cut the tuna into thick strips and serve with additional

sauce. This is delicious cold the next day, served as is, or mixed with warm pasta.

    Yield: 4 servings

    "*Aïoli concentrates all the warmth, the strength, the sun-loving gaiety of Provence in its essence, but it also has a particular virtue: It keeps flies away. Those who don't like it, those whose stomachs rise at the thought of our oil and garlic, won't come buzzing around us, wasting our time. There will only be family.***"**

    —FRÉDÉRIC MISTRAL

THON À L'AIL ARRANTZALEAK, SAUCE PIPÉRADE

Arrantzaleak's Grilled Tuna with Garlic and Sauce Pipérade

I love tuna any way it's cooked, but I think that grilled is my favorite. Tuna's a fatty fish, and I find that, contrary to what one might think, fatty fish needs to be eaten with a little more fat. I like the idea of spooning a touch of oil and garlic over the top of the grilled tuna, adding a voluptuous quality to what seems to have become such a common fish. I sampled this on my first visit to Arrantzaleak, a lively fisherman's bistro on the waterfront in Saint-Jean-de-Luz, in Basque country. With it, I like a chilled rosé, from either Spain or southern France.

1 pound (500 g) tuna steak, cut 1
   inch (2.5 cm) thick, rinsed and
   patted dry
3 tablespoons peanut oil
Freshly ground black pepper
20 large garlic cloves, thinly sliced
1 tablespoon best-quality red wine
   vinegar
Salt
Sauce Pipérade Basquaise (recipe follows)

1. Preheat the broiler.
2. Lightly brush both sides of the tuna with some of the oil. Season generously with pepper. Broil until the flesh begins to turn opaque, about 5 minutes per side. The fish should still be pink in the center.

3. Meanwhile, in a large, non-reactive deep-sided skillet, heat 2 tablespoons of the oil over medium-high heat. When the oil is hot but not smoking, add the garlic and stir to coat with oil. Sauté until light golden, 3 to 4 minutes. Add the vinegar and deglaze the pan, scraping up any bits that cling to the bottom.
4. Sprinkle the tuna with salt. Transfer the fish to a warmed platter and pour the garlic sauce over all. Serve immediately, with a warmed bowl of *pipérade* alongside.

Yield: 4 servings

Pipérade Basquaise Arrantzaleak

Arrantzaleak's Sauce of Tomatoes, Onions, and Chiles

Pipérade is one of my favorite food words. Like *ratatouille, raïto,* and *estouffade,* it's a word that sort of races off the edge of the tongue, suggesting a dish that will be full of energy and life. And that it is. One of the best versions I ever tasted was served on my first visit to Arrantzaleak, a no-nonsense fish restaurant in the Pays Basque. Here, fish jump from the water to the grill, and each day the assortment varies according to the catch.

That day, fresh red tuna was the fish of the day, and we sampled it grilled, along with this marvelous, sun-filled sauce. If, like me, you have a passion for tomatoes, peppers, and onions, you may want to double this, to have plenty on hand to serve with grilled fish, meat, or tossed into an omelet pan to be held together with a few scrambled eggs.

2 small, mildly hot green chiles (optional)
6 tablespoons extra-virgin olive oil
2 pounds (1 kg) tomatoes, peeled, cored, seeded, and chopped
2 medium onions, coarsely chopped
3 large green bell peppers, cored, halved, seeded, and cut lengthwise into thin slices
3 garlic cloves, minced
Salt and freshly ground black pepper

1. If using chiles, put on rubber gloves to protect your hands. Cut the tops from the chiles, slice in half lengthwise, and remove all of the seeds. Cut the chiles into very thin strips. Set aside.

2. In a large nonreactive skillet, heat 2 tablespoons of the oil over medium-high heat. When the oil is hot but not smoking, add the tomatoes and simmer, uncovered, for about 10 minutes.

3. In a medium-size skillet, heat 2 tablespoons of the oil over medium heat. When the oil is hot but not smoking, add the onions and cook until light golden, about 10 minutes.

4. In another medium skillet, heat the remaining 2 tablespoons oil until hot but not smoking. Add the chiles and bell peppers and cook until soft and tender, about 10 minutes.

5. Add the onions and peppers to the tomato mixture. Stir in the garlic and season with salt and pepper to taste. Cook, uncovered, over low heat for 1 hour, stirring from time to time. This pipérade can be served warm or cold, as an accompaniment to grilled fish or meat.

Yield: 4 servings

ESCALOPE DE SAUMON FRAIS RÔTI À L'HUILE D'OLIVE

Fresh Roasted Salmon with Olive Oil

This pleasant and simple salmon recipe comes from Guy Jullien, one of my favorite chefs in Provence. His little country restaurant, La Beaugravière, specializes in wine and truffles and good times (need we ask for more!). Jullien loves to upset tradition, and one day he served this light roast salmon, sauced with a touch of cream, tomatoes, and basil, with a red Châteauneuf-du-Pape from Vieux Télégraphe. (Later, he confessed that he hadn't tasted the combination before serving it. The palate in his mind just told him it would work!) Red wine with fish? Why not? The fatty, full-flavored nature of the salmon stands up well to this vigorous, meaty wine.

1⅔ *tablespoons extra-virgin olive oil*
2 shallots, finely minced
4 medium tomatoes, peeled, cored, seeded, and chopped
½ cup (12.5 cl) crème fraîche (see Index) or heavy cream
4 salmon fillets, with skin attached, each weighing about 4 ounces (125 g)
Salt
1 large bunch of fresh basil

1. Heat 1 tablespoon of oil in a small nonreactive skillet over high heat. When the oil is hot but not smoking, add the shallots and sauté until soft, but not browned, 2 to 3 minutes. Add the tomatoes and continue cooking until much of the liquid has cooked away, about 10 minutes. Reduce the heat to low and add the crème fraîche. Cook just long enough to heat the cream through; set the sauce aside.

2. Preheat the oven to 325°F (165°C).

3. Brush the salmon and skin with the remaining 2 teaspoons olive oil on all sides. Preheat a 12-inch (30 cm) dry nonstick pan over medium-high heat. Adding no fat, cook the salmon, skin side down, for 2 minutes. Season with salt. Turn the salmon over and cook for 2 minutes more. Season again with salt.

4. Remove the salmon to a

roasting pan. Bake until the salmon is opaque through, about 5 minutes more.

5. To serve, mince the basil and stir it into the sauce. Spoon several tablespoons of sauce in the center of a warmed dinner plate and place the salmon on top of the sauce. Serve immediately.

Yield: 4 servings

TRUC

Chef Gérard Allemandou of Paris's La Cagouille prefers the double cooking method for whole fish as well as fillets: Brown the fish first in a nonstick pan with very little sunflower oil, about 2 minutes each side. Then complete the cooking process in a warm (about 325°F; 165°C) oven for 3 to 4 minutes.

SAUMON À L'UNILATERAL CHARDENOUX

Chardenoux's Salmon Cooked with Its Skin

S*aumon à l'unilateral* has become almost a cliché, but what a delicious cliché. This recipe comes from Chardenoux, a lovely turn-of-the-century bistro in Paris's newly fashionable 11th arrondissement. I like to serve it as is, with perhaps a sprinkle of lemon, some buttered fresh pasta, and a lovely white, such as a Vouvray sec. Because the salmon is served rare, make certain that your salmon is absolutely fresh.

---

4 salmon fillets with skin attached (each about 5 ounces; 150 grams)
1 teaspoon extra-virgin olive oil
3 tablespoons (1½ ounces; 45 g) unsalted butter
Coarse sea salt

1. Brush the salmon skin with the oil, so it will not stick to the pan while cooking.

2. In a large skillet, melt the butter over medium-high heat. When the foam begins to subside, add the salmon fillets, skin side down. Cook,

without turning, until the skin is brown and crusty and the salmon has just begun to turn color, about 6 minutes. The salmon will be quite rare. (For salmon that is cooked through, put a lid on the skillet and cook for 2 to 3 minutes more.) Sprinkle with the salt. Serve immediately.

Yield: 4 servings

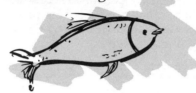

SMOKED POTATOES

Chef José Lampreia of Paris's Maison Blanche suggests baking potatoes—washed but not peeled—in a covered casserole with a thick slice of smoked country bacon. Cook for an hour, at about 400°F (205°C). Finely chop the bacon and serve with the potatoes to accompany grilled or roasted salmon.

DAURADE GRILLÉ, SAUCE AU POIVRONS, CÂPRES, ET CUMIN WILLI'S WINE BAR

Willi's Wine Bar's Grilled Porgy with Red Peppers, Capers, and Cumin

One wintry Saturday morning my husband and I set off for B.H.V., the gigantic Parisian department store that specializes in hardware and things for the home. Of course Saturday is the worst day to go, for that's when every Parisian, handy or not, decides he needs a nail, a lightbulb, a ladder, or an electric extension cord. I hate going there: The crowds are suffocating and the clerks nasty.

I didn't want the day to be a total waste, so I suggested we stop at Willi's Wine Bar for a late lunch. That day, I sampled this wonderful grilled porgy: It was so fresh it tasted as though it had jumped from the water only moments earlier, and it was so perfectly cooked—light and flavorful as could be. I loved the sauce, a pretty and lively, fragrant blend of cubed red peppers, faintly salty capers, and a touch of toasted cumin. The sauce, of course, could be served with any small fish, which I actually pan-fry rather than grill. Good substitutes include sea bream or rainbow trout. With this, sample a nice sturdy white, such as a Châteauneuf-du-Pape from Beaucastel.

5 to 6 tablespoons extra-virgin olive oil
2 large red bell peppers, cored, seeded, and diced
2 tablespoons drained capers
2 teaspoons cumin seeds
4 whole porgy, each weighing about 10 ounces (300 g), cleaned, with heads on (or substitute sea bream, or rainbow trout)
Salt and freshly ground black pepper

1. In a medium-size nonstick skillet, heat 1 tablespoon of the oil over medium heat. When the oil is hot but not smoking, add the peppers and sauté until cooked through, 4 to 5 minutes. Off the heat, stir in the capers and cumin. The sauce can be prepared ahead and reheated at serving time.

2. Rinse the fish and pat dry. Generously season the cavity of each porgy with salt and pepper. Generously brush the fish with oil.

3. In a large nonstick skillet heat 2 tablespoons of oil over medium-high heat. When hot but not smoking, add 2 of the fish and cook until opaque through but not firm or dry, 4 to 5 minutes per side. Keep the fish warm while you cook the other 2 fish, adding more oil as needed.

4. Meanwhile, reheat the sauce. Also, heat 4 dinner plates until very hot and brush the hot plates with olive oil.

5. When the fish are cooked, season with salt and pepper and place them on the hot oiled dinner plates. Spoon the warmed sauce alongside and serve immediately.

Yield: 4 servings

EFFEUILÉE D'AILE DE RAIE AU CHOU L'AMBROISIE

L'Ambroisie's Skate Wing with Cabbage and Spring Onions

L'Ambroisie, one of Paris's top restaurants, is far from a bistro. But in truth, it began as a very small restaurant serving simple food, and this dish—which uses both skate wing and cabbage, an authentic bistro combination—has been on the menu since the restaurant's earliest days. The skate is cooked in a thyme and garlic infused stock, which gives nice flavor to the delicate meat. Cooked in this manner, the skin peels off easily. Be sure not to overcook the fish, and drain it well so it isn't soggy.

4 skate wings, each weighing about 1 pound (500 g)
2 large yellow onions, halved
1 large bunch of fresh thyme, or 2 tablespoons dried thyme
1 whole head of garlic, crushed but not peeled
Salt and freshly ground black pepper
½ small Savoy cabbage, cut lengthwise into eighths
½ cup (12.5 cl) best-quality sherry wine vinegar
8 tablespoons (4 ounces; 120 g) unsalted butter, chilled and cut into small pieces
2 to 3 small white onions, cut into julienne, or 2 to 3 scallions, cut into thin rings

> **"**Young couples would hold hands while they ate a delicious raie au beurre noir or a vol-au-vent. Between bites of food they would exchange passionate kisses. No one sitting near pretended to notice, but everyone looked pleased, and there was a glow of happiness about the place . . . It was a very romantic Prix-Fixe.**"**
>
> —JOSEPH WECHSBERG
> *Blue Trout & Black Truffles*

1. Rinse the fish and pat them dry. Combine the yellow onions, thyme, garlic, and salt and pepper to taste in a large, deep skillet. Add the skate wings and cover with cold water. Cover and bring to a boil over high heat. As soon as the water boils remove the pan from the heat. Remove 1 cup (25 cl) of the cooking liquid to a small nonreactive saucepan; set aside. Cover the skillet and set aside off the heat until the fish is cooked through, about 10 minutes.

2. Meanwhile, steam the cabbage until cooked, about 10 minutes.

3. Bring the reserved 1 cup (25 cl) cooking liquid to a boil over high heat. Boil until reduced by half, about 5 minutes. Add the vinegar and boil for 1 minute. Swirl in the butter a few pieces at a time, and keep the sauce warm over very low heat.

4. To serve, drain the skate on a towel. Remove the skin from both sides. Place 2 wedges of cabbage on each of 4 warmed dinner plates. Place the skate on top of the cabbage. Spoon the sauce over the fish, sprinkle with the raw onions or scallions, and serve immediately.

Yield: 4 servings

LE TURBOT AU VINAIGRE CIDRE

Turbot in Cider Vinegar Sauce

Odile Engel is one of Normandy's best-known cooks, offering a very simple, homey, uncomplicated *cuisine de femme*. She's passionate about fish, treats her turbot, brill, Saint-Pierre, and sole ever so delicately, and doesn't like to smother them in overly complicated sauces. This dish—from her small village restaurant Le Pavé d'Auge in Beuvron-en-Auge—is rich with the flavors of Normandy, combining delicate turbot, rich local butter, and the region's favored apple cider vinegar.

1 pound (500 g) flatfish fillets, either turbot, brill, sole, or flounder
¼ cup (6 cl) best-quality apple cider vinegar
12 tablespoons (6 ounces; 180 g)

unsalted butter, chilled and cut into small pieces
Salt and freshly ground black pepper

1. In a steamer or fish poacher, bring 2 cups (50 cl) of water to a boil over high heat. Place the fish fillets in the steamer, reduce the heat to medium, cover, and cook until they are just opaque throughout, 4 to 5 minutes.

2. Meanwhile, in a nonreactive small saucepan, bring the cider vinegar to a boil over medium-high heat. Add the butter, a few pieces at a time, whisking constantly after each addition, moving the pan on and off the heat as necessary, until all of the butter is added and the sauce is smooth and creamy. Season with salt and pepper to taste.

3. Place the fish fillets on warmed dinner plates and spoon the sauce over.

Yield: 4 servings

A SUPPER FROM NORMANDY

◆

Apples are, of course, one of the stars of Normandy's cuisine. Here's a trio of recipes with a Norman touch. You could drink cider with the meal, or a white Bordeaux such as a young Graves.

CRÊPES AUX COURGETTES LA MÈRE POULARD
La Mère Poulard's Zucchini Crêpes

◆

LE TURBOT AU VINAIGRE DE CIDRE
Turbot in Cider Vinegar Sauce

◆

TARTE AUX POMMES À LA CRÈME
Golden Cream and Apple Tart

MOULES MARINIÈRE BRADERIE DE LILLE

◆

The Lille Festival's Steamed Mussels

Each fall the city of Lille in the north of France sponsors a festive weekend *braderie*, literally a free-for-all in the streets, when thousands of people flood the old town to take part in the citywide garage sale that goes on throughout the night. The festival is accompanied by a mussel and French fry feast: Each café and restaurant serves the specialty, and discarded shells are piled into mounds on the street, as a sign of the diners' gastronomic fortitude.

During one of the *braderies,* I sampled this version at one of Lille's prettiest restaurants, A l'Huitrière. The addition of thyme and pepper add a wonderful punch to an ordinary, but always delicious, preparation. It's an ideal casual lunch, especially when served with fresh baguettes spread with sweet butter, and plenty of chilled white Muscadet. When preparing the dish, be sure to be generous with the pepper. Last time I prepared it, I counted 40 turns of the mill.

4 pounds (2 kg) fresh mussels
2 cups (50 cl) dry white wine, such as Riesling
2 large onions, finely minced
1 celery rib, finely minced
2 large sprigs of fresh thyme, or 2 generous teaspoons dried thyme
Freshly ground black pepper
1 large bunch of fresh parsley, finely minced

plenty of buttered bread and chilled white wine.

Yield: 4 to 6 servings

1. Thoroughly scrub the mussels and rinse with several changes of water. Beard the mussels. (Do not beard the mussels in advance, or they will die and spoil.)

2. Combine the mussels, wine, onions, celery, and thyme in a non-reactive 6-quart (6 l) Dutch oven. Bring the wine to a boil over high heat. Cover and cook just until the mussels open, about 5 minutes; do not overcook. Discard any mussels that do not open. Leave the cooked mussels in their shells.

3. Spoon the mussels and sauce into a large bowl. Sprinkle generously with black pepper and the parsley and serve immediately, with

❝*Pepper, as much used as a condiment, facilitates digestion . . . As it is one of the most powerful stimulants, it is only used in moderation in good cooking; and nervous, susceptible people should even abstain from using it. This does not apply to country people, the sensibility of whose stomachs has become dulled by their habitually eating coarse food.***❞**

—ALEXANDRE DUMAS
Dumas on Food

MOULES SAUCE POULETTE CHEZ TOUTOUNE

Chez Toutoune's Mussels with Cream Sauce

This is a wonderful, classic bistro dish, and one that I first sampled one warm summer's night at the lively Parisian bistro, Chez Toutoune. I'm crazy about briny mussels and love eating them from the shell. In the country, this has become a favorite Saturday afternoon lunch, since it's such a snap to prepare. Be sure to have plenty of grilled country bread on hand to soak up the rich and creamy *sauce poulette,* flavored with just a hint of thyme.

This dish is not quite a soup, but almost, so it's best to serve it out of shallow soup bowls. With it, drink the same wine used in cooking the mussels, either a chilled white Muscadet or a dry white Graves.

2 large egg yolks
½ cup (12.5 cl) crème fraîche (see Index) or heavy cream
2 pounds (1 kg) fresh mussels
3 tablespoons (1½ ounces; 45 g) unsalted butter
2 shallots, finely minced
1 cup (25 cl) dry white wine, such as Muscadet or a white Graves
2 teaspoons fresh thyme leaves
Freshly ground black pepper
2 tablespoons minced fresh parsley

1. Preheat the oven to 225°F (105°C). Warm 4 soup bowls and a large soup terrine in the oven.

2. Combine the egg yolks and crème fraîche in a small bowl, and whisk until well blended. Set aside.

3. Thoroughly scrub the mussels and rinse with several changes of cold water. Beard the mussels. (Do not beard the mussels in advance, or they will die and spoil.)

4. Melt the butter in a nonreactive large skillet over medium heat. Add the shallots and cook just until soft and translucent, about 2 minutes. Add the mussels, wine, and thyme. Increase the heat to high, cover, and cook, stirring from time to time, just until the mussels open, 3 to 4 minutes. Do not overcook, or the mussels will become tough.

5. Remove from the heat. Using a slotted spoon, scoop out the mussels and place the cooked mussels in

their shells in the warmed soup tureen. Discard any mussels that do not open. Cover the tureen and place in the warm oven.

6. Strain the mussel cooking liquid through several thicknesses of dampened cheesecloth. Return the mussel cooking liquid to the skillet (be sure to wipe it out first, to remove any traces of sand from the mussels), then whisk in the crème fraîche and egg yolk mixture. Reheat the sauce gently, without boiling. Pour over the cooked mussels. Sprinkle generously with pepper and the parsley and serve.

Yield: 4 servings

MOULES "BRÛLE DOIGTS" LA CAGOUILLE

La Cagouille's "Burn Your Fingers" Mussels

Some recipes are so simple, one almost feels silly giving specific instructions. This is one of the quickest, easiest, and best ways I know to serve fresh, fresh mussels. Gérard Allemandou, the crazy, talented chef/owner of Paris's fish bistro, La Cagouille, almost always has this dish on his menu. Like many favorite foods, it goes back to childhood days: When Allemandou was growing up in the fish and Cognac-rich region of the Charente, housewives always opened mussels directly over the heat, on cast-iron wood-burning stoves. No wine, no shallots, no complex preparations, just mussels pure and simple, sprinkled with a touch of freshly ground black pepper at the end. The mussels were traditionally eaten right from the stove as they opened, thus the name *brûle doigts* or "burn your fingers."

1½ pounds (750 g) fresh mussels
Freshly ground black pepper

1. Thoroughly scrub the mussels; rinse with several changes of water. Beard the mussels. (Do not beard the mussels in advance or they will die and spoil.)

2. Using no fat, heat a large cast-iron skillet over high heat. When a drop of water sizzles and evaporates immediately, the pan is sufficiently hot to use. Spoon all of the mussels

into the skillet and shake the pan. The mussels should begin to open immediately. Continue shaking the pan until all of the mussels have opened. If the pan becomes thoroughly dry, sprinkle on a bit of water to moisten it. When all of the mussels have opened, sprinkle generously with freshly ground black pepper and serve immediately, either bringing the pan right to the table, or spooning the mussels into serving dishes.

Yield: Serves 4 as a first course, 2 as a main course

> **❝***In cooking, as in all the arts, simplicity is the sign of perfection.***❞**
>
> —CURNONSKY

MOULES À LA PROVENÇALE

Mussels with Tomatoes, Garlic, Olive Oil, and Wine

I think if I had to list my favorite ingredients in the world they would include mussels, tomatoes, garlic, olive oil, and white wine. Well, here you have them all together in a single dish, a simple mussels Provençale-style. I love serving this in shallow ocher-hued soup bowls: The colors sing of the sun, making you want to run, dance, swim, eat! Serve with freshly toasted bread and a nice chilled white or rosé.

1½ pounds (750 g) fresh mussels
1 cup (25 cl) dry white wine
4 garlic cloves, coarsely chopped
2 imported bay leaves
4 shallots, coarsely chopped
1½ pounds plum tomatoes, peeled, cored, seeded, and chopped (off season, substitute 1 can (28 ounce;

794 g) imported plum tomatoes, drained)
¼ teaspoon hot red pepper flakes
1 tablespoon extra-virgin olive oil
3 tablespoons minced flat-leaf parsley

1. Thoroughly scrub the mussels; rinse with several changes of water. Beard the mussels. (Do not beard the mussels in advance or they will spoil and die.)

2. Place the mussels in a non-reactive large skillet along with the wine, garlic, bay leaves, and shallots. Cover and cook just until the mussels begin to open, 3 or 4 minutes. Do not overcook. Remove from the heat. Remove the mussels from the pan with a slotted spoon. Discard any mussels that do not open. Strain the cooking liquor through several thicknesses of dampened cheesecloth; reserve.

3. When the mussels are cool enough to handle, remove only the top shells from the mussels. Arrange the mussels in their shells in 4 shallow soup bowls.

4. Wipe out the saucepan to remove any traces of sand or grit. Return the strained liquor to the saucepan and add the tomatoes and red pepper flakes. Bring to a boil over high heat. Cook for 2 to 3 minutes. Add the olive oil and stir to blend.

5. Spoon the sauce over the mussels. Sprinkle with the parsley and serve.

Yield: 4 first-course servings, or 2 main-course servings

LES PRAIRES FARCIES LOU BACCHUS

◆───────◆

Broiled Clams with Garlic and Parsley

L ou Bacchus is a tiny Parisian café turned into a fish bistro, an intimate spot that for a time was run by a young woman chef who trained under Gérard Allemandou of Paris's wonderful La Cagouille. She served this classic dish one evening, and it sent me swooning. Just be careful not to overcook the clams the first time around, or they will be tough. And this is one time to go easy on the garlic: don't let it overpower the gentle iodine-rich essence of the clams. With this, sample a crisp, chilled Muscadet.

36 *littleneck, butter, or Manila clams,*
  shells well scrubbed under cold
  running water
Salt (optional)
2 cups (50 cl) dry white wine, such
  as Aligoté
1 small onion, finely minced
3 garlic cloves, finely minced
Small bunch of flat-leaf parsley, finely
  minced

1. Steam open a clam to check for grit. If there is none, proceed with the recipe. If they are sandy, place them in a large bucket filled with cold salted water (⅓ cup salt to 1 gallon of water) and let sit for 2 hours. Scrub the shells thoroughly under water with a stiff brush.

2. Preheat the oven to 500°F (260°C).

3. Combine the clams and wine in a large nonreactive saucepan over medium-high heat. Cover and cook, shaking the pan from time to time, until the clams begin to open, 3 to 4 minutes. Remove the clams with a slotted spoon just as soon as they open. Discard any clams that do not open. Add the onion, increase the heat to high, and boil to reduce the liquid by half, about 10 minutes.

4. Meanwhile, open the clams, discarding the top half of the shell. Loosen the clams from the bottom shell by sliding the blade of a sharp knife under the meat to cut the muscle. Place the clams in a single layer in an ovenproof baking dish (use 2 dishes if necessary).

5. Carefully strain the reduced liquid through several thicknesses of dampened cheesecloth. Spoon the liquid over the clam shells. Sprinkle on the garlic and parsley. Bake the clams in the oven until warmed, 2 or 3 minutes.

Yield: 4 servings

❝My waiter was Gaston, an old, asthmatic man who suffered from rheumatism. On days when the weather was about to change, he was ill-tempered and disinclined to listen to the guest's orders. Instead, he would bring the guest what he himself liked to eat. But his taste was excellent and usually he made a better choice than I should have done.**❞**

—JOSEPH WECHSBERG
Blue Trout & Black Truffles

Huîtres et Saucisses L'Huître Joyeuse

Oysters and Spicy Sausages from the Happy Oyster Restaurant

I had long heard of this traditional fisherman's snack, oysters and spicy sausages washed down with white wine, but it took a trip to Bordeaux to find the real thing. Chef Francis Garcia—now of Le Chapon Fin—prepared these one cold wintry afternoon, and educated me on how to properly eat this welcoming combination: First, down a cool oyster, then take a bit of the sausage, and then a sip of chilled white wine. The sausage serves to soften the brininess of the oyster, leaving a lovely blending of flavors lingering on the palate. It's one of my very favorite food and wine combinations, full of crisp, spicy flavors that wake up and keep you going for hours!

You'll find various versions of this dish: I've seen them with very spicy sausage patties, with sausage links, served hot and served cold. Although the dish goes by many names (the most common is *huîtres à la charentaise*) I decided to name these after the oyster festival I attended one August in the Atlantic coast oyster-growing village of Gujan-Mestras. The festival restaurant was called, fittingly, L'Huître Joyeuse, the Happy Oyster! Try this with a young, chilled white Graves.

1 dozen oysters, shells well scrubbed under cold running water, shucked
Crushed ice
8 ounces (250 g) bulk pork sausage meat
1 tablespoon fresh thyme leaves or 1 teaspoon dried
1 teaspoon crushed hot red pepper flakes
¼ teaspoon sea salt

1. Place the oysters on a plate of crushed ice. Arrange the oysters balancing them so they do not lose any of their liquid. Cover loosely with aluminum foil and refrigerate. Remove the oysters 10 minutes before serving.

2. In a medium-size bowl, blend the sausage meat with the thyme, pepper flakes, and salt. Mix well with your hands to blend thoroughly.

3. Shape the pork mixture into 4 equal-size round patties about ½

inch (1.5 cm) thick.

4. In a medium-size skillet, cook the patties over medium-high heat until golden brown on the outside and cooked all the way through, about 5 minutes on each side. Drain on paper towels.

5. Serve the sausages immediately, accompanied by the oysters, slices of buttered, crisp-crusted bread, and chilled white wine.

Yield: 4 servings

> **"**As I ate the oysters with their strong taste of the sea and their faint metallic taste that the cold white wine washed away, leaving only the sea taste and the succulent texture, and as I drank their cold liquid from each shell and washed it down with the crisp taste of the wine, I lost the empty feeling and began to be happy, and to make plans.**"**
>
> —ERNEST HEMINGWAY
> *A Moveable Feast*

CROMESQUIS D'HUÎTRES, "SAUCE TARTARE"

Fried Oysters with Creamy Tartar Sauce

Nothing could be more common than fried fish and tartar sauce. But, boy, is this an uptown version! The recipe comes from L'Ambroisie, one of Paris's top restaurants. While it may seem like a beyond-bistro recipe, when served at home, it's a nice, light, homey starter. Be sure to have all the ingredients ready to go, and even invite your guests to the table so they can be served their oysters piping hot! I love the crispness of the light, golden batter surrounding briny fresh oysters, making for a crunchy exterior and soft, moist interior. The mild pungency of the fried leeks adds a wonderful flavor, as does the lighter version of tartar sauce, prepared with stiffly whipped cream instead of mayonnaise.

1 quart (1 l) peanut oil, for deep-frying
1 leek (white part only) trimmed and rinsed well
12 large fresh oysters, shells well scrubbed
½ cup (70 g) superfine flour, such as Wondra
2 whole eggs
2 egg yolks
1 cup (140 g) fresh bread crumbs

Tartar Sauce:
2 tablespoons very finely chopped cornichon or dill pickle
2 tablespoons drained capers, very finely chopped
1 teaspoon imported Dijon mustard
½ teaspoon paprika
½ cup (12.5 cl) very finely minced flat-leaf parsley
½ cup (12.5 cl) crème fraîche or heavy cream, well chilled

1. Place the oil in a heavy metal 2-quart (2 l) saucepan. Heat to 280°F (140°C) to fry the leek slices.

2. Cut the leek into very, very thin julienne about 3 inches (7.5 cm) long and as thin as possible. In several batches, drop the leek slices into the oil and fry until golden brown, 4 to 5 minutes. The oil should not be too hot, or the leeks will fry too quickly and will burn. Drain on paper towels and set aside. This step can be done

LET'S CALL IT A BORDEAUX COUNTRY FÊTE

I've put together some of my favorite recipes from what I call "Bordeaux Country"—both the city and the villages within a short drive. The oysters and the scallops call out for a crisp, chilled white (a white Graves would make me very happy), and with the duck stew, sample a very young Sauternes.

HUÎTRES ET SAUCISSES L'HUÎTRE JOYEUSE
Oysters and Spicy Sausages from the Happy Oyster Restaurant

◆

PÉTONCLES AU FOUR LA TUPIÑA
La Tupina's Oven-Roasted Scallops

◆

CIVET DE CANARD AU SAUTERNES
Duck Stew in Sauternes

◆

MON GÂTEAU AU CHOCOLAT
Marie-Claude Gracia's Chocolate Cake

up to 2 hours in advance. Reserve the oil for the oysters.

3. Open the oysters, reserving

the oyster liquor. Strain the liquor to remove any shell or sand. Place the liquor in a small saucepan and bring to a boil over high heat. Add the oysters and poach for just 30 seconds. Drain, reserving the oysters and liquor separately. When the oysters and the liquor have cooled, combine them again, to keep the oysters moist and plump. This step can be done up to 2 hours in advance.

4. Set up 3 shallow plates for coating the oysters: Place the flour in one, whisk the eggs and egg yolks in another, and place the fresh bread crumbs in the third.

5. Prepare the tartar sauce: In a small bowl, combine the cornichons, capers, mustard, paprika, and parsley. In a medium-size bowl, whip the crème fraîche or heavy cream until stiff. Carefully fold the cornichon mixture into the cream. Adjust the seasoning if necessary. Set the tartar sauce aside.

6. Reheat the reserved oil to 375°F (190°C) to fry the oysters.

7. Drain the oysters and dredge them, one at a time, in the flour. Dip them into the egg mixture, then dredge them in the bread crumbs. Fry the oysters, 3 or 4 at a time, until nicely browned, about 1 minute.

8. To serve, place the oysters on a platter, top with a "nest" of fried leeks, and place a spoonful of tartar sauce alongside.

Yield: 6 appetizer or 2 main-course servings

HUÎTRES FROIDES NAPÉES D'UNE CRÈME D'HUÎTRE LÉON DE LYON

Léon de Lyon's Cold Oysters Wrapped in Spinach and Sauced with Oyster Cream

The last time I lunched at Léon de Lyon, one of my favorite restaurants in all of France, chef Jean-Paul Lacombe insisted I sample this delicious first course. I love the blend of oysters, spinach, and cream, a marriage of soft textures and delicate but lively flavors. At home, the dish is mildly time-consuming to prepare, but can be done in advance. I love the idea of returning the chilled oysters to their shells, making for a lovely presentation.

18 fresh oysters in the shell
1¾ cups (43.5 cl) heavy cream
2 teaspoons best-quality sherry vinegar
Salt and freshly ground black pepper
About 12 large spinach leaves
Fresh seaweed, for serving (optional)
A pinch of sweet paprika

1. Carefully open the oysters, reserving the oyster liquor. (Your fishmonger can do this for you, but the oysters should be opened no more than a few hours before preparing the dish. If so, it is best to reserve the oysters in their liquid, in their shells, for maximum freshness.) Strain the liquor through several thicknesses of dampened cheesecloth. Keep the oysters chilled.

2. Measure the oyster liquor. If there is ½ cup (12.5 cl) or less, go to Step 3. If there is more than ½ cup, reduce the oyster liquor over medium heat to about ½ cup (12.5 cl).

3. In a small saucepan, reduce the cream over medium heat to about ½ cup (12.5 cl). Combine the cream and oyster liquor. Chill.

4. Pass 6 of the oysters through a fine-mesh sieve or strainer.

5. Once the cream and oyster liquor mixture is chilled, whisk in the sieved oysters and the vinegar. Adjust the seasoning, adding salt and pepper to taste. Chill.

6. Clean the spinach leaves; re-move the tough stems. Blanch the leaves in a large pot of boiling, salted water, to make the leaves more flexible, about 30 seconds. Drain thoroughly. Lay each leaf flat on a cutting board. Cut out the tough central stem. Reserving the oyster shell, place 1 fresh oyster on each spinach leaf. Fold the end and sides of the leaf over the oyster, and roll up from the stem end to make a neat package. (Each package should contain as little spinach as possible, just enough to neatly wrap the oyster.) Return the

wrapped oyster to its shell. Repeat with the remaining 11 oysters.

7. Place several leaves of fresh seaweed on a platter. (If fresh seaweed is not available, you may set the oysters in special indented oyster plates, or, on a thick bed of coarse salt.) Arrange the oysters on the platter, spoon the cream and oyster sauce over the wrapped oysters, and sprinkle with the paprika. Serve immediately—this dish should be eaten chilled.

Yield: 4 servings

COQUILLES SAINT-JACQUES À LA PROVENÇALE L'AMI LOUIS

L'Ami Louis's Scallops with Garlic, Tomatoes, Basil, and Thyme

I generally dislike recipes that make you refer back to several others, but bear with me on this one, it's worth it. I can't remember a wintertime visit to Paris's L'Ami Louis when I didn't sample their gigantic, sizzling portions of *coquilles Saint-Jacques*. I have to confess, I've altered their recipe a bit, adding the thyme and the basil, and cooking the garlic a bit longer. When garlic is cooked a good long while in oil, I find it's much more digestible. At home I serve this with a crisp white wine from Provence, say a Château Simone.

Provençal Roast Tomatoes (see Index)
Garlic Confit (recipe follows)
1 tablespoon poultry fat
12 large sea scallops
Salt and freshly ground black pepper
Pinch of thyme
24 fresh basil leaves, rinsed and patted dry

1. An hour or so before you plan to serve the scallops, prepare and bake the Provençal Roast Tomatoes. At the same time, prepare the Garlic Confit or warm the previously prepared garlic in a small saucepan and keep warm.

2. In a large nonstick skillet over medium-high heat, heat the poultry

fat until hot but not sizzling. Add the scallops and cook until almost opaque all the way through, about 3 minutes on each side. Once cooked, season the scallops generously with salt, pepper, and thyme. You may want to cook the scallops in batches. If so, keep the cooked scallops warm next to the stove, but don't place in the oven or they will toughen.

3. Place 3 scallops on each of 4 warmed dinner plates. Cut the basil leaves with scissors and sprinkle the basil on top of the scallops. Spoon several cloves of garlic and a touch of oil alongside each. Place 2 baked tomatoes alongside and serve immediately.

Yield: 4 servings

L'AIL CONFIT

♦

Garlic Confit

1 cup (25 cl) large garlic cloves
About 1 cup (25 cl) extra-virgin olive
oil

1. Peel the garlic cloves and combine with oil to cover in a small saucepan. Bring to a simmer and cook over medium-low heat until the garlic is tender, about 20 minutes.

2. The garlic can be served immediately, or preserved indefinitely. To store, allow the mixture to cool and transfer to a jar, making sure the garlic is covered with the oil. Refrigerate. To serve, remove the garlic from the oil and warm in a sauté pan over low heat. The oil can be used to prepare a flavorful vinaigrette.

Yield: 1 cup (25 cl)

PÉTONCLES AU FOUR LA TUPIÑA

♦

La Tupiña's Oven-Roasted Scallops

One very cold winter night in Bordeaux, as the snow was beginning to fall (and even before we knew that we were in for a major week-long storm), we took a fireside table at La Tupiña and feasted as though this might be our last decent meal for weeks. From the oven came a steaming platter of *pétoncles*, those tiny, pink-shelled Atlantic scallops, sweet, sea-fresh, and succulent. Served alongside was a fragant mixture of shallots, sherry wine vinegar, and fruity olive oil, making for a marvelously sensual marriage of scents, colors, textures, and tastes. This is a version I've adapted at home. I find that it is delicious with either clams or scallops, whichever is freshest at hand. With this, a crusty baguette and sip of chilled white Graves should send us all to heaven.

2 pounds (1 kg) bay scallops in their shells or littleneck or butter clams, shells well scrubbed under cold running water
¼ cup (6 cl) extra-virgin olive oil
2 shallots, finely minced
2 tablespoons best-quality sherry wine vinegar
Freshly ground black pepper to taste

1. Preheat the oven to 450°F (230°C).

2. Place the scallops or clams in a large, ovenproof baking dish. Bake until they open, 8 to 10 minutes.

3. Meanwhile, whisk together the remaining ingredients in a small bowl. Divide the sauce between 2 small dishes or ramekins.

4. To serve, place the scallops or clams, in their shells, in a large, shallow bowl. Use a small fork or your fingers to remove the meat from the shells and dip them into the sauce.

Yield: 4 servings

GAMBAS GRILLÉ AU SEL DE GUÉRANDE CHEZ GÉRAUD

Chez Géraud's Giant Shrimp Grilled with Brittany Sea Salt

One Friday morning a friend called to tell me about a new Paris bistro he'd been to. It was Chez Géraud, run by Géraud Rongier, the outgoing owner of Paris's popular wine bar, Le Val d'Or. We headed there immediately, and that evening my husband sampled a delicious first course of these superbly simple grilled gambas.

After several experiments, I've decided that the best way to deal with any of these creatures, fresh or frozen, is to try to cook them with their shells intact, if you can find them in the shell, and to marinate them for a few hours before, so they don't dry out too much as they cook. Voilà! A successful dish that I now try to recreate as often as the pocketbook allows. With the grilled gambas, serve a white wine: A dry Loire Valley Vouvray would be delicious.

16 extra-large shrimp, preferably with shells intact, heads removed
2 tablespoons extra-virgin olive oil
1 teaspoon fresh thyme, or ½ teaspoon dried
2 tablespoons coarse sea salt, preferably from Brittany

1. Rinse the shrimp and pat dry. In a shallow bowl, combine the shrimp, oil, and thyme. Cover securely and refrigerate for at least 2 hours before cooking. Remove from the refrigerator 10 minutes before cooking.

2. Preheat the broiler.

3. Scatter the sea salt on a shallow baking pan. Place the shrimp on top of the salt in a single layer. Broil about 5 inches (12.5 cm) from the heat until the meat is opaque but still tender, 1 to 2 minutes. (You should be able to smell when the shrimp is cooked—it will be fragrantly sweet and briny.) Turn the shrimp and cook the other side 1 to 2 minutes more.

4. Divide the shrimp among 4 warmed serving dishes. Shrimp cooked in this manner is so delicious, you need no sauce. Not even lemon juice! Allow each diner to peel his

A WEEKEND BARBECUE, BISTRO-STYLE

◆

Try out this menu on family and friends when the sun is shining and you're in the mood for colorful fare with straightforward flavors. With it, serve a sturdy, oaky red, perhaps a good Rioja from Spain.

SALADE MESCLUN LA MÈRE BESSON
La Mère Besson's Mixed Summer Salad

◆

GAMBAS GRILLÉ AU SEL DE GUÉRANDE CHEZ GÉRAUD
Chez Géraud's Giant Shrimp Grilled with Brittany Sea Salt

◆

THON GRILLÉ SAUCE VIERGE
Grilled Tuna with Tomato, Garlic, Oil, and Lemon Sauce

◆

TARTE AUX FIGUES GEORGETTE
Georgette's Fig Tart

own shrimp. Offer finger bowls, with a touch of lemon, for guests to cleanse their fingers, and a small bowl for discarding the shells.

Yield: 4 first-course servings or 2 main-course servings

SALADE DE CALMARS MARINÉS

Marinated Squid Salad

My local fish market has an enormous selection of freshly prepared foods, ranging from a fish *choucroute* to gorgeous fish terrines sold by the slice. While marketing I often pick up something for my lunch. One of my favorites is their marinated squid salad, which always seems to hit the spot. I've created my own variation, adding tomatoes and a touch less oil. This makes a wonderful summer lunch dish, served with fresh country bread and a glass of chilled rosé, such as the fine offering from Domaine Tempier in Bandol.

The squid could also be spooned on top of a simple tossed green salad for a more substantial *salade composée*. Even in the winter months, this salad reminds me of sunshine and summer. Remember that squid cooks in seconds. If cooked too long those tender little critters turn to rubberbands. So be vigilant while cooking them!

1 teaspoon best-quality red wine vinegar
2 tablespoons plus 1 teaspoon fresh lemon juice
Salt
¼ cup (6 cl) extra-virgin olive oil
2 tomatoes, peeled, cored, seeded, and chopped
3 tablespoons finely minced fresh flat-leaf parsley

Pinch of hot red pepper flakes
Pinch of thyme
1 scallion, sliced into rings
1 pound (500 g) squid, cleaned (see Index) and sliced into thin rings, tentacles reserved

1. In a medium-size nonreactive

bowl, combine the vinegar and 1 teaspoon of lemon juice. Add salt to taste and stir to dissolve the salt. Add 3 tablespoons of the oil, the tomatoes, parsley, pepper flakes, thyme, and scallion, and stir to blend. Set aside.

2. Bring 3 quarts (3 l) of water to a boil. Once it has boiled, add 2 tablespoons salt. Add the squid rings and tentacles and cook just until the squid loses its translucency and turns opaque, not more than 1 minute. (I usually begin tasting the squid as soon as they hit the water, and as soon as they taste right I flip them all into a giant colander.) Drain the squid well, but do not rinse.

3. Add the drained squid to the marinade and toss to blend. Stir in the remaining olive oil and 2 tablespoons lemon juice. Taste the mixture and add salt to taste as necessary. Refrigerate for at least 3 hours before serving.

4. Serve on small salad plates, or on a bed of dressed greens. (Since the marinated squid is quite colorful, they look beautiful set atop a bed of arugula or lamb's lettuce mixed with a touch of vibrant red radicchio.) Serve with fresh country bread and a glass of chilled rosé.

Yield: 4 servings

LES VOLAILLES

◆———————◆

Poultry: Chicken, Duck, Guinea Hen, and Rabbit

I don't think that I gave poultry proper respect until I began gathering recipes for this book. Like most families, ours generally repeated the same three or four chicken recipes, mostly sautéed variations using cut-up chicken parts. But that was about it.

Today, if you asked me to name one of my ten favorite dishes in all the world, it would certainly be a plump golden chicken or farm-raised guinea hen, simply roasted in the oven or carefully turned on a spit. I owe a special debt of gratitude to a number of bistro chefs, namely the late Antoine Magnin of Paris's L'Ami Louis and Marie-Louise Auteli of Lyons' Chez Tante Paulette, for demonstrating the glories of the common chicken.

I have included a healthy selection of poultry or poultry-like bistro classics, such as the ever-favorite rabbit with mustard sauce, Paris's famed duck with olives from Chez Allard, and two different versions of chicken with vinegar—one of those marriages definitely made in heaven.

Poulet Rôti L'Ami Louis

L'Ami Louis's Roast Chicken

I f the dozens of bistro dishes I have sampled again and again over the years, it is the roast chicken at L'Ami Louis that remains at the top of my list. What is so delightful is that this is such an overwhelmingly simple dish to prepare. The secret is to rub the chicken with goose or other poultry fat before roasting it. The chicken is roasted in a hot oven, then melted butter and water are blended with the rich cooking juices. The firm, fresh, pungent watercress leaves serve as a great foil.

1 whole roasting chicken (3 to 4 pounds; 1.5 to 2 kg), well rinsed and patted dry, at room temperature
1 tablespoon (½ ounce; 15 g) poultry fat, or substitute butter
Salt
4 tablespoons (2 ounces; 60 g) unsalted butter
1 bunch of fresh watercress

1. Preheat the oven to 425°F (220°C).
2. Place the liver, gizzard, heart, and neck inside the cavity of the chicken. Truss with household string. Place the chicken in a roasting pan just large enough to hold it. Rub the chicken all over with the poultry fat. Season with salt.
3. Place the roasting pan in the center of the oven. Roast, basting every 10 minutes or so to ensure even browning without drying out, until the juices run clear when the thigh is pierced with a fork, about 1½ hours for a 4-pound (2 kg) chicken.
4. Remove the chicken from the oven. Pour any juices from the chicken cavity into the roasting pan. Allow the chicken to rest for 10 minutes before carving.
5. Meanwhile, add the butter and 3 tablespoons of water to the roasting pan, and deglaze the pan over high heat, scraping up any caramelized bits of skin that stick to the pan. Cook until the liquid is reduced to a syrup, 2 to 3 minutes.
6. Carve the chicken and place the pieces on a warmed platter. Pour the sauce over the chicken. Arrange the watercress around the chicken pieces. Serve immediately.

Yield: 4 to 6 servings

CALL IT CHICKEN SALAD

Chef and cooking teacher Jacques Pépin serves a simple tossed green salad with his roast chicken. For a great marriage of flavors, after the salad has been tossed, sprinkle 1 tablespoon of reserved chicken juices on top, and toss once more. As for the chicken itself, he advises: "Cook it at a high temperature so it's crusty, baste it, take care of it, and then serve it right away. A chicken that's been sitting for over half an hour will start tasting reheated."

POULET RÔTI AUX HERBES PILE OU FACE

Herb-Crusted Roast Chicken Pile ou Face

One of the best roast chickens in Paris is found in the marvelous restaurant Pile ou Face, where a trio of restaurateurs have made a specialty of *produits de la ferme,* fresh products from their Normandy farm. Chef Claude Udron and his partners, Alain Dumergue and Philippe Marquet, raise not only chickens and rabbits, but also grow a wonderful assortment of fresh herbs, including the sorrel, tarragon, chervil, parsley, and dill that go into this fragrant and flavorful crust.

The essential ingredient here is fresh sorrel, as well as a plump, farm-fresh roasting chicken. The bird is basted with egg yolks, to help the herbs adhere to the chicken as it roasts. Don't worry if some of the herbs fall off while basting, for they'll end up in the flavorful sauce in the end!

3 ounces (90 g) fresh sorrel leaves (about 4 cups or 1 l) loosely packed)

1½ ounces (about 20 g) fresh tarragon (about 1 cup or 25 cl, loosely packed)

1½ ounces (about 20 g) fresh chervil (about 1 cup or 25 cl, loosely packed)

1½ ounces (about 20 g) fresh flat-leaf parsley (about 1 cup or 25 cl, loosely packed)

1½ ounces (about 20 g) fresh dill (about 1 cup or 25 cl, loosely packed)

1½ ounces (about 20 g) fresh curly-leaf parsley (about 1 cup or 25 cl, loosely packed)

1 chicken, 3 to 4 pounds (1.5 to 2 kg), at room temperature

2 egg yolks, beaten

Salt and freshly ground black pepper

3 tablespoons (1½ ounces; 45 g) unsalted butter

1. Preheat the oven to 425°F (220°C).

2. Wash and thoroughly dry all of the sorrel and herbs. Carefully remove the stems from the sorrel. Place the sorrel and herbs in a food processor and process until the herbs are very finely chopped.

3. Place the liver, gizzard, heart, and neck inside the cavity of the chicken. Truss with household string. Place the chicken in a roasting pan; brush it all over with the egg yolks. Season generously with salt and pepper to taste. Sprinkle the chicken with the herb mixture, patting them to evenly cover the bird. Dot with the butter.

3. Place the roasting pan in the center of the oven. Roast, basting every 10 minutes or so, so the chicken is evenly browned and does not dry out. The chicken is cooked when the juices run clear when pierced with a fork. It should take about 1½ hours for a 4-pound (2 kg) chicken.

4. Remove the chicken from the oven, removing the gizzard, heart and liver to a serving platter. Pour any juices from the interior of the chicken into the roasting pan. Allow the chicken to rest for 10 minutes before carving.

5. Meanwhile, add 3 tablespoons of water to the roasting pan and set over high heat. Deglaze, scraping up any caramelized bits of skin that may stick to the pan. Boil over high heat, until the liquid is reduced to a syrup.

6. Carve the chicken and place the pieces on a warmed platter. Pour the sauce over the chicken. Arrange the chicken gizzard, heart, and liver around the chicken pieces and serve immediately.

Yield: 4 to 6 servings

POULET AU VINAIGRE LE PETIT TRUC

Le Petit Truc's Chicken with Tarragon Vinegar

While the regional bistro shares many common traits with its Parisian counterpart—the decor borders on the haphazard, the ambiance is frankly familial, the rarely varying menu could well be engraved in stone—each manages to take on a character all its own, reflecting the gastronomic style and rhythm of every section of France. Often, as in the now defunct Burgundian bistro Le Petit Truc, it's also the personality of the owner. Here, the youthful, blonde Edith Remoissenet-Cordier ran her tiny restaurant with a will of iron. If you didn't reserve a table, you just didn't get in! But if you played by the rules, all usually went well.

At Le Petit Truc Madame Remoissenet-Cordier offered a medley of homey fare, including this special version of chicken with tarragon vinegar.

3 tablespoons extra-virgin olive oil
3 tablespoons (1½ ounces; 45 g) un-
    salted butter
1 chicken (3 to 4 pounds; 1.5 to 2
    kg), well rinsed, patted dry, cut
    into 8 serving pieces, at room tem-
    perature
Salt and freshly ground black pepper
½ cup (12.5 cl) dry white wine, such
    as Mâcon-Villages
4 shallots, minced
2 medium tomatoes, peeled, cored,
    seeded, and chopped
½ cup (12.5 cl) white wine tarragon
    vinegar
1 bunch of tarragon leaves, minced

> **❝Poultry is for the cook what canvas is for the painter. ❞**
> —BRILLAT-SAVARIN

1. In a deep-sided nonreactive, 12-inch (30 cm) skillet, heat the oil with 1 tablespoon (½ ounce; 15 g) of the butter over high heat. Season the chicken liberally with salt and pepper. When the fats are hot but not smoking, add the chicken and cook on both sides until the skin turns an even, golden brown and the chicken is cooked to the desired doneness,

about 12 minutes on each side. Carefully regulate the heat to avoid scorching the skin. (If you do not have a pan large enough to hold all of the chicken pieces in a single layer, do this in several batches.)

2. Transfer the chicken to a serving platter; cover loosely with aluminum foil. Keep warm.

3. Pour off the fat in the skillet. Return the skillet to medium-high heat and add the wine. Deglaze the pan, scraping up any bits that cling to the bottom. Add the shallots and tomatoes and cook for several minutes. Raise the heat to high and slowly add the vinegar. Cook for an additional 2 to 3 minutes. Whisk in the remaining 2 tablespoons (1 ounce; 30 g) butter; cook for 1 more minute. Return the chicken to the skillet; coat well with the sauce. Cover and continue cooking over medium heat until the chicken absorbs some of the sauce, just 2 or 3 minutes. Sprinkle with the tarragon and turn the chicken pieces to coat. Serve immediately, accompanied by sautéed potatoes.

Yield: 4 to 6 servings

A BURGUNDIAN DINNER

This is typical of the meals served in Burgundian family homes, starting with cheese puffs and a chilled white Chablis, finishing off with a young red Burgundy.

GOUGÈRE FRANÇOISE POTEL
Françoise Potel's Cheese Puffs

POULET AU VINAIGRE LE PETIT TRUC
Le Petit Truc's Chicken with Tarragon Vinegar

QUARTIERS DE POMMES DE TERRE SAUTÉS DANS LEUR PEAU
Potato Quarters Sautéed in Their Skins

TARTE AUX POMMES FRANÇOISE POTEL
Françoise Potel's Apple Tart

POULET BASQUAISE

Chicken with Hot Peppers, Ham, Tomatoes, and Onions

Poulet basquaise—along with couscous, *blanquette de veau,* and *gigot aux flageolets*—is standard plat-du-jour fare in Paris cafés. Unfortunately, when you order this dish, named after the hot-pepper-rich Basque region of southwestern France, what you usually get is a soggy piece of chicken topped with some greasy, mysterious tomato sauce. But what a joy a great *poulet basquaise* can be: Fresh farm chicken, perfectly browned, embellished with a mix of piquant peppers, good country ham, garden fresh tomatoes, and onions. Serve this with plain boiled rice and you've got a superb one-dish meal. As with all spicy dishes, adjust the amount of hot peppers to suit your palate! Note that this dish tastes even better the next day.

4 small, mildly hot green chiles (such as serrano), or 2 hot green chiles (or substitute ½ teaspoon hot red pepper flakes)

1 chicken (3 to 4 pounds; 1.5 to 2 kg), well rinsed, patted dry, cut into 8 serving pieces, and at room temperature

Salt and freshly ground black pepper

5 tablespoons vegetable oil

12 fat garlic cloves, cut into thin slices

2 pounds (1 kg) red bell peppers, cored, seeded, and thickly sliced

4 thick slices (about 8 ounces; 250 grams) unsmoked ham, such as prosciutto, cubed

2 large onions, coarsely chopped

2 pounds (1 kg) tomatoes, peeled, cored, seeded, and chopped (or substitute 1 large can (28 ounces; 794 g) imported plum tomatoes, drained)

1. When preparing chiles, be sure to wear rubber gloves to protect your hands. Core and seed the chiles. Slice into ⅛-inch (3.5 mm) strips; set aside.

2. Season the chicken liberally with salt and pepper. In a nonreactive, deep-sided 12-inch (30 cm) skillet, heat 3 tablespoons of the oil over high heat. When the oil is hot but not smoking, add the chicken and brown on one side until the skin turns an even, golden brown, about 5 minutes. Be careful to avoid scorching the skin. Turn the pieces and brown them on the other side, for an additional 5 minutes. Work in batches, if necessary.

3. Return all of the chicken to the skillet (it's okay to crowd them all in). Add the garlic, bell peppers, chiles, and ham, burying the ingredients amidst the chicken pieces. Cook, covered, over medium heat, until the chicken is cooked through, and the peppers are meltingly soft, about 45 minutes to 1 hour. The pan will make a lot of crackling noises as the peppers give off much of their liquid. Turn the mixture from time to time, and adjust heat to avoid scorching. You want a tender sauce.

4. Meanwhile, in another large skillet, heat the remaining 2 tablespoons of oil over high heat until hot but not smoking. Add the onions. Reduce the heat to medium-low and cook until very soft, about 5 minutes. Add the tomatoes and continue cooking for another 30 minutes. The mixture should be soft and well-

blended. Season to taste with salt. (The dish can easily be made ahead to this point. Reheat both mixtures separately.)

5. To serve, layer the tomato and onion mixture on a preheated platter. Cover with the chicken mixture, and serve immediately, with white rice.

Yield: 4 to 6 servings

POULET SAUTÉ AUX ECHALOTES

Chicken Sautéed with Shallots

T his is a wonderfully simple and homey recipe, a first cousin of the popular chicken with 40 cloves of garlic. Instead of garlic, one uses a generous portion of shallots, those tiny onion-like bulbs that turn sweet and soft when cooked in this manner. Serve this dish with baked or steamed rice, so all of the delicious sauce will be absorbed into the rice, and not a drop wasted.

3 tablespoons extra-virgin olive oil
1 tablespoon (½ ounce; 15 g) unsalted butter
1 chicken (about 3 to 4 pounds; 1.5 to 2 kg), well rinsed, patted dry, cut into 8 serving pieces, at room temperature
Salt and freshly ground black pepper
About 60 shallots (2 generous cups, about 14 ounces; 400 g), peeled
3 garlic cloves
2 tablespoons Cognac
4 tomatoes, peeled, cored, seeded, and chopped
Hot, cooked rice
A handful of fresh parsley, minced

1. In a deep-sided nonreactive, 12-inch (30 cm) skillet, heat the oil and butter over high heat. Season the chicken liberally with salt and pepper. When the fats are hot but not smoking, add 3 or 4 pieces of chicken and cook on one side until the skin turns an even, golden brown, about 5 minutes. Do not crowd the pan; brown the chicken in several batches. Carefully regulate the heat to avoid scorching the skin. Turn the pieces and brown them on the other side, an additional 5 minutes.

2. Reduce the heat to medium-high. Add the shallots and garlic, burying them under the chicken at

the bottom of the skillet. Add all of the chicken to the pan. Sauté, covered, shaking the pan frequently, until the shallots are soft and begin to brown, and the chicken is cooked through, about 20 minutes.

3. Heat the Cognac in a very small saucepan over medium-high heat for 20 to 30 seconds. Ignite with a match and pour over the chicken. Shake the pan until the flames subside. Cook, shaking the pan, for an additional 2 to 3 minutes.

4. Stir in the tomatoes and continue cooking until the sauce is nicely blended, about 5 minutes more.

5. To serve, place a bed of cooked rice on a large serving platter, cover with the sauce, then arrange the chicken pieces on top. Sprinkle with the parsley; serve immediately.

Yield: 4 servings

LA VOLAILLE AU VINAIGRE DE VIN BISTRO D'À CÔTÉ

Bistro d'à Côté's Chicken in Wine Vinegar

One quality of many bistro dishes is that they take well to reheating. I almost insist you prepare this chicken 24 hours ahead and then reheat it, for it seems to improve with a bit of age. I have to admit I've enjoyed this dish at quite a few wintertime lunches, a preparation I sampled on my very first visit to Michel Rostang's neighborhood (my neighborhood!) bistro called Bistro d'à Côté. The name's an easy one, for right next door—*a côté*—is his "grand" restaurant, known as Michel Rostang. On many nights, you can see him bouncing back and forth between both spots, chatting with regulars who also seem to bounce back and forth between establishments. He serves this with a *gratin dauphinois,* a nice and cheesy potato gratin. With it, sample a fruity red wine, a Beaujolais perhaps, or a red from the Loire or the Rhône.

3 tablespoons extra-virgin olive oil
4 tablespoons (2 ounces; 60 g) un-salted butter
1 chicken (3 to 4 pounds; 1.5 to 2 kg), well rinsed, patted dry, cut into 8 serving pieces, and at room temperature
Salt and freshly ground black pepper
1 cup (25 cl) best-quality red wine vinegar
2 medium tomatoes, peeled, cored, seeded, and chopped
¾ cup (18.5 cl) chicken stock, preferably homemade (see Index)
About 3 tablespoons minced fresh parsley

1. In a deep-sided nonreactive, 12-inch (30 cm) skillet, heat the oil with 1 tablespoon (½ ounce; 15 g) of the butter over high heat. Season the chicken liberally with salt and pepper. When the fats are hot but not smoking, add some of the chicken and brown on one side until the skin turns an even, golden brown, about 5 minutes. Carefully regulate the heat to avoid scorching the skin. Turn the pieces and brown them on the other side, for an additional 5 minutes. Do not crowd the pan. Cook the remaining chicken pieces in the same manner.

A BURGUNDIAN FETE TO CELEBRATE BEAUJOLAIS NOUVEAU

Come November, it's time to put together a Beaujolais feast to celebrate the year's new vintage. The menu is typically Lyonnais, hearty fare to welcome those cooler fall days.

SALADE HARENGS—POMMES DE TERRE LA MEUNIÈRE
La Meunière's Herring and Potato Salad

◆

LA VOLAILLE AU VINAIGRE DE VIN BISTRO D'À CÔTÉ
Bistro d'à Côté's Chicken in Red Wine Vinegar

◆

GALETTE LYONNAISE
Lyonnaise Potato Galette

◆

TARTELETTES AUX POMMES LIONEL POILÂNE
Lionel Poilâne's Individual Apple Tarts

2. When all the chicken has been browned, remove it from the skillet and pour out the cooking fat. Return the chicken to the skillet. Very slowly add the vinegar. (If the pan is hot, and you add it too rapidly, the fumes will chase you out of the kitchen!) Over medium-high heat, reduce the vinegar roughly by half, turning the chicken from time to time to coat it with the vinegar, about 10 minutes.

3. Add the tomatoes and chicken stock. Cover and simmer gently over medium-low heat until all the juices mingle nicely and the chicken is cooked through, about 20 more minutes. (The chicken can and should be prepared ahead of time up to this point.)

4. To prepare the chicken for serving, remove it from the sauce and place it on a warm serving platter. Cover and keep warm. (If reheating the dish, heat the chicken through in the sauce, then remove to a warmed platter. Cover). Remove the warmed sauce from the heat and whisk in the remaining 3 tablespoons (1½ ounces; 45 g) butter. Adjust the seasoning. Pour the sauce over the chicken; sprinkle on the parsley. Serve, accompanied by a *gratin dauphinois.*

Yield: 4 to 6 servings

POULET MISTRAL LE PRIEURÉ

Mistral's Chicken with Garlic

T his thoroughly Provençal dish—chicken smothered with garlic—is named after the the region's favorite native son, the poet Frédéric Mistral. Chef Michel Gonod, of the restaurant Le Prieuré outside Avignon, says this is one of the most popular dishes on his menu. With it, sample a chilled rosé de Provence.

2 tablespoons extra-virgin olive oil
1 tablespoon (½ ounce; 15 g) unsalted butter
1 chicken (3 to 4 pounds; 1.5 to 2 kg), well rinsed, patted dry, cut into 8 serving pieces, and at room temperature

Salt and freshly ground black pepper
About 40 large garlic cloves
½ cup (12.5 cl) dry white wine, such as Cassis
½ cup (12.5 cl) chicken stock, preferably homemade (see Index)

1. In a deep-sided nonreactive, 12-inch (30 cm) skillet, heat the oil and butter over high heat. Season the chicken liberally with salt and pepper. When the fats are hot but not smoking, add the chicken pieces and cook on one side until the skin turns an even, golden brown, about 5 minutes. Carefully regulate the heat to avoid scorching the skin. Turn the pieces and brown them on the other side, for an additional 5 minutes. Work in batches, if necessary.

2. Reduce the heat to medium. Bury the garlic cloves under the chicken to make sure they settle in one layer at the bottom of the skillet. Sauté, shaking the pan frequently, until the garlic is lightly browned, about 10 minutes. Slowly pour in the wine and stock. Shake the pan and scrape up any browned bits from the bottom of the pan. Cover and continue cooking until the juices run clear when a thigh is pricked, 10 to 12 more minutes.

3. Serve the chicken with the garlic and pan juices, with sautéed potatoes or rice.

Yield: 4 servings

BOUILLABAISSE DE POULET CHEZ TANTE PAULETTE

◆

Tante Paulette's Chicken Stew with Fennel and Saffron

Chez Tante Paulette is one of my favorite bistros in the world. It's an authentic, old-fashioned spot on a small side street in Lyons, run by the elderly Marie-Louise Auteli, better known as Tante Paulette. Her most famous dish is chicken with garlic, and following that, fans flock to her little upstairs dining room to feast on the unusual *bouillabaisse de poulet*. Like its more famous counterpart—which is prepared with the freshest of Mediterranean fish—this bouillabaisse is infused with onions, garlic, tomatoes, a touch of fennel, and a wave of saffron.

While Madame Auteli serves hers with the classic red pepper mayonnaise known as *rouille* and slices of grilled bread, I tend to prefer my chicken stew as is, with a few sips of chilled white wine, such as a white Cassis from the fishing village not far from Marseilles.

4 tomatoes, peeled, cored, seeded, and
    chopped
2 large onions, quartered
4 garlic cloves, crushed
4 large fennel bulbs with feathery
    leaves attached, coarsely chopped
3 tablespoons extra-virgin olive oil
⅓ cup (8 cl) licorice-flavored aperitif,
    such as Ricard or Pernod
Generous pinch of saffron
Small handful of fresh thyme, or sev-
    eral teaspoons dried thyme
4 imported bay leaves
Salt and freshly ground black pepper
4 chicken legs with thighs attached,
    skin removed
1 pound (500 g) boiling potatoes,
    peeled and quartered
2 cups chicken stock, preferably home-
    made (see Index)

1. The day before you plan to serve the dish, combine the tomatoes, onions, garlic, fennel, olive oil, licorice-flavored aperitif, saffron, herbs, and seasonings in a nonreactive large covered casserole or Dutch oven. Stir to blend. Add the chicken legs and thighs, and stir to coat the chicken. Cover and refrigerate for at least 8 hours to blend the seasonings.

2. At least 1 hour before you begin to prepare the dish, remove the chicken from the refrigerator. Stew the chicken in its marinade, covered, over medium heat, stirring from time to time, for about 30 minutes. Add the potatoes and chicken stock and simmer until the potatoes are cooked, an additional 30 to 45 minutes. Taste for seasoning. Serve in warmed shallow soup bowls.

Yield: 4 servings

FRICASSÉE DE POULET AUX CHAMPIGNONS CHEZ ROSE

◆

Chez Rose's Chicken Fricassee with Mushrooms

I sampled this the first time I ever visited Chez Rose, one of Lyons' most traditional family bistros. It reminded me very much of the very simple sort of chicken dishes my mother made when I was a child. With it, serve a good Beaujolas, lightly chilled.

6 tablespoons extra-virgin olive oil
2 garlic cloves, minced
*1 chicken (about 2½ pounds; 1.25
    kg), well-rinsed, patted dry, cut
    into 8 serving pieces, at room tem-
    perature*
¼ cup (35 g) all-purpose flour
*1 pound (500 g) fresh mushrooms,
    washed, trimmed, patted dry; caps
    separated from stems, caps halved
    or quartered if large*
*1 large can (28 ounces; 794 g) im-
    ported plum tomatoes, well
    drained, halved*
Salt and freshly ground black pepper
Chopped fresh parsley, for garnish

1. Heat 3 tablespoons of the oil in a large, heavy nonreactive skillet over medium heat until hot but not smoking. Add the garlic; reduce the heat to low. Sauté the garlic, stirring frequently, until soft but not browned, about 2 minutes.

2. Lightly dredge the chicken pieces with the flour. Increase the heat under the skillet to medium. Add the chicken pieces. (If you do not have a skillet large enough to hold all of the chicken pieces in a single layer, sauté the chicken in 2 batches.) Sauté until well browned on both sides, about 20 minutes. Carefully regulate the heat to avoid scorching the skin.

3. Meanwhile, heat the remaining 3 tablespoons of oil in a separate skillet over medium heat until hot but not smoking. Add the mushroom caps and stems; sauté, stirring occa-

sionally, until lightly browned, 5 to 6 minutes

4. When the chicken is browned, stir in the tomatoes and mushrooms; season with salt and pepper. Reduce the heat to medium-low. Cook the chicken, covered, for 20 minutes. Uncover and cook for another 10 minutes, or until the chicken is tender.

5. To serve, arrange the chicken pieces on a warmed platter. Ladle the sauce and vegetables over all. Garnish with the parsley and serve immediately.

Yield: 4 servings

LAPIN, POULET, AND THEIR FRIENDS . . .

The French language has numerous expressions relating to poultry. A womanizer might be known as "un chaud lapin" or warm rabbit, while a "poule aux oeuf d'or" (a hen with golden eggs) is a hen that will never be killed, for it would mean sacrificing future profits for immediate pleasure. If you "donner un canard à moitié" (give someone half a duck), it means you've sold something without selling anything at all. In other words, you've cheated someone.

PINTADE DE LA DRÔME AUX OLIVES DE NYONS

Guinea Hen from the Drôme with Black Olives from Nyons

This recipe combines many of the finest ingredients of the Drôme, a sparsely populated area of northern Provence that includes the village of Nyons, a lovely town surrounded by rolling fields of olive trees. The Drôme also includes numerous farms that raise tender lamb, as well as the delicious, prized guinea hen known as *pintade*.

I love the full-flavored stuffing, a blend of pungent thyme, slightly salty bacon, delicate shallots, rich poultry liver, and of course the large, meaty olives from Nyons. If a guinea hen is unavailable, this recipe could also be made with chicken. Serve with a good red Côtes-du-Rhône, such as Cru de Coudelet.

3 ounces (90 g) lean slab bacon, rind removed, trimmed of fat and minced
4 shallots, minced
1 guinea hen (about 3 pounds; 1.5 kg), barded (ask your butcher to do this), liver trimmed and reserved
1 tablespoon minced fresh thyme
¾ cup (about 3 ounces; 90 g) black olives, preferably from Nyons, pitted and minced
1 tablespoon extra-virgin olive oil

1. Preheat the oven to 425°F (220°C), or prepare a rotisserie for roasting.
2. Place the bacon and shallots in a large nonstick skillet. Cook, stir-ring frequently, over medium-high heat until the bacon is crisp and shallots are browned in the bacon fat, about 4 minutes. Set aside.
   3. In the same pan, add the liver and quickly sauté for just a minute or 2 on each side. Set aside.
   4. When the liver has cooled, chop it very finely. Add the liver to the bacon and shallot mixture, along with the thyme and olives. Taste the stuffing; adjust the seasoning.
   5. Fill the cavity of the guinea hen and sew the opening closed with kitchen string. Brush the bird with the olive oil. If roasting, place on a roasting rack and roast until the juices run clear when you pierce a thigh with a skewer, about 1 hour. Baste the bird from time to time. If

roasting on a rotisserie, baste about every 10 minutes. The bird should roast in about 40 minutes.

6. Remove the bird from the oven, and let rest for 10 minutes.

Place the stuffing in a warmed serving bowl and carve the guinea hen. Serve with a green salad and a potato gratin or a potato purée.

Yield: 4 to 6 servings

CANARD AUX OLIVES CHEZ ALLARD

◆━━━◆

Chez Allard's Roast Duck with Olives

C hez Allard, one of Paris' longtime popular bistros, has had this dish on the menu for decades. The recipe comes from the notebooks of Marthe Allard, the restaurant's first cook. While many recipes for duck with olives simply call for olives to be tossed into a warm sauce at the last minute, this version offers a more intense reduction of flavors, a subtle blending of herbs, wine, stock, tomatoes, and delicious green olives—a perfect sauce to serve with the simplest roast duck. With this, sample a fruity red, such as a Beaujolais cru, Fleurie.

━━━

2 tablespoons rendered chicken fat (or substitute 1 tablespoon oil and 1 tablespoon butter)

2 pounds (1 kg) chicken wings or backs, cut up

1 duck (about 4 pounds; 2 kg), well-rinsed, patted dry, and trussed, with neck and gizzard reserved

3 onions, minced

1½ tablespoons superfine flour

2 cups (50 cl) dry white wine

2 quarts (2 l) chicken stock, preferably homemade (see Index)

1 bouquet garni: 12 parsley stems, 8 peppercorns, ¼ teaspoon thyme, ¼ teaspoon fennel seed and 1 im-

ported bay leaf tied in a double thickness of cheesecloth

⅓ cup (8 cl) tomato paste

8 ounces (250 g) brine-cured green olives, pitted

2 tablespoons (1 ounce; 30 g) unsalted butter, softened

━━━

1. In a large nonreactive stockpot or stovetop casserole, melt the chicken fat over medium heat. Add the chicken pieces and reserved duck neck and gizzard. Cook, stirring over medium-high heat, until golden,

about 8 minutes. Add the onions and cook until softened, about 5 minutes. Sprinkle on the flour and cook, stirring, for 1 minute. Stir in the wine, stock, bouquet garni, and tomato paste. Simmer, uncovered, over low heat for 2 hours, stirring occasionally. Strain the sauce through a fine-mesh sieve into a nonreactive saucepan; discard the solids.

2. In a medium saucepan, bring 1 quart (1 l) of water to a boil. Add the olives and boil over high heat for 2 minutes; drain and rinse under cold running water; drain well. Taste an olive. If it still is very salty, repeat the blanching. Add the olives to the strained sauce. Set over low heat and simmer, uncovered, until the sauce is just thick enough to coat a spoon, 1 to 1½ hours.

3. Preheat the oven to 425°F (220°C).

4. Pierce the duck skin all over with a knife; rub the skin with the butter. Place the bird, breast side down, on a rack in a roasting pan and roast for 30 minutes. Reduce the oven temperature to 350°F (175°C); turn the duck breast-side up. Continue to roast the duck until the juices run clear when you pierce the thigh with a skewer, about 1 hour more. If you find that the breast is brown before the bird is cooked through, shield the breast by covering it loosely with aluminum foil.

5. To serve, carve the duck. Arrange the meat on a large serving platter and surround it with the green olives and sauce.

Yield: 8 servings

LEFT BANK BISTRO; TABLE FOR TWO

◆

Familiar bistro fare, a menu designed to celebrate romance, love, or simply the fact that you're alive and well. With this, try a Saint-Véran or a Mâcon-Villages.

SAUCISSON CHAUD POMMES À L'HUILE
Warm Poached Sausage with Potato Salad

◆

CANARD AUX OLIVES CHEZ ALLARD
Chez Allard's Roast Duck with Olives

◆

TARTE AUX POMMES À LA CRÈME
Golden Cream and Apple Tart

Canard Rôti à l'Ancienne Brasserie Flo

Brasserie Flo's Roast Duck with Tomatoes, Olives, and Mushrooms

What a wonderful way to prepare duck! Simply roast it, so you have all the advantage of that crispy wonderful skin. Then serve it with a vibrant sauce of tomatoes, mushrooms, and olives. This recipe, from the popular Paris restaurant, Brasserie Flo, is not complicated to make, but takes some coordinating in the kitchen. I like to prepare it when a group of us is cooking together, so each cook can take a different assignment. With this, serve a young, chilled red wine, such as a Beaujolais cru, Juliénas.

Duck:
3 tablespoons extra-virgin olive oil
1 carrot, peeled and cubed
1 onion, coarsely chopped
1 roasting duck (about 4½ pounds;
    2.25 kg), trussed
Salt and freshly ground black pepper

Vegetable sauce:
1 pound (500 g) onions, minced
1 pound (500 g) mushrooms, cleaned,
    trimmed, and sliced
4 pounds (2 kg) tomatoes, peeled,
    cored, quartered, and seeded
1 tablespoon Herbes de Provence (see
    Index)
2 garlic cloves, chopped
1 bouquet garni: Several sprigs of
    fresh parsley and fresh thyme,

8 whole peppercorns and 2
    imported bay leaves tied in a
    double thickness of cheesecloth
½ cup (100 g) green olives, preferably
    picholine, pitted
½ cup (100 g) oil-cured black olives,
    preferably from Nyons, pitted

Chopped fresh parsley

1. Preheat the oven to 400°F (205°C).
2. Prepare the duck: Place a rack in a roasting pan and scatter the carrot and onion over the bottom of the pan. Season the duck generously with salt and pepper. Place the bird, breast side down, on the rack. Roast for 30 minutes, basting the bird every

5 or 10 minutes.

3. Reduce the oven temperature to 325°F (165°C) Turn the duck, breast side up. Continue to roast and baste until the juices run clear when you pierce the thigh with a skewer, about 45 more minutes. If you find that the breast is brown before the bird is cooked through, cover it loosely with foil.

4. Meanwhile, prepare the sauce: In a large nonreactive skillet, heat the oil over medium heat until hot but not smoking. Add the onions and cook until soft but not browned, 5 minutes. Add the mushrooms, tomatoes, herbs, garlic, olives, and bouquet garni. Season with salt and pepper. Lower the heat, cover, and simmer, stirring from time to time, for 1 hour.

5. When the duck is cooked, remove it and the rack to a carving board. Place the roasting pan over medium-high heat, and add several tablespoons of water. Deglaze, scraping up any browned bits from the bottom of the pan. Boil, uncovered, for 5 minutes.

6. To serve, transfer the vegetable sauce, removing the bouquet garni, to a large, warmed platter. Carve the duck and place the duck pieces on top. Sprinkle with the parsley and serve. Strain the pan drippings into a sauceboat and pass separately. Serve immediately.

Yield: 4 to 6 servings

> **❝***Côte Rôtie was my darling. Drinking it, I fancied I could see that literally roasting but miraculously green hillside, popping with goodness, like the skin of a roasting duck, while little wine-colored devils chased little nymphs along its simmering rivulets of wine.***❞**
>
> —A.J. LIEBLING
> *Between Meals: An Appetite for Paris*

CIVET DE CANARD AU SAUTERNES

Duck Stew in Sauternes

This is actually a "fancy restaurant" dish I clipped from a French magazine and transformed into a rustic autumn specialty. The first time I tested this was one early fall evening in the country. By the time we sat down to eat on the terrace it was so dark we could barely see what it was was we were eating. But that didn't stop us from feasting on this delightful marriage of duck and distinctive Sauternes wine. The perfect acidity of the apples serves to gently gild the lily! My sister, who patiently helped test the bulk of the recipes noted: "The family's favorite. So far . . . !" The wine to drink with this is, of course, a young Sauternes.

1 duck (3 to 4 pounds; 1.5 to 2 kg), well rinsed, patted dry, cut into 8 to 10 serving pieces, at room temperature
Salt and freshly ground black pepper
2 tablespoons extra-virgin olive oil
1 carrot, peeled and finely minced
1 onion, finely minced
2 cups (50 cl) Sauternes
2 cups (50 cl) duck stock or chicken stock, preferably homemade (see Index)
Bouquet garni: 12 parsley stems, 8 peppercorns, 1 imported bay leaf, ½ teaspoon fresh thyme, and ¼ teaspoon fennel seed tied in a double thickness of cheesecloth
4 Golden Delicious apples
3 tablespoons (1½ ounces; 45 g) unsalted butter

1. Season the duck breast pieces and duck legs liberally with salt and pepper. Heat the oil in a nonreactive deep-sided skillet over medium-high heat. When the oil is hot but not smoking, add the duck breasts and brown on the skin side only. Brown the legs on both sides. Remove the duck from the skillet. Add the carrot and onion and brown for 3 to 4 minutes.

2. Return the duck to the skillet. Add the wine, stock, and the bouquet garni. Cover, reduce heat, and simmer gently about 40 minutes.

3. Remove the duck pieces to a dish and keep warm. Strain the sauce through a fine-mesh sieve. Pour the sauce over the duck. Adjust the seasoning, if necessary.

4. Peel and core the apples; cut lengthwise into eighths. Melt the butter in a large skillet. Add the apples and sauté over medium heat until lightly browned, 4 to 5 minutes.

5. Divide the apples among 4 heated dinner plates. Place a piece of duck on each plate and cover with the sauce.

Yield: 4 servings

PETIT SALÉ DE CANARD LE PETIT MARGUERY

Le Petit Marguery's Salt-Cured Duck with Cabbage

T his is one of my favorite bistro dishes, one that seems to be enjoying new popularity. *Petit salé aux lentilles,* salt pork with lentils, is a traditional bistro favorite, and now duck marinated in a herb-filled brine shows up more and more often. This recipe, from the Parisian bistro Le Petit Marguery, appears complicated, but in the end does not take a great deal of time, for much of the work is done in advance. And trust me, the effort is worth it!

I don't know which of the three elements I love more, the meltingly tender duck, the buttery cabbage, or the rich, golden sauce that accompanies it. You might want to also serve this with boiled potatoes—often dull on their own, but perfect here, for absorbing the rich flavors.

Brine and duck:
2 teaspoons fresh thyme
2 garlic cloves, sliced
6 juniper berries
6 black peppercorns
2 whole cloves
¾ cup (about 150 g) coarse sea salt or kosher salt
2 tablespoons sugar
4 duck legs, with thighs attached, or 1 whole duck, cut into 4 portions, with skin and bones intact, trimmed of excess fat

Stock:
4 tablespoons (2 ounces; 60 g) unsalted butter
2 leeks (white and tender green portions) trimmed, well-rinsed, and minced

2 carrots, peeled and minced
2 onions, minced
1 celery rib, minced
1 whole head of garlic, cloves separated and peeled
About 3 cups (75 cl) dry white wine, such as Savennières

Sauce and cabbage:
¼ cup (6 cl) crème fraîche (See Index) or heavy cream
2 large egg yolks
Salt and freshly ground black pepper
1 head of Savoy cabbage, cut into thin strips, ribs removed
4 tablespoons (2 ounces; 60 g) unsalted butter

1. Six days before you plan to serve the duck, prepare the brine: In a small saucepan, combine the thyme, garlic, juniper berries, peppercorns, cloves and 2 cups (50 cl) of water. Bring to a boil over high heat. Reduce the heat, cover, and simmer for 10 minutes. Set aside to cool.

2. Meanwhile, in another saucepan, combine the salt, sugar, and 2 cups (50 cl) of water. Cook over low heat, stirring just until the salt dissolves. Set aside to cool.

3. When the mixtures are cool, combine them in a large nonreactive bowl. Add the duck. Cover securely and refrigerate for 6 days.

4. The morning of the day you plan to serve the duck, drain it, discarding the brine. Cover the duck with fresh cold water and set aside for 6 hours, at room temperature.

5. Prepare the stock: Melt the butter in a large nonreactive skillet over medium heat. Add the vegetables and the garlic and cook, stirring occasionally, just until the onions are translucent, about 10 minutes. Be very careful not to let them brown.

6. Drain the duck, discarding the soaking liquid. Add the duck to the skillet. Add the wine and an equal amount of water, enough to cover the duck pieces. Cover and simmer gently until the meat is very soft and tender and almost falling off the bone, about 2 hours. Remove the skin from the duck. Return the duck pieces to the stock and keep it warm over low heat.

7. Prepare the sauce and cabbage: Transfer 3 cups (75 cl) of the stock to a small nonreactive saucepan. Bring to a boil over high heat and boil until reduced by half, about 15 minutes. Reduce heat to low, stir in the crème fraîche, then quickly stir in the egg yolks. Season with salt and pepper to taste. Keep warm over very low heat or in a *bain marie.*

8. Cook the cabbage in a large pot of vigorously boiling salted water until tender and crisp, about 5 minutes. Refresh under cold water and drain thoroughly.

9. Melt the butter in a large skillet over medium-high heat. Add the cabbage and sauté, tossing to coat with the butter, cooking until the cabbage has absorbed the butter, about 2 minutes.

10. To serve, transfer the cabbage to a warmed serving platter. Arrange the pieces of duck next to the cabbage and spoon the sauce over both. Serve immediately.

Yield: 4 servings

She died with a knife in her hand in her kitchen, where she had cooked for 50 years, and her death was solemnly listed in the newspaper as that of an artist.

—JANET FLANNER (GENÊT), WRITING ABOUT THE DEATH OF MOTHER SORET OF LYONS, WHOSE "CHICKEN IN HALF MOURNING" WAS FAMOUS ALL OVER FRANCE.

LAPIN MONSIEUR HENNY

Monsieur Henny's Rabbit with Mushrooms and Thyme

R abbit is a favorite French bistro dish. While testing recipes for this book, I made, of course, frequent visits to my local butcher, Monsieur Henny. Inevitably, no matter what I was ordering, chicken, rabbit, leg of lamb, oxtail, he would ask me what I was going to do with it. Then, as soon as I would explain my recipe, he would rattle off instructions for his own mouth-watering dish using whatever cut of meat or piece of poultry I happened to have in my hand. He is not only a great cook, but a superb salesman, for often I would end up taking home two chickens, two oxtails, two legs of lamb, testing my own recipe, and then Monsieur Henny's.

Here's one that I scratched on the back of an envelope one sunny day in September, as Monsieur Henny dictated from behind the counter, and a trail of customers waited patiently for us to complete our social business. It's been a family favorite ever since.

1 fresh rabbit (2½ to 3 pounds; 1.25 to 1.5 kg), cut into 7 or 8 serving pieces, liver reserved (you can substitute chicken)
Salt and freshly ground pepper
3 tablespoons extra-virgin olive oil
2 medium onions, coarsely chopped
5 ounces (140 g) salt pork, cubed
2½ cups (62.5 cl) dry white wine, such as Aligoté, Riesling, or a white Côtes-du-Rhône
8 ounces (250 g) fresh mushrooms, thinly sliced
4 imported bay leaves, tied with 1 sprig of fresh thyme
3 tablespoons imported Dijon mustard

⅓ cup (⅕ ounce; 8 g) fresh thyme leaves
½ cup (70 g) fresh bread crumbs

1. Season the rabbit pieces liberally with salt and pepper. Heat the oil in a deep-sided nonreactive skillet over medium-high heat. When the oil is hot but not smoking, add the rabbit, without crowding, and turn the pieces until all are thoroughly browned.

2. Remove the rabbit to a dish. Add the onions and salt pork and

brown in the fat for 3 to 4 minutes. Very slowly add the wine. Add the rabbit, mushrooms, and bay leaves. Cover, reduce the heat to medium, and cook until the rabbit is cooked through, about 20 minutes.

3. Remove rabbit to a warm platter. Cover and keep warm.

4. Combine the reserved rabbit liver, mustard, thyme leaves, and bread crumbs in a food processor. Process until puréed. Stir the mixture into the sauce remaining in the pan. Pour over the rabbit. Serve with pasta or rice.

Yield: 4 servings

LAPIN À LA MOUTARDE CAFÉ DES FÉDÉRATIONS

Café des Fédérations' Rabbit with Mustard Sauce

Rabbit with mustard sauce is one of the great, all-time bistro dishes. And no wonder, it's such a mellow combination of delicate and assertive flavors. I love this version from the Café des Fédérations in Lyons, because the rabbit remains superbly moist and full-flavored. I like to serve this with fresh noodles bathed in just a touch of sweet butter. At the Café des Féderations they serve a young Morgon with just about everything, so feel free to follow suit.

1 fresh rabbit (about 2½ pounds; 1.25 kg), cut into 7 to 8 serving pieces (or substitute chicken)
½ cup (12.5 cl) imported Dijon mustard
Salt and freshly ground black pepper
3 tablespoons peanut oil
1 tablespoon (½ ounce; 15 g) unsalted butter
1 bottle (75 cl) dry white wine

2 medium onions, finely chopped
1 tablespoon superfine flour, such as Wondra
Several branches of fresh thyme, or 1 teaspoon dried thyme
1 imported bay leaf
Chopped fresh parsley

1. Evenly brush one side of each rabbit piece with some of the mustard. Season generously with salt and pepper. Heat the oil and butter in a large nonreactive skillet over medium heat. When the fat is hot but not smoking, add several of the rabbit pieces, mustard side down; do not crowd the pan. You will have to cook this in several batches. Cook until brown, about 10 minutes. Turn the rabbit and brush the second side with additional mustard. Season with salt and pepper. Cook until golden brown, another 10 minutes. Transfer the rabbit to a large platter and continue cooking in this manner until all the rabbit is browned.

2. Add several tablespoons of the wine to the skillet and scrape up any browned bits that stick to the pan. Add the onions and cook, stirring, until golden brown, about 5 minutes. Remove the skillet from the heat. Sprinkle the flour over the onions and stir to coat. Pour in the remaining wine, the thyme, and bay leaf. Add all of the rabbit pieces. Return the skillet to medium heat and simmer until the rabbit is very tender and the sauce begins to thicken, about 1 hour.

3. Transfer the rabbit and sauce to a warmed platter and sprinkle with parsley. Serve immediately, over buttered fresh noodles or rice.

Yield: 6 servings

LYONS, LYONS, BISTRO HEAVEN

The selection of bistro recipes would be slight, indeed, without the familiar fare of Lyons. This menu includes some of my favorites from some very special bistros. The wine of choice is, as ever, Beaujolais.

SALADE LYONNAISE LA MEUNIÈRE
La Meunière's Salad of Escarole, Potatoes, Herring, and Eggs

♦

LAPIN À LA MOUTARDE CAFÉ DES FÉDÉRATIONS
Café des Fédérations' Rabbit with Mustard Sauce

♦

TARTE AUX FRAMBOISES CAFÉ DU JURA
Café du Jura's Raspberry Tart

LAPIN AUX OLIVES VERTES

Rabbit with Green Olives

T his is one of my favorite *plat ménager,* a solid and simple housewife's dish, the sort you can put on the stove and all but forget. I call it duck with olives without the fat. In fact, I've come to prefer the rabbit dish to the more traditional duck preparation, for it is lighter and more flavorful. Try to find good-quality unpitted green olives, if possible the picholine green olives from Provence. I've found that even when using rather salty varieties, the olives do not need to be blanched to rid them of excess salt.

The dish takes well to long cooking—an hour on the stove will give the sauce a bit more depth and won't overcook the rabbit—but when you're pressed, it can be put together in under an hour. Light and hearty at the same time, it's good year-round. If serving with pasta, serve the plain noodles as a side dish, rather than mixing the sauce in. The pasta will absorb too much of the liquid and make for a dry dish.

1 fresh rabbit (2½ to 3 pounds; 1.25 kg to 1.5 kg), cut into 7 or 8 serving pieces (or substitute chicken)

Salt and freshly ground black pepper

3 tablespoons olive oil

2 medium onions, coarsely chopped

1 tablespoon all-purpose flour

2½ cups (62.5 cl) dry white wine, such as Aligoté, Riesling, or a white Côtes-du-Rhône

4 tomatoes, peeled, cored, seeded, and chopped

2 imported bay leaves

3 tablespoons minced fresh herbs, preferably a blend of rosemary, thyme, and parsley

1 generous cup (185 g) green olives, pitted

1. Season the rabbit pieces liberally with salt and pepper. Heat the oil in a deep-sided nonreactive skillet over medium-high heat. When the oil is hot but not smoking, add the rabbit, without crowding the pan, and cook, turning the pieces to make sure that each is thoroughly browned. Continue until all of the rabbit is browned. Remove the rabbit to a plate.

2. Add the onions to the fat and

brown for 3 to 4 minutes. Sprinkle on the flour and stir to make a thick paste. Very slowly stir in the wine. Add the rabbit, tomatoes, bay leaves, herbs, and olives. Cover, reduce the heat to medium, and cook until the rabbit is cooked through, about 20 minutes. (The dish can cook longer, and can be prepared ahead and reheated.)

3. To serve, discard the bay leaves. Serve the rabbit hot, accompanied by rice or fresh pasta.

Yield: 4 to 6 servings

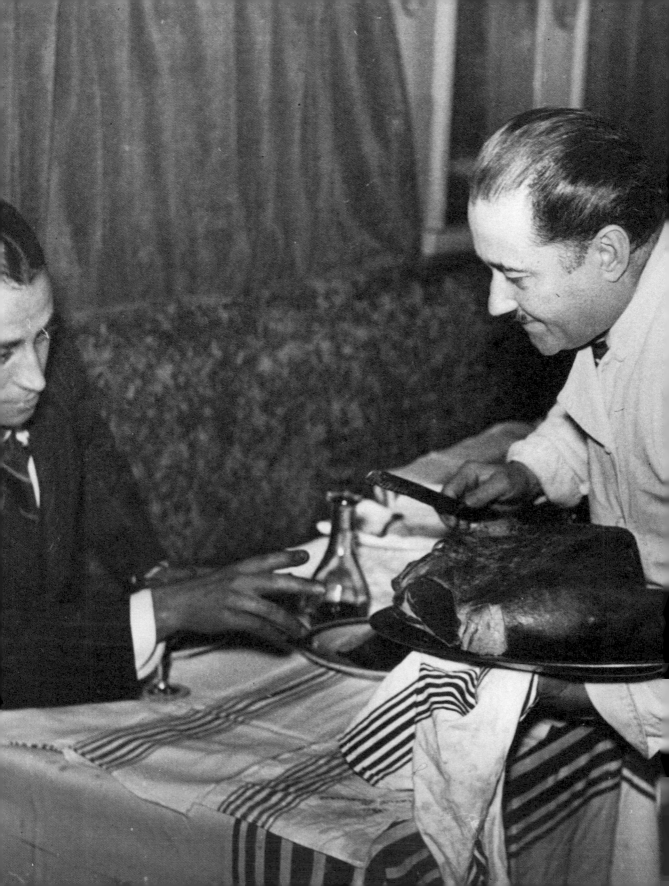

Les Viandes, Les Rôtis, et Plats du Jour

*Meats, Roasts,
and Daily Specials*

Meaty daubes, warming stews, boiled beef, and vegetables are all synonymous with the word "bistro." In this chapter I've tried to show the breadth and variety of fare served today, ranging from a spicy dish of red beans and sausages from France's Basque country to the distinctly Parisian veal sautéed with carrots. Many combinations, such as lamb with white beans, are bistro standards, while Le Caméléon's Braised Veal with Fresh Pasta serves as a totally modern interpretation. Almost all the dishes share two common, pleasing traits: They feed a crowd and take well to reheating.

POT-AU-FEU AUX DEUX VIANDES CHEZ ADRIENNE

Chez Adrienne's Two-Cut Boiled Beef

Most French cooks agree that a good *pot-au-feu*, or boiled beef and vegetables, requires at least two cuts of beef, preferably a meaty cut, such as short rib, rump, or top round, and a gelatinous one, such as beef shank. Some cooks also add gelatinous and flavorful oxtail, half a stewing chicken, and a whole variety of wintry vegetables, among them carrots, celery root, cabbage, leeks, and potatoes. Chef Adrienne Biasin, of the Paris bistro Chez La Vieille, says she loves to add turnips to the *pot-au-feu*, but finds that most customers just leave them on the plate.

At Adrienne's the *pot-au-feu* is served from a large, warmed platter, with the beef sliced and arranged in the center, the vegetables all around. Just as Adrienne brings the platter to the table, she spoons a bit of meat broth and bit of vegetable cooking broth over all. Note that the beef broth can be chilled, skimmed of fat and reserved to poach a beef tenderloin. With this sample a Pierre Ferraud Beaujolais, preferably Fleurie.

Approximately 1½ pounds (750 g) beef marrow bones, cut into 2-inch (5 cm) lengths
4 whole leeks (white and green parts separated), trimmed and rinsed well
2 pounds (1 kg) short ribs of beef
2 pounds (1 kg) boned beef shank
Coarse sea salt or kosher salt
3 medium onions, each studded with 1 clove
Bouquet garni: 12 parsley stems, 8 peppercorns, ½ teaspoon fresh thyme, ¼ teaspoon fennel seeds, and 1 imported bay leaf tied in a double thickness of cheesecloth
1 cabbage (about 1¼ pounds; 625 g), quartered
6 carrots, peeled
1 small celery root (celeriac), peeled and cubed

1. Wrap each piece of marrow bone in a green leek stem and tie with kitchen string. Set aside.

2. Tie the beef ribs and boned beef shank in two separate bundles, arranging them so they retain their shapes and fit compactly into a large stockpot. Cover the meat completely with cold water. Bring just to a simmer over medium-high heat. The water should barely simmer, never boil.

3. After about 10 minutes, skim the stock very carefully, removing all traces of impurities or grease. Careful skimming is essential to producing a fine *pot-au-feu*.

4. When the impurities have turned to foam, skim again. Move the pot to halfway off the heat so that the foam rises on one side only. making it easier to skim. Continue cooking for another 30 minutes.

5. Season the liquid lightly with about 1 tablespoon of coarse salt.

Add the clove-spiked onions, the bouquet garni, and the remaining dark green portion of the leeks. Skim again and simmer gently, skimming frequently, for 2 hours more. The meat should be very moist and tender, falling off the bone. (The meat can be cooked ahead to this point, then brought back to a simmer before serving time).

6. About 30 minutes before serving, add the marrow bones, submerging them in the liquid.

7. Meanwhile, cook the vegetables, using two pots, one for the cabbage and one for the carrots, the white portion of the leeks, and the celery root. Cover the vegetables with cold water. Cover and bring to a boil. Cook until tender, about 20 minutes for the leeks, 35 to 45 minutes for the carrots and celery root, and about 15 minutes for the cabbage. As the vegetables cook, remove them to a large platter kept warm in the oven.

8. Remove the twine from the

DES RESTES

Adrienne Biasin's special *pot-au-feu* tip, and one I've readily adopted, is to cook the vegetables separately from the meat. In this way, you can cook as many vegetables as you need for each serving, and end up with a less fatty dish in the end. She advises that you cook the cabbage separately. The remaining vegetables can be cooked together in one large pot.

meat. Cut it into chunks; place on the warmed platter. Discard the onions, bouquet garni, and green portions of the leek. Remove and discard the leek wrappers from the marrow bones. Place the marrow bones alongside the meat. Arrange the cooked vegetables all around. Ladle several spoonfuls of both the meat broth and the vegetable broth over the *pot-au-feu*. Serve immediately. Pass the condiments, such as coarse salt, cornichons, and imported hot Dijon mustard.

Yield: 8 to 10 servings

DES RESTES

A cooking tip for leftover *pot-au-feu* from Colette Dejean at Paris's Chez Toutoune: Line ramekins with thin slices of cooked leeks. Layer with finely diced cooked carrots, chopped leftover beef, and a mixture of chopped parsley and cooked onion. Repeat until the ramekin is full. Press down firmly, cover with a purée of turnips, then cover with additional slices of leek. Cook in a 350°F (175°C) oven in a bain-marie. Serve warm, using leftover bouillon as a sauce.

DAUBE DE BOEUF AUBERGE DE LA MADONE AUX CÈPES ET À L'ORANGE

Auberge de la Madone's Beef Stew with Wild Mushrooms and Orange

I am convinced that in Provence there are as many recipes for *daube*, or beef stew, as there are households. This version, flavored with mushrooms and orange, comes from a favorite family restaurant— Auberge de la Madone—situated just north of Nice, in the village of Peillon. Although chef Christian Millo uses wild cèpe mushrooms, I find that when they are not available, fresh domestic mushrooms are a worthy substitute. Serve with the same wine used in cooking, a sturdy red such as Nice's Bellet, Château de Crémat.

4½ *pounds (2.25 kg) stewing beef,
preferably a combination of beef
round and beef chuck, cut into
large pieces (each weighing about
4 ounces; 125 g)*
4 *carrots, peeled and cut into rounds*
3 *medium onions, coarsely chopped*
2 *garlic cloves*
1 *sprig of fresh parsley*
1 *celery rib, thickly sliced*
3 *imported bay leaves*
1 *tablespoon fresh thyme or 1 teaspoon
dried*
¼ *cup (6 cl) marc de Provence or Cognac*
1 *bottle (75 cl) sturdy red wine, such
as Côtes-du-Provence*
¼ *cup (6 cl) plus 1 tablespoon extra-
virgin olive oil*
1 *teaspoon whole black peppercorns*
3 *whole cloves*
3 *tablespoons (1½ ounces; 45 g) unsalted butter*
1 *pound (500 g) fresh wild cèpe
mushrooms or cultivated mushrooms*
1 *tablespoon tomato paste*
Salt and freshly ground pepper
Grated zest and juice of 1 orange

1. One day before serving the stew: In a large nonreactive bowl, combine the meat with the carrots, onions, garlic, parsley, celery, bay leaves, thyme, marc, red wine, and the 1 tablespoon olive oil. Tie the peppercorns and cloves in a piece of cheesecloth; add to the bowl and toss well. Cover and refrigerate for 24 hours, stirring once or twice.

2. Let the meat and vegetables return to room temperature. With a slotted spoon, remove the meat from the marinade. Drain well; pat dry on paper towels. Set the vegetables aside. Transfer the liquid and the cheesecloth bag to a nonreactive large heatproof casserole. Bring to a boil over medium-high heat. Boil for 5 minutes to reduce slightly. Remove from the heat.

3. In a large skillet, melt the butter in the remaining ¼ cup (6 cl) olive oil over high heat. When the foam subsides, add half of the meat. Sauté, tossing, until browned all over, about 5 minutes. With a slotted spoon, transfer the meat to the liquid in the casserole. Repeat with the remaining meat.

4. In the same skillet, sauté the reserved vegetables until browned, about 7 minutes. Transfer the vegetables to the casserole. Add the mushrooms to the skillet. Sauté until lightly browned, about 5 minutes; set aside.

5. Stir the tomato paste into the casserole. Bring to a simmer over medium-low heat. Reduce the heat to very low and simmer, skimming occasionally, until the meat is very tender, 3½ to 4 hours. Stir in salt and pepper to taste, the mushrooms, and the orange zest and juice. Discard the cheesecloth bag of cloves and peppercorns. (The recipe can be prepared 2 to 3 days ahead and refrigerated. Reheat before serving.) Serve with potatoes, rice, or pasta.

Yield: 8 servings

ESTOUFFADE PROVENÇALE

Provençal Beef Stew

F or decades, this has been the Monday special at La Mère Besson, a traditional family bistro in the sun-drenched city of Cannes. Recipes don't come any easier: You combine all the ingredients one day, cook them the next, let them ripen one more day, spoon off any unwanted fat that rises to the surface, reheat, and eat. All this with only a single pot to wash! It's a lovely, moist beef stew, marinated with all the best ingredients of Provence: dense red wine, herbs of the fields, garlic, onions, and carrots. At the end, you add a touch of orange zest—fresh or dried—and you have a marvelous main course. With the *estouffade,* serve either La Macaronade (see Index), a simple gratin of macaroni and Parmesan softened with the cooking liquid from the stew, or simply serve buttered noodles and pass a bowl of grated Parmesan.

2½ pounds (1.25 kg) stewing beef, cut into 1½-inch (4 cm) chunks (a butcher can do this for you)
2 medium onions, coarsely chopped
2 garlic cloves, crushed
1 carrot, peeled and cut into ½-inch (1 cm) rounds
1 celery rib, minced
Salt and freshly ground black pepper
2 tablespoons extra-virgin olive oil
1 bottle (3 cups; 75 cl) red wine, preferably Provençal
1 bunch of fresh thyme
3 imported bay leaves
1 strip of orange zest (about 2 inches; 5 cm), chopped

1. Two days before serving the stew, combine all of the ingredients,

except the orange zest, in a large enameled casserole. Cover and refrigerate overnight.

2. The next day, bring the mixture to a simmer over low heat. Simmer gently, until the meat is very tender, 3 to 4 hours.

3. Allow the stew to cool down. Refrigerate until the fat rises to the top and can be easily scraped off with a small spoon, about 12 hours.

4. At serving time, scrape off any additional fat. Reheat until the meat is heated through, 10 to 15 minutes. Adjust the seasonings. To serve, remove the bay leaves and thyme; stir in the orange zest.

Yield: 8 servings

GARDIANE LA CAMARGUE

La Camargue's Beef Stew with Black Olives

In France's cowboy country, the Camargue, south of Arles, one of the most popular regional dishes is the *gardiane,* a meaty stew that combines beef (or, more often, bull meat), the sturdy black olives of Nyons, and the vibrant red wine of Provence. I know of few more pleasant spots than the small village bistro called La Camargue, in Aigues-Mortes. Here, along with the tiny *tellines,* or minature clams sautéed in olive oil and garlic, diners feast on a flavorful, wine-infused meat stew, which simmers away for hours until the meat is meltingly tender. With this, sample a heady red Côtes-du-Rhône, such as Vacqueyras.

4½ pounds (2.25 kg) stewing beef, preferably a combination of beef round and beef chuck, cut into large pieces each weighing about 4 ounces (125 g)
5 garlic cloves
2 to 3 medium onions (about 12 ounces; 360 g), cut into rounds
4 carrots, peeled and cut into 1-inch (2.5 cm) lengths

1 bottle (75 cl) full-bodied red wine, such as Côtes-du-Rhône
2 tablespoons olive oil
2 sprigs of fresh thyme or ½ teaspoon dried
3 imported bay leaves
1 cup (4 ounces; 125 g) oil-cured black olives, preferably from Nyons
Salt and freshly ground black pepper

1. One day before serving the stew: Combine the meat, garlic, onions, carrots, and wine in a large, nonreactive bowl. Cover and refrigerate for 24 hours, stiring once or twice.

2. Three hours before cooking, remove the meat from the refrigerator and let come to room temperature. Remove the meat from the marinade; drain well.

3. In a very large, heavy-bottomed nonreactive casserole, heat the oil over medium-high heat. Add the meat and brown on all sides, working in several batches, if necessary. Do not crowd the meat. Add the thyme, bay leaves, and olives, and season with salt and pepper. Pour the marinade ingredients over the meat. Cover and bring to a boil. Reduce the heat and barely simmer, half-covered, for 2 hours.

4. Discard the bay leaves and thyme sprigs. Transfer the stew to a deep serving platter. Serve with boiled white rice, potatoes, or pasta.

Yield: 6 servings

> **"***What a nice Sunday!***"** *A beef stew simmering in the low-ceilinged, blue-tiled kitchen, the whole house fragrant with the scent of herbs. . .*
>
> —GEORGES SIMENON
> *The Patience of Maigret*

SAUTÉ DE VEAU AUX CAROTTES LA BOUTARDE

La Boutarde's Sautéed Veal with Carrots

One of the great joys of French bistro cooking lies in its simplicity. This main-course dish depends upon just three basic ingredients—veal, wine, and carrots—and when carefully prepared, it is a meal fit for a king, a meltingly tender marriage of delicately flavored veal and soft, sweet carrots that joyfully simmer away in the flavorful cooking juices.

This version of the classic bistro preparation comes from La Boutarde, a small bistro that serves as a lunchtime *cantine* for the editors and writers from the International Herald Tribune. When I prepare this dish at home, I like to make it a day ahead, so the flavors have plenty of time to mature. I also find that because the dish shines with such simplicity, it doesn't even need to be boosted along by rice or potatoes. A nice mixed green salad and a crisp baguette will do just fine. With it, sample the same wine used in cooking. I'd recommend an Atlantic Coast Muscadet de Sèvre-et-Maine.

¼ *cup (6 cl) extra-virgin olive oil*
2 *pounds (1 kg) boneless veal rump,*
    sirloin roast, or stewing veal, cut
    into rather large (2 ounce; 60 g)
    cubes
Salt and freshly ground black pepper
2 *onions, cut into thin rounds*
1 *bottle (75 cl) white wine, such as*
    Muscadet de Sèvre-et-Maine
3 *imported bay leaves*
2 *teaspoons Herbes de Provence (see*
    Index)
2 *small tomatoes, cored, peeled, seeded,*
    and chopped
2 *pounds (1 kg) tender young carrots,*
    peeled and cut into thin rounds

1. In a deep-sided, nonreactive, 12-inch (30 cm) skillet, heat the oil over medium-high heat. When the oil is hot, begin to brown the cubes of veal on all sides. Do not crowd the pan, and be patient when browning. Good browning is essential, so the veal retains all of its flavor. The meat should be browned in several batches, taking about 5 minutes to brown each batch. Carefully regulate the heat to avoid scorching the meat.

As each batch is browned, remove the veal to a platter and season generously with salt and pepper.

2. When all of the veal is browned, return all of the meat to the skillet. Add the onions and cook over medium-high heat just until the onions are soft and translucent, 2 to 3 minutes. Reduce the heat to medium; add 1 cup (25 cl) of the wine. Using a metal spatula, scrape up any cooked-on bits of meat from the bottom of the pan and stir them in with the wine. Stir in the bay leaves, herbs, and tomatoes. Cover and bring just to a simmer. Simmer for about 5 minutes. Pour 1 more cup (25 cl) of the wine. Cover and simmer very gently, over low to medium heat, for 1 hour. Stir in the remaining wine. Cover and simmer for 1 more hour.

3. Remove the veal from the pan; set aside. Add the carrots to the skillet. Cover and simmer until soft, 40 to 45 minutes. By this point, the carrots will have absorbed much of the sauce. Return the veal to the skillet and reheat until warmed through. Serve immediately.

Yield: 4 to 6 servings

TENDRONS DE VEAU LE CAMÉLÉON

Le Caméléon's Braised Veal with Fresh Pasta

I n France, one of the most popular cuts of veal for stewing is *tendron,* the portion of the breast that contains the cartilaginous rib-like portions that visually resemble pork spare ribs when cooked. For this recipe, you can choose from any number of good cuts of stewing veal, including the breast (known in France as *poitrine* or *tendron*), the short ribs *(haut de côtes),* veal shoulder and shoulder chops (*épaule* or *côtes découvertes*), and the heel of round or shank (*gîte à la noix* or *jarret*). This is one of my favorite bistro dishes (both to prepare and to eat!) and I order it often when I go to the popular Paris bistro Le Caméléon. With it, I usually drink the fruity red Saumur-Champigny from the Loire.

2 tablespoons peanut oil
2 pounds (1 kg) breast of veal with the bone (ask your butcher to cut across the lower breast portion to make several strips of equal width)
Salt and freshly ground black pepper
1 cup (25 cl) dry white wine
4 medium carrots, peeled and cut into rounds
2 medium onions, cut into rings
4 garlic cloves, coarsely chopped
2 imported bay leaves
1 teaspoon dried thyme
1 large can (28 ounces; 794 g) Italian plum tomatoes, with their liquid
1 pound (500 g) fresh fettuccine
Small handful flat-leaf parsley, finely chopped

1. Heat the oil in a nonreactive, deep-sided, 12-inch (30 cm) skillet over medium-high heat. When the oil is hot, begin to brown the veal in batches on both sides; do not crowd the pan. Be patient when browning; good browning is essential for the veal to retain all of its flavor. The meat should take about 5 minutes to brown each batch. Carefully regulate the heat to avoid scorching the meat. As each batch is browned, remove the veal to a platter and season generously with salt and freshly ground black pepper.

2. When all of the veal is browned, pour out the fat from the skillet. Return all of the meat to the pan. Add the wine, carrots, onions, garlic, bay leaves, thyme, and tomatoes. Bring to a boil over high heat. Reduce the heat to low. Cover and

simmer until the meat is very tender and the liquid is transformed into a thick, delicious sauce, about 1½ hours. Keep an eye on the pan, making sure the liquid remains at a quiet, gentle simmer.

3. Meanwhile, bring a large pot of water to a rolling boil. Salt the water, add the pasta, and cook just until tender. Drain. Place the pasta on a large, warmed serving platter.

4. Using a flat metal strainer, remove the veal from the pan; place on top of the pasta. Strain the sauce through a sieve. Pour the sauce over the veal. Sprinkle on the parsley. Serve immediately, on warmed dinner plates.

Yield: 6 to 8 servings

> **❝***Standing there I wondered how much of what we felt on the bridge was just hunger. I asked my wife and she said, 'I don't know, Tatie. There are so many kinds of hunger . . . memory is hunger.'***❞**
> —ERNEST HEMINGWAY, OUTSIDE THE RESTAURANT MICHAUD

BAECKEOFE CAVEAU D'EGUISHEIM

Alsatian Mixed-Meat Stew

I don't know of any more "meat and potatoes" type of dish than *baeckeofe,* which translates literally as "baker's oven." In Alsace, this dish was traditionally prepared on Monday, when the housewives did their weekly washing and had little time to cook. In the morning, they would take their prepared casseroles to the *boulangerie,* where the baker would fill his wood-fired oven with the assortment of colorful, hand-decorated clay casseroles. At lunchtime, the washing done, the women would fetch the steaming casserole for lunch.

Baeckeofe is indeed a meat-eater's delight. With it, serve the same wine used in preparing the *baeckeofe,* an Alsatian white. If you do not have a large clay baking dish use a cast-iron casserole with a good, secure cover.

Meat and marinade:

1 pound (500 g) boneless beef shoulder, trimmed of fat, cut into 3-inch (7 cm) cubes
1 pound (500 g) lamb shoulder or lamb shoulder chops, boned, cut into 3-inch (7 cm) cubes
1 pound (500 g) pork shoulder or pork cutlets, trimmed of fat, cut into 3-inch (7 cm) cubes
1 bottle (75 cl) white Alsatian Sylvaner, Tokay, or Riesling wine
4 carrots, peeled and thinly sliced
2 medium onions, thinly sliced
3 garlic cloves
2 imported bay leaves
2 tablespoons dried thyme
Salt to taste

Vegetables:

4 pounds (2 kg) waxy boiling potatoes, peeled and thinly sliced
1 pound (500 g) onions, thinly sliced
3 leeks, trimmed slightly, well rinsed, and cut into thin rings
Salt and freshly ground black pepper

1. One day before serving the *baeckeofe*, marinate the meats: In a very large nonreactive bowl, combine the meats and all of the marinade ingredients. Toss to mix. Cover securely with plastic wrap; refrigerate overnight.

2. The next day, preheat the oven to 375°F (190°C).

3. Cook the vegetables and meat: Scatter about one-third of the potatoes, onions, and leeks over the bottom of a very large, nonreactive casserole.

4. Drain the meat, reserving the marinade and seasonings. Place half of the meat on top of the vegetables. Season with salt and pepper to taste. Repeat with another layer of the vegetables, and then the rest of the meat. Season again. Top the meat with the remaining vegetables; season to taste. Pour the marinade and seasonings over all.

5. Cover the casserole securely and bake until the meat is very tender, about 3 hours. Traditionally, the casserole is hermetically sealed with a paste of flour and water, so that no steam escapes, but I don't find this essential. In principle, the dish should need no tending during the 3 hours of baking, but I have to confess that I like to give it a little peek every now and then to make sure the liquid hasn't cooked away.

6. To serve, tilt the casserole and spoon off any excess fat. Serve immediately, spooning portions of meat and vegetables on large, warmed dinner plates.

Yield: 8 to 10 servings

DAUBE DE QUEUE DE BOEUF

Oxtail Stew

Oxtail is one of the most economical and most flavorful cuts of meat, and one that takes well to marinating for days in a hearty mixture of red wine, herbs, and vegetables. The longer you marinate the mixture, the more flavorful it will be, but be sure it marinates at least 3 days. Oxtail is also a fatty cut—give yourself plenty of time to allow the stew to cook and then cool, so all the fat can be skimmed off. Serve this with thick noodles in warmed soup bowls, accompanied by a tossed salad, and of course, a robust red wine.

Marinade and oxtail:
4 whole cloves
1 pound (500 g) onions, peeled and
    quartered
1 head of garlic, cloves peeled and halved
8 ounces (250 g) shallots, peeled
1 pound (500 g) carrots, peeled and
    cut into ¾-inch (2 cm) slices
3 bottles (each 75 cl) red wine, such
    as Côtes-du-Rhône
1 bunch of fresh parsley
4 imported bay leaves
1 bunch of fresh thyme
1 teaspoon black peppercorns
5 pounds (2.5 kg) oxtail, cut into 4-
    inch (10 cm) pieces

Stew:
10 ounces (300 g) salt pork, cubed
1 pound (500 g) carrots, peeled and
    cut into ¾-inch (2 cm) slices
Salt and freshly ground black pepper

For serving:
Coarse (kosher) salt
8 ounces (250 g) rigatoni or large
    macaroni

1. Stick a clove into 4 onion quarters. Place all of the marinade ingredients through the peppercorns in a large nonreactive casserole or Dutch oven. Add the oxtail pieces. Cover and refrigerate for up to 5 days. Remove the pan from the refrigerator from time to time to stir and evenly distribute all the ingredients.

2. The day before you plan to serve the stew, remove the casserole from the refrigerator. Remove the pieces of oxtail from the marinade and drain well.

3. In a heavy skillet, brown the salt pork over medium-high heat

until evenly browned. Add the pieces of oxtail, in batches, and brown on all sides.

4. Return the oxtail and salt pork to the marinade, adding, if necessary, enough water to cover generously. Bring to a simmer over medium heat. Carefully skim any impurities or grease that rise to the top. Simmer, keeping the mixture bubbling gently, until the meat is falling off the bone, at least 2 to 2½ hours.

5. Remove from the heat to cool. Cover and refrigerate overnight. The next day, use a small spoon to remove and discard all the fat that has solidified on top of the stew. Add the fresh carrots, salt, and

pepper, and cook again until the mixture is heated through, checking for seasoning from time to time.

6. To serve, bring a large pot of water to a boil. Add salt and the pasta. Cook the pasta just until firm. Drain well. Evenly divide the pasta among shallow soup bowls.

7. With a two-pronged fork, carefully remove the pieces of oxtail from the stew. Drain, and place on a carving board. Remove the meat in big chunks, and place them on top of the pasta. Carefully spoon the sauce and the vegetables on top of the meat, sprinkle with just a bit of coarse salt. Serve immediately.

Yield: 8 to 12 servings

GÎGOT D'AGNEAU À LA SEPT HEURES AMBASSADE D'AUVERGNE

Ambassade d'Auvergne's Seven-Hour Leg of Lamb

Cook lamb for seven hours? For those of us who have religiously followed the rule that "the only good lamb is a rare lamb," this recipe is sheer heresy! I first sampled it years ago at Paris's Ambassade d'Auvergne, and decided that the slow cooking—almost like a pot roast—really worked well with a large leg of lamb.

By now, I've lost track of the number of places, and number of times I've prepared this dish. The first time I tried it, I baked the lamb in our brick-lined bread oven, and the sweet, tender aromas of the lamb filled our courtyard for the long afternoon. Once, a friend prepared it for me, using red wine, and it was delicious. Traditionally, the dish was prepared with tougher mutton, but I find any size leg of lamb can be used. With this, try a good red, such as Côteau d'Auvergne, or a Gigondas.

6 *medium onions, quartered*
6 *carrots, peeled and quartered*
1 *whole head of garlic, cloves peeled and halved*
6 *imported bay leaves*
1 *bunch of fresh thyme or several tea-spoons dried*
1 *leg of lamb, bone-in, 6 to 7 pounds (3 to 3.5 kg)*
Salt and freshly ground black pepper
2 *bottles (75 cl each) dry white wine, such as Aligoté*
5 *pounds (2.5 kg) large boiling potatoes, peeled and quartered*
5 *tomatoes, peeled, cored, seeded, and chopped*

1. Preheat the oven to 425°F (220°C).

2. Layer the onions, carrots, garlic, bay leaves, and thyme on the bottom of a covered nonreactive roaster large enough to hold the lamb. Place the lamb on top and roast, uncovered, for 30 minutes. Remove the roaster from the oven and generously season the lamb with salt and pepper. Return it to the oven and roast for 30 more minutes.

3. Remove the roaster from the oven. Leave the oven on. Place the roaster on top of the stove, slowly pour the wine over the lamb, cover, and bring the liquid to a boil. Return

---

HARVEST TIME SUPPER

This is a menu that reminds me of fall and winter, when days are short and you want to be with friends. Turn the open-face sandwiches into tiny bite-size appetizers, and then dig into one of my favorite lamb preparations, the incredible "seven hour" leg of lamb. All this calls for a warming red, such as southwestern Cahors.

LA TARTINE CHAUDE AU BLEU DES CAUSSES ET JAMBON CRU LES BACCHANTES
Les Bacchantes' Blue Cheese and Ham Sandwich

♦

GIGOT D'AGNEAU À LA SEPT HEURES AMBASSADE D'AUVERGNE
Ambassade d'Auvergne's Seven-Hour Leg of Lamb

♦

RIZ AU LAIT
Rice Pudding

---

the roaster, covered, to the oven and roast the lamb until the meat is very tender, still juicy, and falling off the bone. Timing will vary according to the size and age of the leg of lamb, and type of roasting pan used. But once the wine has been added, it will generally take 4 to 5 additional hours of baking. Obviously, it is best to check on the lamb from time to time, reducing the oven heat if the lamb begins to burn or the liquid begins to evaporate too much.

4. One hour before serving, bury the potatoes and tomatoes in the liquid. Cover, and roast until the potatoes are cooked through, about 1 hour more. The lamb should be very moist and tender and falling off the bone. As the French say, you should be able to eat it with a spoon.

Yield: 12 servings

TRANCHE DE GIGOT LA BOUTARDE

La Boutarde's Pan-Fried Leg of Lamb Slices

F rench lamb is wonderful: tender, fragrant, flavorful. It's one of my favorite meats, and so I order it often, and prepare it with frequency. I first sampled this version—one that takes literally seconds to make—at the small Parisian bistro La Boutarde. I've embellished it a bit with one of my favorite ingredients, garlic. The garlic can, of course, be separated earlier in the day, leaving almost no last-minute labor. Serve this with a rich potato gratin and a hearty red wine, such as Gérard Chave's red Hermitage.

3 tablespoons extra-virgin olive oil
40 garlic cloves, in their skins
1 tablespoon fresh thyme
4 slices leg of lamb (each weighing
*   about 5 ounces; 150 g)*
Salt and freshly ground pepper
¼ (6 cl) cup dry white wine, such as
*   Cassis*

1. In a large, cast-iron skillet, heat the oil over medium-high heat. Add the garlic and thyme and sauté, shaking the pan back and forth, until the garlic begins to soften, 5 to 6 minutes. Adjust the heat to keep the garlic skins from burning.

2. Remove the garlic and thyme to a warmed platter. Cover and keep warm.

3. Place the slices of lamb in the hot skillet and brown quickly on both sides. (For rare lamb, this will take just 1 to 2 minutes on each side. For well-cooked meat, cook 3 to 4 minutes on each side.)

4. Divide the lamb among 4 dinner plates. Season generously with salt and pepper.

5. Deglaze the pan with the wine, scraping up any browned bits from the bottom of the skillet. Return the garlic and thyme to the pan and toss in the sauce. Spoon the sauce over the lamb and serve immediately.

Yield: 4 servings

GIGOT D'AUTOMNE GUY SAVOY

Guy Savoy's Fall Leg of Lamb

L amb is, hands down, my favorite meat, and leg of lamb my favorite cut. This is a variation on many popular bistro preparations—*boeuf à la ficelle, navarin printanier,* and the classic *pot-au-feu.* When I prepare this dish, the biggest problem is finding a pot big enough to hold it all! A large oval pot is better than a round one. Also note, the size of lamb can vary according to the number of people you intend to serve. I find that if you cook the lamb for about 10 minutes per pound, the lamb will be slightly, but perfectly, rare. The recipe comes from one of my favorite Paris chefs, Guy Savoy, who runs both the elegant restaurant that bears his name, as well as Le Bistro de l'Etoile, right across the street from it.

1 leg of lamb, bone-in (6 to 7 pounds, 3 to 3.5 kg)

½ medium cabbage (about 1½ pounds; 750 g), tied with string to keep its form

1 pound (500 g) carrots, peeled and cut into rounds

1 pound (500 g) turnips, peeled and halved or quartered, depending on size

8 ounces celery root (celeriac), peeled and cubed

3 whole leeks, rinsed well, trimmed slightly, and tied together with a string

1 pound (500 g) white pearl onions or boiling onions

1 large onion pierced with 2 cloves

3 garlic cloves, unpeeled

2 shallots, unpeeled

1 bouquet garni: 12 parsley stems, 8 peppercorns, 1 imported bay leaf, ¼ teaspoon fennel seed, and ¼ teaspoon dried thyme tied in a double thickness of cheesecloth

1 tablespoon salt

10 black peppercorns

½ cup (12.5 cl) crème fraîche (see Index) or heavy cream

½ cup (12.5 cl) drained prepared horse-radish

1. Carefully tie the leg of lamb with household string, so it holds its shape while cooking. Place the lamb in a large nonreactive pot. Add the vegetables, garlic, shallots, bouquet garni, and salt. Cover completely with cold water. Bring just to a boil, partially covered, over medium-high heat. This should take 20 to 25 min-

utes. All the while, skim very carefully to remove all traces of impurities or grease.

2. When the liquid begins to boil, note the time on a clock. Reduce the heat to low. Add the peppercorns and simmer gently. Simmer the lamb for about 10 minutes per pound (500 g) to produce sliced lamb that is pink inside. At the end of the cooking time, turn off the heat. Allow the lamb to rest in the bouillon for 15 minutes.

3. Meanwhile, prepare the horseradish sauce. Combine the crème fraîche and horseradish. Season to taste with salt and pepper.

4. To serve, transfer the lamb to a carving board. Remove the string; cut the lamb into slices, placing them in the center of a large platter. Cut the cabbage into 8 pieces. Halve the leeks lengthwise. Surround the lamb with the vegetables. Serve with the horseradish sauce.

Yield: 8 servings

DES RESTES

Another cooking tip for leftover leg of lamb from Colette Dejean at Paris's Chez Toutoune: Brown chopped shallots in butter, moistening them with a touch of bouillon. Add freshly ground bread crumbs and a bit of red wine vinegar. Cook over low heat until well blended, then toss in a few diced sour pickles. Serve warm, over sliced lamb, which can be served at room temperature or reheated.

GIGOT RÔTI AU GRATIN DE MONSIEUR HENNY

Roast Lamb with Monsieur Henny's Potato, Onion, and Tomato Gratin

This is a simple, satisfying dish to make—the sort of one-dish meal that French village women used to bring to the local baker for cooking in the community's bread oven. In Provence, it's become our "house special." In this recipe offered to me by my village butcher Monsieur Roland Henny, the lamb's wonderful juices drip into the gratin, a mixture of tomatoes, potatoes, and onions, as it cooks. While more traditional recipes call for baking the lamb right in the gratin, I like to let it sit an inch or so above the gratin on a sturdy cake stand or oven rack that rests atop the gratin dish. This allows the lamb to roast and not steam. Serve with a solid red wine, such as a Côtes-du-Rhône-Villages or a Châteauneuf-du-Pape.

---

6 garlic cloves, 1 clove split, the rest
  chopped
2 pounds (1 kg) baking potatoes, such
  as russets, peeled and very thinly
  sliced
Salt and freshly ground black pepper
1 tablespoon fresh thyme
2 large onions, very thinly sliced
5 medium tomatoes (about 1 pound;
  500 g), cored and thinly sliced
⅔ cup (16 cl) dry white wine
⅓ cup (8 cl) extra-virgin olive oil
1 leg of lamb, bone-in (6 to 7 pounds;
  3 to 3.5 kg)

---

1. Preheat the oven to 400°F (205°C).

2. Rub the bottom of a large oval porcelain gratin dish about 16 × 10 × 2 inches (40.5 × 25.5 × 5 cm) with the split garlic clove. Arrange the potatoes in a single layer. Season generously with the salt, pepper, and some of the thyme and chopped garlic. Layer the sliced onions on top; season as with the potatoes. Layer the tomatoes on top of the onions. Season with salt, pepper, and the remaining thyme and garlic. Pour on the white wine, and then the oil.

3. Trim the thicker portions of fat from the leg of lamb. Season the meat with salt and pepper. Place a sturdy cake rack or oven rack directly on top of the gratin dish. Set the lamb on the rack, so that the juices will drip into the gratin.

4. Roast, uncovered, for about 1 hour and 15 minutes for rare lamb. (For well-done lamb, roast an additional 30 to 40 minutes.) Turn the lamb every 15 minutes, basting it with liquid from the dish underneath. Remove from the oven and let the lamb sit for 20 minutes before carving.

5. To serve, carve the lamb into thin slices and arrange on warmed dinner plates or on a serving platter, with the vegetable gratin alongside.

Yield: 8 to 10 servings

> **"***Gourmandise is a capital sin. So, therefore, my brothers, let us guard against being gourmands. Let's be gourmets.***"**
> —SAINT IGNATIUS OF LOYOLA, founder of the Jesuit order

LE SAUTÉ D'AGNEAU AUX FLAGEOLETS LE PERRAUDIN

Le Perraudin's Braised Lamb with White Beans

In many cases, there is no distinction between a classic bistro dish and a recipe coming from a classic French housewife. This recipe, in which lamb is sautéed quickly, drowned in liquid, then simmered gently with the traditional trio of carrots, onions, and tomatoes, could be found in home, as well as restaurant kitchens. White beans are cooked separately, and served as a welcome accompaniment. It's soothing cold weather fare, easy to make and just as easy to eat. As the French say, *"Ça se mange tout seul!"* Literally, "It eats all by itself."

When Le Perraudin's owner, Hubert Gloaguen, sent along this recipe, he added, "To accompany this rustic dish, why not drink a Loire Valley white or a Côtes-du-Rhône? The wine should be fruity and served at room temperature. *Bon appétit.*" Need I say more?

Beans:

*1 pound (500 g) dried lima beans or
    small dried white beans*
3 carrots, peeled and sliced
2 onions, peeled and chopped
*1 bouquet garni: Several thyme and
    parsley sprigs and several imported
    bay leaves tied with a string or in
    a double thickness of cheesecloth*
2 ounces (60 g) diced, smoked bacon
Salt

Lamb:

2 tablespoons peanut oil
*2 pounds (1 kg) lean shoulder of
    lamb, meat and bones cut into 2-
    inch (5 cm) cubes*
Salt and freshly ground black pepper
*¾ cup (95 g) superfine flour, such as
    Wondra*
*2 cups (50 cl) dry white wine, such
    as Sauvignon Blanc*
4 onions, peeled and chopped
3 carrots, peeled and sliced
*5 small tomatoes, peeled, cored, seeded,
    and chopped (or substitute 3 table-
    spoons tomato paste)*
2 imported bay leaves
*Several sprigs of fresh thyme or 1 tea-
    spoon dried*
Several sprigs of fresh parsley
Finely minced fresh parsley, for garnish

1. Prepare the beans: Rinse the beans and place them in a large saucepan. Cover with cold water. Cover the pan and bring the water to a boil over high heat. Once boiling, remove the pan from the heat. Leaving the cover in place, let rest for 40 minutes.

2. Drain the beans, discarding the cooking liquid. Rinse the beans and cover again with cold water. Add the carrots, onions, bouquet garni, and bacon. Bring just to a simmer over medium heat. Cook, covered, over medium heat until tender, about 1 hour. (Cooking time will vary according to the freshness of the beans. Older beans take longer to cook.) The beans should not be mushy, but firm-tender. Add salt to taste. (The beans may be cooked in advance then reheated.)

3. Prepare the lamb: Heat the oil in a large nonreactive skillet over medium-high heat. When the oil is hot but not smoking, add the lamb and the bones in batches, without crowding, and brown on all sides, about 10 to 15 minutes for each batch. Season the lamb with salt and pepper to taste.

4. When all of the lamb is browned, return it to the casserole. Sprinkle on the flour and stir until the lamb is well coated. Pour in the wine. Bring to a boil, stirring constantly to blend. Add 6 cups (1.5 l) of water (the lamb should literally be drowning in liquid), along with the onions, carrots, tomatoes, bay leaves, thyme, and parsley sprigs. Season with salt and pepper. Cover and simmer for 1 hour.

5. To serve, place 3 or 4 pieces of lamb on a warmed dinner plate. With a slotted spoon, place the beans alongside. Spoon the sauce from the lamb over the lamb and the beans. Sprinkle with the parsley, and serve immediately.

Yield: 6 servings

BLANQUETTE D'AGNEAU AU VIN BLANC

Lamb Stew in White Wine

I love this dish, served from time to time at the Parisian restaurant L'Aquitaine. The *blanquette* is so simple, subtle, and lovely, and is such a cinch to prepare, I really look forward to making—and eating—it. If you can get your butcher to bone and cube the meat for you, there's almost nothing left to do but set the table and uncork a nice bottle of white wine, such as a fruity Burgundian Aligoté.

As an accompaniment, serve the lamb with oven-baked rice, seasoned with a touch of thyme. I have to admit that I always thought of *blanquette* as a pale, dull dish. But try this version, with its luscious lemon and thyme-flavored sauce, and you'll be converted too! As the French say, *Miam! Miam!* (Yum, yum, of course.)

3 tablespoons (1½ ounces; 45 g) unsalted butter
2 pounds (1 kg) boned leg of lamb, fat and tendons removed, meat cut into 1½-inch (4 cm) cubes (ask your butcher to do this for you)
Salt and freshly ground black pepper
4 fresh garlic cloves, crushed
2 tablespoons superfine flour, such as Wondra
1 bottle (75 cl) dry white wine, such as an Aligoté
2 imported bay leaves
1 teaspoon dried thyme
1 large egg yolk
1 tablespoon freshly squeezed lemon juice
2 tablespoons crème fraîche (see Index) or heavy cream

1. In a deep-sided, nonreactive 12-inch (30 cm) skillet, melt the butter over medium-high heat. When the butter is hot but not smoking, add some of the lamb and brown on all sides. Be patient when browning, and don't hurry the meat along. Good browning is essential, so the lamb retains all of its flavor. The meat should be browned in several batches, taking about 5 minutes to brown each batch. Carefully regulate the heat to avoid scorching the meat. As each batch is browned, remove the lamb to a platter and season generously with salt and pepper

2. When all of the lamb is browned, return all of the meat to the skillet. Add the garlic and cook over medium-high heat, just until

you begin to smell the garlic, 2 to 3 minutes. Sprinkle on the flour; stir vigorously with a wooden spoon to evenly coat the lamb. Reduce the heat to medium and stir in 1 cup (25 cl) of the wine, the bay leaves, and thyme. Cover and bring just to a simmer. Simmer for about 5 minutes. Add 1 more cup (25 cl) of the wine. Cover and simmer over medium heat for 1 hour.

3. Add the remaining wine. Cover and simmer for 15 minutes more. (The dish can be prepared ahead of time up to this point. Refrigerate, covered, for up to 1 day, then very gently reheat and proceed with the recipe.)

4. Whisk together the egg yolk, lemon juice, and crème fraîche in a small bowl.

5. With a slotted spoon, remove the lamb to a heated platter. Off the heat, quickly whisk the egg yolk mixture into the wine sauce in the skillet until the sauce is very smooth and rich-looking. Do not allow the egg yolk to cook. Pour the sauce over the lamb. Serve immediately, with oven-baked rice.

Yield: 4 servings

HARICOTS ROUGES AUX BOUDIN NOIR ET CHORIZO

◆━━━━━━━◆

Spicy Chorizo Sausage and Blood Sausage with Red Beans

Whew! You can't get much earthier than this, three robust ingredients that together form a dish that's wonderfully hearty, and yes, a bit heavy. But taken in small, appreciative doses, this is an ideal wintertime one-dish meal. Just make sure that your sausage is top-rate. The recipe was shared with me by Aroxxa Aguirre, a young woman chef who once ran Euskalduna, a small Basque bistro in Bayonne.

2½ cups (1 pound; 500 g) dried red kidney beans
7 ounces (200 g) slab bacon, rind removed, cut into 1½ × 1 inch (4 × 2.5 cm) pieces
1 large onion, minced
2 large carrots, peeled and finely diced
4 garlic cloves, crushed
2 to 3 cups (50 to 75 cl) dry red wine, such as a Spanish rioja
Salt and freshly ground black pepper
8 ounces (250 g) chorizo sausages
8 ounces (250 g) blood sausages
2 tablespoons extra-virgin olive oil
About ½ cup (12.5 cl) pickled mild green chiles, chopped, for garnish

---

1. Rinse the beans carefully, picking them over to remove any pebbles. Place the beans in a non-reactive large heavy saucepan. Add boiling water to just cover and let sit for 1 hour.

2. Meanwhile, place the bacon in a large nonstick skillet. Cook, stirring frequently over medium-high heat, for 3 to 4 minutes. Add the onion, carrots, and garlic; sauté until the bacon is crisp and the onions are soft but not browned, about 5 minutes.

3. Drain the beans, discarding the water. Return the beans to the saucepan and add enough of the red wine to cover. Bring to a slow boil over medium heat, skimming off any foam that rises to the top. Add more wine or water if necessary. When all the foam has been skimmed off, add the sautéed bacon mixture. Cover and simmer for about 30 minutes. Stir in 1 tablespoon of salt. Continue cooking until the beans are tender. The cooking time will vary depending upon the freshness of the beans; fresher beans cook more quickly than older ones. They usually take about 2 hours of total cooking time.

4. As the beans cook, prepare the sausages. (The beans can be prepared several hours ahead of time and reheated at serving time.) Prick the chorizo and blood sausages evenly with a fork. Heat the oil in a large heavy skillet over medium heat.

When the oil is hot but not smoking, reduce the heat to low and add the sausages. Sauté the sausages, turning frequently, until evenly browned on all sides, about 10 minutes.

5. Reheat the beans if necessary, then turn off the heat. Season with salt and pepper. Transfer the beans with their cooking liquid to a serving platter. Cut the sausages into thick rounds, and remove the casings if desired. Arrange the sausages around the beans. Pass the pickled chiles separately. Serve immediately.

Yield: 6 to 8 servings

LES DESSERTS MAISON

Homemade Desserts

Bistro cooking is based, quite frankly, on everyday home cooking. So it's no surprise to find that bistro desserts tend to be uncomplicated affairs that require little technique and make use of ingredients readily at hand. A number of the desserts, such as prunes in red wine or chocolate mousse, know no season and thus can be served throughout the year. For others, like the raspberry tart from the Café du Jura, you'll have to wait until the summertime berries are ripe. Typically, fruit tarts make up the bulk of the selection, for apple and pear tarts lead the bistro hit parade wherever you go. I've added, as well, some typically regional favorites, including the lemon verbena custard from Marie-Claude Gracia in the southwest, the delicate local cheesecake from a *ferme-auberge* in Alsace, and the sweet pear omelet from Lyons' Chez Tante Paulette.

Mon Gâteau au Chocolat

Marie-Claude Gracia's Chocolate Cake

I firmly believe that one can never have too many chocolate cakes in one's repertoire. I love the pureness and simplicity of this one— it's moist, rich, not cloying. This recipe comes from the kitchens of one of my favorite French cooks, Marie-Claude Gracia of La Belle Gasconne in the southwestern village of Poudenas. It's one of those cakes you can make with your eyes closed: All you need to add is a dash of confectioner's sugar to dress it up a bit.

12 ounces (360 g) bittersweet choco-
    late, preferably Lindt or Tobler,
    broken into pieces
⅔ cup (5⅓ ounces; 150 g) unsalted
    butter
¾ cup (160 g) granulated sugar
5 large eggs, separated
⅓ cup (45 g) unbleached all-purpose
    flour
About 2 teaspoons confectioner's sugar,
    for decoration (optional)

> **Life is so brief that we should not glance either too far backwards or forwards . . . therefore study how to fix our happiness in our glass and in our plate.**
>
> —Grimod de la Reynière

1. Preheat the oven to 350°F (175°C). Butter a 9½-inch (24 cm) springform pan or deep, nonstick cake pan.

2. Combine the chocolate, butter, and granulated sugar in the top of a double boiler placed over simmering water. Melt over medium heat, stirring until the ingredients are thoroughly blended. Set the mixture aside to cool.

3. Whisk the egg yolks into the chocolate. Whisk in the flour.

4. Beat the egg whites in a large bowl just until they form firm peaks; do not overbeat.

5. Add one-third of the egg whites to the chocolate batter and mix vigorously. Gently fold in the remaining whites. Do this slowly and patiently. Do not overmix, but be sure that the mixture is well blended and that no streaks of whites remain.

6. Pour the batter into the prepared pan. Bake until the cake is firm and springy, 35 to 40 minutes.

7. Cool on a rack for several hours before unmolding. The cake is traditionally served without icing (though you may want to dust it with the confectioners' sugar), and with a glass of sherry, a sweet Sauternes, or Banyuls.

Yield: 8 to 12 servings

GÂTEAU AU CHOCOLAT LE MAS DE CHASTELAS

Le Mas de Chastelas' Chocolate Cake

N ow this is my idea of a real chocolate cake, a chocolate "pound" cake. I guess that you can't get much richer than this. The recipe comes from a beautiful restaurant near Saint-Tropez, situated in a restored *magnanerie*, or silkworm factory. Make this cake on a day that you intend to serve a hungry group of chocolate lovers! The cooking process—baked for just 15 minutes, then left to "steam" for another 12—may seem bizarre, but the result is a very moist, mousse-like cake.

1 pound (500 g) bittersweet chocolate, preferably Lindt or Tobler brand
½ pound (8 ounces; 250 g) unsalted butter, cut in small pieces
10 large eggs, separated
¼ cup (50 g) sugar
¼ cup (35 g) unbleached all-purpose flour

1. Preheat the oven to 400°F (205°C). Butter a 10½-inch (27 cm) springform pan or deep nonstick cake pan.

2. Break the chocolate into pieces. Melt in the top of a double boiler placed over boiling water, stirring from time to time.

3. Off the heat, stir the butter into the chocolate, stirring until the butter and chocolate are combined. Transfer to a large mixing bowl.

4. In a large bowl, beat the egg whites just until they form firm peaks; do not overbeat.

5. In a medium-size mixing bowl, whisk the egg yolks and the sugar until frothy and lemon-colored. Add the flour to the yolk mixture and mix thoroughly.

6. Fold the egg yolk mixture into the chocolate mixture. Add one-third of the egg whites to the chocolate batter and blend thoroughly. Very gently fold in the remaining whites. Do this slowly and patiently

until no streaks of white remain.

7. Pour the batter into the prepared pan. Bake for just 15 minutes. Remove from the oven. Cover the pan with a plate for an additional 12 minutes to keep the cake very moist and supple. Serve at room temperature.

Yield: 8 to 12 servings

QUATRE-QUARTS AUX POIRES

Pear Pound Cake

Quatre-quarts is the French equivalent of our pound cake, essentially equal parts of eggs, butter, flour, and sugar. This is a very homey favorite—I think of it as pears cooked with a vanilla and pear-flavored cake topping. For an evening meal, I like to serve it warm, with a decadent side serving of whipped crème fraîche, laced with a touch of pear brandy or eau-de-vie de poire.

½ cup (100 g) Vanilla Sugar (see Index)
2 to 3 ripe pears (about 1½ pounds; 750 g), peeled, cored and quartered, with each quarter cut into 4 slices
2 tablespoons pear brandy or eau-de-vie
7 tablespoons (3½ ounces; 105g) unsalted butter, at room temperature
2 large eggs, at room temperature
¾ cup (90 g) plain cake flour

1. Preheat the oven to 325°F (165°C). Generously butter the inside of a 10½-inch (27 cm) springform pan. Sprinkle with 1 tablespoon of the vanilla sugar.

2. Arrange the pear slices in a circle just inside the outer edge of the pan, slightly overlapping them. Fill in the interior ring, overlapping the remaining slices. Sprinkle with 1 tablespoon of the pear brandy.

3. In a medium-size bowl, cream the butter and the remaining 7 tablespoons of sugar with an electric mixer. Add the eggs, one at a time, mixing well after each addition. Add the flour and mix just until combined. Mix in the remaining 1 tablespoon pear brandy.

4. Spoon the batter over the

pears in a thin even layer. Do not be concerned if the batter does not completely cover the pears; it will spread out as it bakes.

5. Bake until the cake is firm and nicely browned, about 45 minutes. Remove from the oven to cool in a rack. To serve, unmold the cake and serve as is, or with a dollop of whipped crème fraîche.

Yield: 8 servings

"By what miracle did I arrive in Autun just as night began to fall? How I had the energy to knock on the door of the Hôtel Saint-Louis et de la Poste, I don't know. But it is true that one hour later, having shaved and bathed, totally refreshed, I was seated at a table in the flower-filled courtyard of the hotel. I will never forget the trout, nor the chicken with tarragon, nor the wild cèpe mushrooms, nor the rabbit terrine—nor the phenomenal chocolate cake, crispy and moist at the same time, nor a certain Meursault, followed by a Nuits, and a little Richebourg to end, and then two glasses of Marc."

—LE GOURMAND VAGABOND
Promenades Gastronomiques, 1928

CAKE AU CITRON

◆

Lemon Cake

The French have many wonderful lemon recipes, and this is one of my favorites. Not a pound cake, not a bread, not a rich *financier* cookie, this very lemony, fine-textured cake is just the thing one needs as a 3 o'clock in the afternoon pick-me-up, with a bracing cup of steaming black coffee or tea. It's just as good as a dessert, served with perhaps a compote of apples or pears or slices of fresh pineapple, and tastes even better the second or third day.

2¼ cups (295 g) unbleached all-purpose flour
1 teaspoon baking powder
5 large eggs
1½ cups (300 g) Vanilla Sugar (see Index)
¾ cup (18.5 cl) crème fraîche (see Index) or heavy cream
7 tablespoons (3½ ounces; 105 g) un-salted butter, melted and cooled
½ cup (12.5 cl) freshly squeezed lemon juice
Grated zest of 4 lemons

1. Preheat the oven to 350°F (175°C). Butter two 9½-inch (24 cm) loaf pans.

2. Combine the flour and baking powder; set aside.

3. In the large bowl of an electric mixer, combine the eggs and sugar and mix until well blended. With the mixer at slow speed, slowly add, in this order: the crème fraîche, the flour and baking powder mixture, the melted butter, lemon juice, and lemon zest. Beat until very smooth.

4. Divide the batter evenly between the loaf pans. Place the pans in the center of the oven and bake until golden and a toothpick inserted in the center comes out clean, about 1 hour.

5. Remove from the oven and cool in the pans on the rack. To serve, unmold and cut the loaves into thin slices. This cake can be stored, carefully covered with plastic wrap, for several days.

Yield: 2 loaves

TARTE AU FROMAGE BLANC FERME D'ALSACE

Alsatian Farm Cheesecake

The French *tarte au fromage blanc* is like a light version of the popular American cheesecake. I've come to prefer this slightly tart, feather-light version. This one is made in memory of the most beautiful tart I ever sampled, at a little farmhouse in Alsace.

2 cups (50 cl) small-curd cottage cheese
2 cups (50 cl) whole-milk yogurt
1 recipe Pâte Sucrée, through Step 1
   only (see Index)
3 large eggs
2 tablespoons crème fraîche (see Index)
   or heavy cream
½ cup (100 g) sugar

1. The day before or on the morning of the day you plan to serve the cheesecake, combine the cottage cheese and yogurt in a food processor. Purée. Transfer the mixture to a large sieve lined with dampened cheesecloth and set over a bowl. Drain at room temperature for 6 to 24 hours, until the mixture is very dry and firm. It is ready to use when no more liquid drips from the sieve.

2. On a lightly floured surface, carefully roll out the dough to a 12-inch (30 cm) circle. Transfer the dough to a 10½-inch (27 cm) spring-form pan, lining the bottom and bringing the pastry halfway up the sides of the pan. Carefully press the pastry into the pan and up the side, trying not to stretch it. Trim neatly with a knife. Prick the bottom of the shell with the tines of a fork. Chill for at least 20 minutes, or wrap well and chill for up to 24 hours.

3. Preheat the oven to 375°F (190°C).

4. Line the shell loosely with heavy-duty foil, pressing well into the edges so the pastry does not shrink while baking. Fill with pie weights, or dry rice or beans—making sure you get all the way into the edges—to prevent shrinkage. Bake just until the pastry begins to brown around the edges and seems firm enough to stand up by itself, about 20 minutes. Remove the weights and foil and continue baking until lightly browned all over, about 10 more minutes for a partially baked shell. Watch the pastry carefully, for ovens vary tremendously and pastry can brown very quickly. Cool on a rack for at least 20 minutes before filling. Leave the oven on.

5. While the pastry is baking, transfer the drained cheese mixture to the bowl of an electric mixer. Add the eggs, one at a time, mixing well after each addition. Beat in the crème fraîche and sugar until well blended.

6. Pour the mixture into the cooled pastry shell. Bake until firm in the center, from 35 to 40 minutes. Cool on a rack. Unmold and serve at room temperature.

Yield: 8 to 10 servings

> **❝***Coffee is to the Frenchman what tea is to the Englishman, beer to the German. . . After one of Vefour's magnificent repasts it enters your stomach in the character of a settler. It leaves you volatile, nimble and quick . . . In a few moments, its miracles begin to be wrought.***❞**
>
> —ISAAC APPLETON JEWETT

FINANCIERS AUX NOISETTES

Hazelnut Butter Cakes

F*inanciers,* tiny little butter cakes flavored with nuts, are among my favorite French sweets. While traditional *financiers* are made with almonds—the best taste as though they're filled with marzipan—this version is prepared with hazelnuts. As with traditional *financiers,* these are cooked first in a very hot oven, to set the crust, and then the heat is reduced to keep the interior chewy and moist. Special *financier* molds, each measuring 2 × 4 inches (5 × 10 cm) can be found in restaurant supply shops. Small oval barquette molds or muffin tins may also be used.

1²⁄₃ cups (210 g) confectioners' sugar
1 cup (90 g) hazelnuts, finely ground
½ cup (70 g) unbleached all-purpose
*   flour*
¾ cup (18.5 cl) egg whites (5 to 6)
¾ cup (6 ounces; 180 g) butter,
*   melted and cooled*

1. Preheat the oven to 450°F (230°C). Generously butter 22 *financier* molds.

2. In a medium-size bowl, combine the sugar, ground hazelnuts, and flour. Sift the flour mixture through a fine mesh sieve into a second bowl. The mixture should be very fine. Stir in the egg whites until thoroughly blended. Stir in the melted butter and mix well.

3. Fill each of the prepared molds with batter to the rim. Place the tins on a heavy baking sheet and place in the center of the oven. Bake for 7 minutes. Reduce the heat to 400°F (205°C) and bake for another 7 minutes. Turn off the heat and let the *financiers* cool for another 7 minutes.

4. Remove the *financiers* from the oven to a cooling rack and unmold as soon as they are cooled. Serve with tea, coffee, ice cream, or sorbet. (Note: Wash the molds immediately with a stiff brush and hot water but no detergent, so they retain their seasoning.) The *financiers* will keep well stored in an airtight container for several days.

Yield: *22 financiers*

TARTE AUX POMMES FRANÇOISE POTEL

Françoise Potel's Apple Tart

I've been fortunate enough to have helped organize several wine tasting dinners at the home of Françoise and Gérard Potel, of the Domaine de la Pousse d'Or in Burgundy. Several times, Françoise Potel—a great home cook and the sort of hostess that instantly puts everyone at ease—served this delicious apple tart. I've added it to my ever-growing "apple pie" repertoire.

1 recipe Pâte-Demi Feuilleté (see Index), prepared through Step 1 only

Filling:
5 Golden Delicious or Granny Smith apples (about 2 pounds; 1 kg)
3 tablespoons freshly squeezed lemon juice
2 tablespoons (1 ounce; 30 g) unsalted butter
¼ cup (50 g) sugar

Topping:
2 eggs
½ cup (100 g) sugar
6 tablespoons (3 ounces; 90 g) unsalted butter, melted
1 teaspoon vanilla extract

1. Remove the prepared dough from the refrigerator. On a lightly floured surface, carefully roll out the dough to a 12-inch (30 cm) circle; transfer the dough to a 10½-inch (27 cm) black tin tart pan with a removable bottom. With your fingertips, carefully press the pastry into the pan and up the sides, trying not to stretch it. Trim the overhang, leaving about a 1-inch (2.5 cm) extending over the rim. Tuck this overhang inside the pan, pressing gently against the side to create a sturdy, double-sided shell. If you build the pastry a bit higher than the height of the pan, you will have less problem with shrinkage. Chill for at least 20 minutes.

2. Preheat the oven to 375°F (190°C).

3. Prick the bottom of the shell with the tines of a fork. Carefully line the shell loosely with heavy-duty foil, pressing well into the edges so the pastry does not shrink while baking. Fill with pie weights, or dry rice or beans—making sure you get all the way into the edges—to prevent shrinkage. Bake just until the pastry

begins to brown around the edges and seems firm enough to stand up by itself, about 20 minutes. Remove from the oven.

4. Meanwhile, peel and core the apples. Cut each apple into 12 even wedges (an apple corer and slicer can be used for this). Toss them in a bowl with the lemon juice to prevent discoloration.

5. In a large skillet, melt the butter over medium-high heat. Add the apples, sprinkle on the sugar, and sauté, shaking the pan from time to time so the apples cook evenly. Cook until lightly browned on all sides,

about 15 minutes.

6. While the apples cook, prepare the topping: Place the eggs and sugar in the bowl of an electric mixer and beat thoroughly until thick and pale. Add the melted butter and vanilla and continue mixing at high speed until the ingredients are thoroughly incorporated.

8. Spoon the apples into the center of the prepared pastry shell, arranging them carefully. Pour the topping over the apples.

9. Bake until golden, about 30 minutes.

Yield: 6 to 8 servings

TARTE AUX POMMES À LA CRÈME

Golden Cream and Apple Tart

T his beautiful, golden, homey apple tart is a joy. Typical of the simple fruit tarts one finds in bistros all over France, this version comes from the Savoy, where apples and cream can be found in abundance. The first time I made it my guests wanted to know where I bought the tart. Was I delighted to tell them it was *fait maison*!

3 large egg yolks
¾ cup (18.5 cl) crème fraîche (see Index) or heavy cream
5 tablespoons (60 g) sugar
1 Pâte Brisée shell (see Index), prebaked and cooled
4 cooking apples such as Granny

Smith (about 1½ pounds; 750 g)

1. Preheat the oven to 375°F (190°C).

2. Place the egg yolks in a large bowl and beat with a fork. Add the

crème fraîche and 3 tablespoons of the sugar. Mix until well blended. Set aside.

3. Peel and core the apples; cut them in half. Cut each half into quarters. Starting just inside the edge of the pastry shell, neatly layer the apple slices—slightly overlapping them—in 2 or 3 concentric circles, working toward the center. Pour the cream mixture over the apples. Sprinkle on the remaining 2 tablespoons sugar.

4. Bake the tart in the center of the oven until the cream filling is set and the apples are very brown, even slightly blackened at the edges, about 45 minutes. Remove to a rack to cool. Serve warm or at room temperature.

Yield: 8 servings

TARTELETTES AUX POMMES LIONEL POILÂNE

Lionel Poilâne's Individual Apple Tarts

There is absolutely no better dessert in the world than a perfect apple tart, and this one is inspired by Lionel Poilâne, France's best-known baker.

1 recipe Pâte Sucrée (see Index), prepared through Step 1 only
4 Golden Delicious or Granny Smith apples (about 1½ pounds; 750 kg)
4 tablespoons (2 ounces; 60 g) unsalted butter

¼ cup (50 g) granulated sugar
1 egg, beaten
1 tablespoon light brown sugar

1. Preheat the oven to 425°F (220°C).

2. Divide the dough into 4 equal portions. On a floured surface, roll out each portion into a 6-inch (15 cm) circle. Place the circles of dough on a baking sheet and refrigerate until ready to bake.

3. Peel and core the apples. Cut each apple into 12 even wedges (an apple corer and slicer can be used for this). In a large skillet, melt the butter over medium-high heat. When it is hot but not smoking, add the apples, sprinkle on the granulated sugar, and sauté until lightly browned, about 15 minutes.

4. Remove the pastry from the refrigerator. Place the apples in the center of each of the pastry rounds. Fold the edges of the dough over the apples to form a 1-inch (2.5 cm) border. Brush the border with the beaten egg.

5. Bake the tartelettes until golden, about 20 minutes. Sprinkle the apples with brown sugar, and serve warm or at room temperature.

Yield: 4 individual apple tarts or 1 large tart (see Note)

Note: Alternatively, to form a single large tart, roll the dough into a 12-inch (30 cm) circle; place all of the apples in the center. Then fold over the dough. Increase the baking time by about 10 minutes to be certain to bake the tart fully.

> **❝**When an orchard in Brittany was picked, one last and best apple was left at the end of the highest branch. If it clung to the branch until all the leaves fell in the autumn winds, there would be a good crop next year, not just on that tree but in the whole orchard, pear trees and plum trees as well.**❞**
>
> —JANE GRIGSON
> *Jane Grigson's Fruit Book*

TARTE TATIN AUX POIRES

Caramelized Upside-Down Pear Tart

This is a pear-filled version of the popular tart Tatin, the upside-down apple pie made famous by the two Tatin sisters from the French village of Lamotte-Beuvron. This is a simple and foolproof tart, and once you have the pastry made (I always prepare it several hours ahead), the rest is child's play. Like an authentic tart Tatin, the pear version consists of nothing but well-caramelized pears and a layer of thin pastry. The pears should remain in huge chunks, making for an honest, rustic tart. The clear glass baking dish allows you to see if any pears are sticking as you turn out the tart. This may seem like a lot of pears for a single tart, but they cook down quickly.

6 *tablespoons (3 ounces; 90 g) unsalted butter*
7 *to 8 firm pears (about 2¾ pounds;
1.75 kg), preferably Bosc or
Anjou, peeled, quartered, and
cored*
½ *cup (100 g) sugar*
1 *recipe Pâte Brisée (see Index), prepared through Step 1 only*
1 *cup (25 cl) crème fraîche (see Index)
or sour cream, for serving*

1. Preheat the oven to 425°F (220°C).

2. Melt the butter in a deep 12-inch (30 cm) skillet over medium-high heat. Stir in the pears and sugar. Cook, stirring carefully from time to time so the pears and sugar do not stick, 20 minutes. Increase the heat to high and cook until the pears and sugar are a deep, golden brown, about 15 more minutes. (If you are like me, the urge will be to stop the cooking a bit soon, so it doesn't burn. But the tart will be much prettier and taste better if you take the time to allow the pears to turn a true golden brown.) Shake the pan from time to time, and watch carefully to be sure that the pears and sugar do not burn. (If you do not have a pan large

enough to cook all of the pears, cook them in 2 smaller pans, dividing the ingredients in half.)

3. Literally pile the pears into an unbuttered round 10½-inch (27 cm) clear glass baking dish or a special tin-lined copper tart Tatin pan.

4. Roll out the *pâte brisée* slightly larger than the dish. Place the pastry on top of the pears, tucking a bit of the dough around the edges and down into the dish. You do not need to prick the dough.

5. Place the tart in the center of the oven and bake until the pears bubble and the pastry is a deep, golden brown, 35 to 40 minutes.

6. Remove the tart from the oven and immediately place a large, flat heatproof serving platter top-side down on top of the baking dish or pan. Invert the pan and give the bottom a firm tap, to release any pears that may be sticking to the bottom. Slowly release the baking dish, so the tart falls evenly onto the serving platter. Serve warm or at room temperature, passing a bowl of rich crème fraîche to spoon over the tart.

Yield: 8 to 10 servings

TARTE AUX FRAMBOISES CAFÉ DU JURA

Café du Jura's Raspberry Tart

I s there anyone who does not love raspberries? In truth sometimes I think it's a shame to eat these berries any way but out of hand. That is, until I come face to face with an exquisitely simple raspberry tart, prepared with a touch of cream and a perfect cookie-like *sablée* crust. This is an easy tart to prepare and can be made several hours ahead to serve later in the day. This version comes from the Café du Jura, an authentic bistro in the heart of Lyons.

3 large egg yolks
¾ cup (18.5 cl) crème fraîche (see Index) or heavy cream
3 tablespoons granulated sugar
1 Pâte Sablée shell (see Index), pre-baked
1 pint (2 cups; 250 g) fresh raspberries
2 teaspoons confectioners' sugar

ers' sugar. Allow to cool thoroughly before serving.
Yield: 8 servings

1. Preheat the oven to 375°F (190°C).

2. Place the egg yolks in a large bowl and beat with a fork. Add the crème fraîche and the granulated sugar; mix until well blended. Pour the mixture into the cooled pastry shell.

3. Carefully arrange the berries in a single layer on top of the cream.

4. Place in the center of the oven and bake just until the cream filling begins to set, about 15 minutes. Sprinkle evenly with the confection-

TARTE AUX FIGUES GEORGETTE

Georgette's Fig Tart

I like to call this Fig Newton tart, for it reminds me of the Fig Newtons my mother used to tuck into my lunch bag as a child. I've always loved the texture of figs and find them especially beautiful as they are presented here, arranged in a pool of vanilla-flavored syrup on top of a crisp cookie-like crust. The recipe was offered to me by Georgette, the owner of the bistro Estaminet des Remparts in Mougins, where she is known as the "queen of tarts and magician of Provençal cuisine!" A touch of crème fraîche serves to properly gild the lily!

2 pounds (1 kg) fresh figs, preferably black figs
¾ cup (160 g) sugar
1 vanilla bean, split lengthwise
1 Pâte Sablée shell (see Index), partially baked and cooled
½ cup (12.5 cl) crème fraîche (see Index) or heavy cream

1. In a heavy saucepan, combine the figs, sugar, vanilla bean, and ½ cup (12.5 cl) water. Stir to dissolve most of the sugar. Bring just to a boil over medium-high heat, shaking the pan gently to keep the sugar from burning. Simmer, uncovered, until the figs are very soft and the syrup is very thick, about 1 hour. Watch carefully, to prevent scorching. (The fig compote can be cooled for about 20 minutes, then used immediately for a tart, or preserved in sterilized jars for use later in the season.)

2. Preheat the oven to 375°F (190°C).

3. Carefully spoon the figs and the syrup into the tart shell in a single layer. Bake in the center of the oven until the syrup is firm, about 20 to 30 minutes.

4. Cool on a rack. Serve at room temperature, with crème fraîche, if desired.

Yield: 8 servings

❝*To eat figs off the tree in the very early morning, when they have been barely touched by the sun, is one of exquisite pleasures of the Mediterranean.*❞

—ELIZABETH DAVID

TARTE AMANDINE LE PETIT MARGUERY

Le Petit Marguery's Fruit and Almond Tart

At Le Petit Marguery, the lively Paris bistro run by the three Cousin brothers, some version of this almond-flavored fruit tart is almost always on the menu. It can be prepared with pears, peaches, cherries, or the tiny yellow plums known as mirabelles. Once you've prepared your pastry, there's not much left to do but sit back and watch it bake!

¼ cup (160 g) whole unblanched almonds
1 large egg, lightly beaten
5 tablespoons (60 g) granulated sugar
2 tablespoons kirsch or cherry eau-de-vie
¾ cup (18.5 cl) crème fraîche (see
  Index) or heavy cream
6 to 7 ripe Bartlett pears (about 2
  pounds; 1 kg)
1 Pâte Brisée shell (see Index), pre-
  baked and cooled
1 tablespoon Vanilla Sugar (see Index)

> **"**You can't distinguish be-
> tween fresh fruits and the very
> freshest ones unless you have
> eaten, let us say, wood straw-
> berries, newly picked in a
> sunny glade, or tasted a ripe
> apricot straight from the tree.
> Yet it is this almost impercep-
> tible difference between fresh
> and freshest that is all-
> important.**"**
>
> —JOSEPH WECHSBERG
> *Blue Trout & Black Truffles*

1. Preheat the oven to 375°F (190°C).

2. In a spice grinder or food processor, grind the almonds to a fine powder. Thoroughly blend the almonds with the egg, granulated sugar, kirsch, and crème fraîche. The mixture should be very smooth.

3. Peel and core the pears. Cut each into 8 even slices. Carefully arrange the pear slices in a spiral in the prebaked tart shell, beginning at the outside edge. Slowly pour the cream filling over the pears.

4. Place the tart in the center of the oven and bake until the cream filling has set and the tart shell is nicely browned, about 45 minutes. Remove from the oven and sprinkle on the vanilla sugar. Serve warm or at room temperature with crème fraîche as an accompaniment.

Yield: 8 servings

TARTE AUX PRUNEAUX ET AUX AMANDES

Prune and Almond Tart

Until moving to France, I really didn't feel one way or the other about prunes. But as I've traveled the country, and discovered the wonders of this sweet, rich, and nutritious dried fruit, I've become a true aficionada. This tart is particularly succulent, for something wonderful happens to the prunes as they bake, turning them into an almost sweet, compact candy. Be sure to make a good, strong tea (I use about 1 tablespoon of loose Earl Grey tea leaves to 2 cups; 50 cl of water) for soaking the prunes.

---

2 cups (50 cl) brewed hot strong black
    tea, such as Earl Grey
1 pound (500 g) prunes, pitted
¼ cup (35 g) whole unblanched al-
    monds
1 large egg, lightly beaten
5 tablespoons (60 g) granulated sugar
2 tablespoons plum eau-de-vie or
    brandy
¾ cup (18.5 cl) crème fraîche (see
    Index) or heavy cream
1 Pâte Sucrée shell (see Index) par-
    tially baked and cooled
1 tablespoon confectioners' sugar

---

1. At least 1 hour before preparing the tart, pour the hot tea over the prunes. Set aside to marinate.

2. Preheat the oven to 375°F (190°C).

3. In a food processor, grind the almonds to a fine powder. Add the egg, sugar, eau-de-vie, and crème fraîche. Process until very smooth.

4. Thoroughly drain the prunes, discarding the soaking liquid. Carefully arrange the prunes in the cooled tart shell. This will seem like a lot of prunes, and you may have to arrange them in 2 layers. Pour the almond filling over the prunes.

5. Place the tart in the center of the oven, and bake until the filling is set and the tart shell is nicely browned, about 45 minutes. Remove from the oven. Sprinkle on the confectioners' sugar. Cool on a rack. Serve at room temperature.

Yield: 8 servings

TARTE AU CITRON MADAME CARTET

Madame Cartet's Lemon Tart

W hen you walk into the minuscule Paris bistro, Cartet, your eyes land immediately on the desserts, arranged in a tidy row along the bar at the entrance. Without fail, this superb and simple lemon tart is there. I love the golden, yellow color, and the puckery tart flavor. As Marie-Thérèse and Raymond Nouaille, current owners, explained, "Madame Cartet used to make it with four eggs. We make it with five." Either way, I always think of it as a delicious end to a copious and satisfying meal.

⅔ *cup (16 cl) freshly squeezed lemon juice (about 4 lemons)*
½ *cup (100 g) sugar*
3 *tablespoons crème fraîche (see Index) or heavy cream*
5 *large eggs*
1 *Pâte Sablée shell (see Index), pre-baked and cooled*

1. Preheat the oven to 375°F (190°C).

2. In a large mixing bowl, whisk together the lemon juice, sugar, and crème fraîche until well blended. Add the eggs, one at a time, mixing well after each addition.

3. Pour the lemon cream into the prepared tart shell. Bake until firm, 15 to 20 minutes. Remove from oven and place on a rack to cool. Serve at room temperature.

Yield: 8 servings

TOURTE AUX BLETTES

Sweet Swiss Chard Torte

I first sampled this traditional dessert from Nice several years ago, while dining at Catherine-Hélène Barale's popular family bistro, Barale. At first the thought of a sweet swiss chard dessert seemed sort of out of kilter, but once I sampled this one, I was ready for more. Now, I make it often in Provence, serving it as a late afternoon snack with a glass of chilled rosé, or as a lovely summer dessert, ideally served with the rare white wine from Nice, the Bellet blanc from Château du Crémat.

The dough, by the way, is a delight, easy to make and devoid of animal fat. Many traditional recipes include pine nuts, though I find I prefer a simpler version. But if you love pine nuts, go ahead and toss them in! (The local torte can be found in most of the pastry shops in old Nice.)

2 cups (280 g) unbleached all-purpose
  flour
½ teaspoon salt
½ cup (12.5 cl) extra-virgin olive oil
1 pound (500 g) swiss chard leaves
  (or substitute spinach)
2 eggs, gently beaten
1 cup raisins
1 tablespoon confectioners' sugar, for
  decoration

1. Preheat the oven to 400°F (205°C).

2. Prepare the pastry: Combine the flour and salt in a medium-size bowl. Stir in ½ cup (12.5 cl) of water and then the oil, mixing until thoroughly blended. Knead briefly. The dough will be very moist and easy to work. Divide the dough in half; press each half into a flat disk.

3. Prepare the filling: Wash and dry the green leafy portion of the chard, discarding the center white stem. Break up the leaves and chop them rather finely, in several batches, in a food processor. Combine the eggs and raisins in a medium-size bowl; mix until thoroughly blended. Stir in the chard, and mix well; reserve.

4. Roll out 1 disk of pastry into a 10½-inch (27 cm) circle. Place on the bottom of a 10½-inch (27 cm) tart tin with a removable bottom; you do not need to build up the sides of the tart.

5. Spoon the chard mixture over the dough. Roll out the remaining disk of dough. Place it on top of the

chard mixture, tucking the ends of the dough down inside the tart.

6. Bake until the crust is golden brown, about 40 minutes. Remove to a rack to cool. Serve at room temperature, sprinkled with confectioners' sugar.

Yield: 8 servings

FLAN À L'ANANAS ADRIENNE

Adrienne's Fresh Pineapple Flan

I sat, so to speak, at chef Adrienne Biasin knee one morning, squeezed into her closet-size kitchen as she prepared the daily lunch for the faithful group of customers at her Paris bistro, Chez La Vieille. Throughout the morning, I sort of danced about her kitchen, jotting down notes and trying to keep out of her way, as the *pot-au-feu* simmered away and Adrienne prepared this wonderfully homey fresh pineapple custard dessert. It's a real winner, gathering points on aroma alone. The beautiful sunshine yellow color makes it an especially rewarding wintertime dessert.

1 *vanilla bean*
2 *cups (50 cl) milk*
1 *fresh pineapple (about 2¾ pounds; 1.75 kg)*
3 *large whole eggs*
3 *large egg yolks*
⅔ *cup (135 g) Vanilla Sugar (see Index)*
2 *tablespoons unbleached all-purpose flour*
2 *tablespoons crème fraîche (see Index) or heavy cream*

1. Preheat the oven to 400°F (205°C). Butter a straight-sided 10½-inch (27 cm) round glass or porcelain baking dish.

2. Cut the vanilla bean in half lengthwise and, using a small spoon, scrape out the tiny black seeds. Combine the milk, vanilla seeds, and vanilla bean pod in a heavy saucepan. Scald over high heat. Remove from the heat. Cover and let steep for 15 minutes. Remove just the vanilla bean pod.

3. Meanwhile, prepare the pine-

apple: Using a large knife, slice off the top and bottom of the pineapple. Slice off the prickly pineapple rind, being sure to remove all the "eyes." Discard the rind and the eyes, leaving a cylinder of pineapple. Cut the pineapple lengthwise into eighths. Remove and discard the pithy core. Cut the eighths into 1-inch (2.5 cm) wedges. (You should have, in all, about 1½ pounds or 750 g of fresh pineapple wedges.)

4. Scatter the pineapple wedges in the prepared baking dish. Bake for about 5 minutes. (Adrienne advised baking the pineapple for a few moments beforehand, so the juices are reabsorbed into the pineapple and don't seep into the custard.)

5. In a large mixing bowl, whisk together the eggs, egg yolks, vanilla sugar, flour, and crème fraîche until well blended. Gradually whisk in the warm milk.

6. Pour the custard mixture over the pineapple wedges. Bake until golden, about 45 minutes. Cool on a rack. Serve at room temperature.

Yield: 8 servings

MILLAS AUX PRUNEAUX

Prune and Armagnac Flan

I love hanging around good cooks: You eat well, of course, but you also learn those little tricks that make all the difference. One morning I was in the kitchen with Marie-Claude Gracia—a favorite cook from the southwest—as she was preparing her delicate prune custard tart. I noticed that she uses sugar the way we use salt! Rather than adding a lot of sugar to a dessert, she sprinkles the bottom and the top of the preparation. This way you get the sugar flavor right at the tip of your tongue, but the dessert won't be overly sweet. Pretty and golden, this flan is served at Madame Gracia's *auberge* La Belle Gasconne, in Poudenas.

1 pound (500 g) dried prunes, pitted
3 tablespoons Armagnac
5 tablespoons (65 g) sugar
3 large eggs

3 tablespoons plus 1 teaspoon unbleached all-purpose flour
2 cups (50 cl) milk

1. Two days before preparing the flan, toss the prunes with the Armagnac in a bowl. Cover securely and set aside to marinate. (If time is limited, the prunes can be marinated for just a few hours, although a 2-day marinade will offer a richer flavor.)

2. Preheat the oven to 375°F (190°C). Lightly butter and flour a 10½-inch (27 cm) straight-sided ceramic baking dish. (You may also use a springform pan, but be certain that it is leakproof.)

3. Toss 1 tablespoon of the sugar with the marinated prunes. Arrange them on the bottom of the prepared baking dish, forming a single, tight layer that thoroughly covers the bottom of the dish.

4. Beat the eggs with 3 table-spoons of the sugar in a large bowl until well blended. Add the flour, and mix well. Add the milk, and mix well. Pour the batter over the prunes. Bake until bubbly and brown, about 45 minutes.

5. Set on a rack. Sprinkle on the remaining 1 tablespoon sugar. Allow to cool. (If using a springform pan, unmold the flan before serving.) Serve at room temperature.

Yield: 8 servings

> **❝Cuisine is when things taste like themselves.❞**
> —CURNONSKY

MOUSSE AU CHOCOLAT AMBASSADE D'AUVERGNE

Ambassade d'Auvergne's Chocolate Mousse

I have to confess to a weakness for chocolate. But it's one of those foods for which I have almost a reverence, so I indulge rarely but with gusto. I happened upon this mousse almost by accident. One night my husband ordered it at the Ambassade d'Auvergne, a favorite Paris restaurant. I knew when the giant white bowl arrived that we were in for a treat! This is rich, there's no question. But why not live it up a little every now and then! The higher proportion of yolks to whites gives it that gooey texture I love.

8 ounces (250 g) bittersweet chocolate,
   preferably Lindt or Tobler, broken
   into pieces
3 tablespoons orange liqueur, such as
   Grand Marnier
2 teaspoons vanilla extract
8 tablespoons (4 ounces; 120 g) unsalted butter, cut into small pieces
8 large egg yolks
½ cup (100 g) sugar
5 large egg whites

1. Place the chocolate, orange liqueur, and vanilla in the top of a double boiler over simmering water. Stir until melted. Remove from the heat. Stir in the butter.

2. Combine the egg yolks and sugar in a large bowl and beat until thick and pale yellow. Beat in the chocolate mixture while still lukewarm.

3. Place the egg whites in a medium-size mixing bowl. Beat until stiff but not dry.

4. Add one-third of the beaten egg whites to the chocolate batter; mix vigorously. Gently fold in the remaining whites. Do this slowly and patiently. Do not overmix, but be sure that the mixture is well blended and that no streaks of whites remain.

5. Pour the mixture into a large serving bowl (I use a plain white, 2-quart, or 2 l, soufflé dish). Cover securely with plastic wrap; refrigerate for at least 6 hours before serving.

6. To serve, pass the bowl with a large serving spoon.

Yield: 8 to 10 servings

TRUC

Never add salt to eggs that have been whipped and will be incorporated with other ingredients. The salt will only liquify the beaten eggs.

LES FLANS À LA VERVEINE DE MA MÈRE

My Mother's Lemon Verbena Custards

I only discovered lemon verbena, the fragrant herb the French call *verveine,* when I moved to France some years ago. My French tutor introduced me to the fresh herb used as an infusion in tea, and soon I was growing *verveine* on my balcony. Many years later I found another use for it when I sampled this superb homey dessert at one of my favorite restaurants in all of France, La Belle Gasconne in Poudenas, in the southwest. The owner, Marie-Claude Gracia, comes from a long line of women cooks and named this dish after her mother. If you don't have fresh or dried verbena, fresh mint is a wonderful substitute.

.2 vanilla beans
3 cups (75 cl) milk
¾ cup (160 g) *Vanilla Sugar (see Index)*
18 leaves of fresh or dried lemon verbena, or fresh mint
6 large eggs

1. Preheat the oven to 350°F (175°C)

2. Cut the vanilla beans in half lengthwise. Using a small spoon, scrape out the tiny black seeds. (Save the vanilla bean pods for vanilla sugar.)

3. Combine the milk, sugar, and vanilla seeds in a large saucepan. Bring to a boil. Remove from the heat. Add 12 of the verbena leaves. Cover and set aside and allow the flavors to infuse for 10 minutes.

4. Place the eggs in a large bowl, and whisk until well blended.

5. Remove the verbena leaves from the milk mixture. Slowly whisk the milk into the eggs.

6. Carefully pour the custard mixture into six 12-ounce (18 cl) custard cups or ramekins. Place 1 verbena leaf in the center of each cup. Place them in a roasting pan and add enough boiling water to the pan to reach halfway up the sides of the ramekins.

7. Bake until the custards are just set in the center but still trembling, from 45 to 50 minutes. Remove the cups from the water bath; set aside to cool. Cover with plastic wrap and refrigerate. The custards should be prepared at least 12 hours and no more than 24 hours before serving.

8. To serve, remove from the refrigerator about 15 minutes before serving.

Yield: 6 servings

CRÈME CARAMEL

Caramel Cream

This is one of my favorite "nursery" desserts, a soothing concoction that is also rewarding to make. Unfortunately this homey dessert has become rather banal in France, for nine times out of ten the crème caramel you are served is insipidly sweet and a faint image of the real thing. So, it's all the more rewarding to serve your guests a caramel cream that is rich and golden, fragrant with vanilla, and creamy, creamy, creamy.

Caramel:
1¼ cups (250 g) Vanilla Sugar (see Index)

Custard:
2 vanilla beans
3 cups (75 cl) milk
¾ cup (160 g) Vanilla Sugar (see Index)
3 large whole eggs
6 large egg yolks

1. Prepare the caramel: Combine the sugar and ¼ cup (6 cl) water in a heavy saucepan. Place over high heat and stir until the sugar dissolves. Bring the syrup to a full boil. Cook, without stirring, until the syrup caramelizes to a medium-dark amber color, about 4 minutes. Immediately immerse the bottom of the pan in cold water to stop the cooking. Divide the caramel among eight 1-cup (25 cl) custard cups or ramekins, working quickly so the caramel does

not solidify and swirling the cups to evenly coat the bottoms. Set aside.

2. Preheat the oven to 325°F (165°C).

3. Prepare the custard: Cut the vanilla beans in half lengthwise, and use a small spoon to scrape out the tiny black seeds. Combine the vanilla seeds, vanilla bean pods, and milk in a heavy saucepan. Bring to a boil over high heat. Remove from the heat, cover, and set aside to steep for 15 minutes. Remove the vanilla pods, which can be dried and used to prepare vanilla sugar.

4. In a large mixing bowl, combine the sugar, eggs, and egg yolks. Gradually whisk in the hot milk. Carefully pour the mixture into the caramel-lined cups.

5. Place the cups in a roasting pan and add enough boiling water to come halfway up the sides of the pan. Place the pan in the center of the oven. Bake until the custards are just set in the center but still trembling, 50 to 60 minutes. Remove the cups

from the water bath and let set for about 15 minutes. Carefully run a knife blade around the edge of each caramel cream and unmold onto a small plate. Serve immediately. Al-ternatively, cover the custards while still in their cups and refrigerate for several hours before serving.

Yield: 8 servings

CRÈME BRÛLÉE

Burnt Cream

This seems to be one of the world's favorite desserts, at least in our time. Everyone seems to have his own version: "the best." Like just about everything else in cooking, this dish depends dearly on the quality of ingredients. The freshest farm eggs, really good cream, au-thentic vanilla, and of course, a careful cook!

1 vanilla bean
1 quart (1 l) heavy cream
½ cup (100 g) Vanilla Sugar (see Index)
6 large egg yolks
½ cup (75 g) firmly packed dark brown sugar

1. Preheat the oven to 300°F (150°C)

2. Cut the vanilla bean in half lengthwise and use a small spoon to scrape out the tiny black seeds. Combine the cream, vanilla seeds, and va-nilla pod halves in a heavy saucepan. Bring to a boil. Remove from the heat, cover, and set aside to steep for 15 minutes. Remove the vanilla pods, which can be dried and used to prepare vanilla sugar.

3. In a medium-size bowl, com-bine the vanilla sugar and egg yolks and whisk until well blended. Add the vanilla cream and mix well.

4. Place 6 shallow 6-inch (15 cm) round baking dishes in a roasting pan. Pour the cream mixture into the dishes. Add enough boiling water to the pan to reach halfway up the sides of the baking dishes.

5. Bake just until the mixture is just set in the center but still trem-bling, about 30 minutes.

6. Refrigerate for at least 1 hour and up to 24 hours. Remove from the refrigerator, sieve the brown sugar evenly over the top of the baked cream, and glaze under the broiler for several seconds, until

the sugar forms a firm crust, watching carefully to see that it does not burn. Return the custards to the refriger- ator until about 15 minutes before serving.

Yield: 6 servings

OMELETTE AUX POIRES CHEZ TANTE PAULETTE

Tante Paulette's Sweet Pear Omelet

One weekday afternoon in the middle of August, I had just completed a major feast in the dining room of Chez Tante Paulette, one of my favorite bistros in Lyons. Her garlic-laden, hearty salad was followed by copious portions of a saffron-rich chicken bouillabaisse, second helpings of meltingly tender Saint-Marcellin cheese, all washed down with plenty of Beaujolais. I was happy and satisfied, so wasn't sure I could sustain the same enthusiasm for dessert. At that point, Tante Paulette approached the table with a golden fruit omelet. Sprinkling the dessert with pear eau-de-vie, she lit a match, flames soared, and *voilà!* it was clear that the only choice remaining was to march on!

The next evening, I prepared this dessert at home, to help remember forever all of the flavors, textures, and colors of this simple dish. Do try to find the freshest, biggest, farm eggs available. You'll taste the difference! Tante Paulette prepares this with apples as well as pears, depending upon her mood and the season.

2 tablespoons (1 ounce; 30 g) unsalted butter
4 firm pears (about 1 pound; 500 g), peeled, quartered, and cored
2 tablespoons sugar
3 large farm-fresh eggs, lightly beaten
3 tablespoons pear eau-de-vie or brandy

1. Melt the butter in a 9-inch (22.5 cm) omelet pan over medium-high heat. Add the pears and 1 tablespoon of the sugar and stir to combine. Cook for 20 minutes, stirring carefully from time to time so the pears and sugar do not stick. Carefully pour the eggs evenly over the pears and tilt the pan from side to

side to allow the eggs to run to the bottom. As the underside of the omelet begins to set, use a fork to lift the edges of the omelet to keep it from sticking. The eggs should take just 2 or 3 minutes to cook and should be only slightly firm.

2. Invert the omelet onto a large serving platter. Sprinkle immediately with the remaining 1 tablespoon sugar. Sprinkle on the pear eau-de-vie. Ignite the eau-de-vie and shake the platter until the flames subside. Cut into wedges and serve immediately.

Yield: 4 servings

TRUC

How do you know if your eggs are fresh? Place them in a bowl of cold, salted water. If they fall to the bottom and stay there, they're fresh enough to eat *à la coque,* or soft-boiled.

RIZ AU LAIT

Rice Pudding

Rice pudding is a sane and happy dessert, one that appears filling and rich without being really so. Satisfying nursery fare, this comes out the way I like the dish, soup on its way to being pudding, very creamy, and not at all dry. The baking time seems excessive, but it takes that long for this tiny bit of rice to absorb all of that liquid. Make this on a cold winter Saturday, and fill the house with the aroma of orange and lemon.

⅓ cup (65 g) raw long-grain white
  rice (do not use instant or quick-
  cooking rice)
1 vanilla bean
3 cups (75 cl) milk
Pinch of salt
Grated zest of 1 orange

Grated zest of 1 lemon
2 tablespoons (1 ounce; 30 g) unsalted
  butter
¼ cup (50 g) Vanilla Sugar (see
  Index)

1. Thoroughly wash and drain the rice. Place the rice in a large saucepan, cover generously with water, and bring to a boil over medium heat. Boil vigorously for about 5 minutes, to blanch the rice. Rinse in warm water and drain again. Set aside.

2. Cut the vanilla bean in half lengthwise. Use a small spoon to scrape out all of the small seeds. (Reserve the pod for vanilla sugar.)

3. Combine the vanilla seeds, milk, salt, and fruit zests in a large saucepan. Bring to a boil over medium heat. Watch the milk carefully and stir from time to time, to make sure it does not boil over.

4. Preheat the oven to 325°F (165°C).

5. Remove the milk from the heat. Stir in the butter and sugar until the sugar dissolves. Set aside to cool for about 10 minutes.

6. Stir the blanched rice into the flavored milk. Pour the mixture into a 1-quart (1 l) baking dish. Cover with foil. Bake, without stirring, until almost all of the liquid is absorbed, about 1 hour and 40 minutes.

7. Transfer the rice to a serving bowl. Serve hot or cold.

Yield: 4 servings

A RICHER RICE PUDDING

Once the rice is cooked, stir in 3 or 4 well-beaten whole eggs and sweeten to taste with sugar. Pour the mixture into a buttered mold and place the mold in a shallow pan. Partially fill the pan with boiling water. Bake in a 350°F (175°C) oven for about 20 minutes.

CLAFOUTIS AUX FIGUES

Fig Clafoutis

One fall weekend years ago we were driving around in the Savoy and walked into a pretty little restaurant for dinner. Sitting on the counter was one of the most beautiful fig tarts one could imagine. I was mentally putting in my order for dessert, when I heard the owner say, *complet*—all booked. There would be no dinner there, what's more, no fig tart. Ever since, fig desserts have reminded me of that mythic tart. This clafoutis, rich with the flavor of honey and figs, always reminds me of Provence. The exact number of figs used will depend on their size.

4 tablespoons (2 ounces; 60 g) unsalted butter
2 heaping tablespoons (about 50 g)
full-flavored honey
½ teaspoon freshly ground cinnamon
10 to 12 (about 2 pounds; 1 kg) large
fresh figs, stemmed and halved
lengthwise
6 large eggs
½ cup (100 g) Vanilla Sugar (see
Index)
1 cup (25 cl) milk
⅔ cup (85 g) unbleached all-purpose
flour
Pinch of salt
Confectioners' sugar

1. Preheat the oven to 400°F
(205°C).
2. Butter and sugar a 10½-inch
(27 cm) ceramic baking dish or pie
plate.
3. Melt the butter in a small
saucepan over low heat. Set aside to
cool.
4. Warm the honey and cinnamon in a large skillet over medium-
high heat. Roll each fig half in the
honey mixture. Arrange them, cut
sides up, in the prepared baking dish.
5. Combine the eggs and sugar
in a bowl and beat with an electric
mixer until frothy. Slowly incorpo-
rate the milk, flour, salt, and melted
butter. Be sure that the mixture is
well blended.
6. Pour the batter over the figs.
Bake until the batter is firm and
golden, from 30 to 35 minutes. Remove to a rack to cool. When slightly

cooled, sprinkle on confectioners'
sugar. Serve warm or at room temperature.
Yield: 8 servings

A SUMMER LUNCH IN PROVENCE, BENEATH THE OLD OAK TREE

◆　　　◆

A medley of full-flavored, uncomplicated summer dishes that call for
a hungry crowd, crispy homemade
bread, and carafes of chilled rosé de
Provence.

ANCHOÏADE CHEZ GILBERT
*Chez Gilbert's Anchovy, Garlic, and
Olive Oil Spread*

◆

**TAPENADO RESTAURANT
MAURICE BRUN**
Restaurant Maurice Brun's Tapenade

◆

**LA BOURRIDE DE BAUDROIE
RESTAURANT LOU MARQUÈS**
*Lou Marquès' Monkfish Soup with
Garlic Cream*

◆

AÏOLI
Garlic Mayonnaise

◆

CLAFOUTIS AUX FIGUES
Fig Clafoutis

CLAFOUTIS AUX POIRES

Pear Clafoutis

I love the golden color of this homey confection, which is, as the French say, *beau et bon*—beautiful as well as good! Prepare it in autumn when pears are at their most flavorful.

½ cup (12.5 cl) pear eau-de-vie or
  brandy
6 Anjou pears (about 2 pounds; 1 kg)
6 large eggs
½ cup (100 g) Vanilla Sugar (see
  Index)
¾ cup (95 g) unbleached all-purpose
  flour
½ cup (12.5 cl) crème fraîche (see
  Index) or heavy cream
Pinch of salt
1 tablespoon confectioners' sugar

1. Pour the pear brandy into a shallow bowl large enough to hold the pears when cut. Peel and core each pear, then cut each into 16 even slices. As they are cut, place the pear slices into the bowl. Gently stir to coat each slice with the pear brandy. When all the pears are cut, stir again, cover, and let marinate for 1 hour. Turn the pears from time to time, so they do not darken.

2. Preheat the oven to 400°F (205°C). Butter and sugar a 10½ inch (27 cm) porcelain baking dish.

3. Combine the eggs and vanilla sugar in the bowl of an electric mixer and beat until frothy. Slowly beat in the flour, cream and salt. Drain the pears and add the marinade liquid to the batter. Mix until well blended.

4. Arrange the pear slices in a spiral in the prepared baking dish. Pour the batter over the pears.

5. Place the baking dish in the center of the oven. Bake until the batter is firm and the top is golden, about 25 minutes. Remove to a rack to cool, then sprinkle on the confectioners' sugar. Serve warm or at room temperature.

Yield: 8 to 12 servings

POIRES AU VIN ROUGE

Pears in Red Wine

Bold, beautiful, vermillion red pears, infused with a spicy, fruity sauce make one of the simplest and yet most impressive desserts. Make these a day in advance, to allow the pears to soak up all of the fragrant, spicy sauce. And use rather green, or unripe pears, or they will fall apart as they cook. For a wine, I'd suggest using a good-quality Beaujolais, such as one from Georges Duboeuf.

*4 large or 6 very small pears, peeled
    with stems intact*
*½ cup (100 g) Vanilla Sugar (see
    Index)*
*1 bottle (75 cl) fruity red wine, such
    as a good Beaujolais*
½ cup (12.5 cl) crème de cassis
*2 tablespoons freshly squeezed lemon
    juice*
1 sprig of summer savory or rosemary
1 vanilla bean, split lengthwise
4 whole cloves
4 black peppercorns

1. In a deep nonreactive saucepan that will hold all the pears snugly, combine all of the ingredients. Cover and bring to a simmer over medium heat. Turn the pears from time to time, so they are evenly coated. Simmer until the pears are cooked through, about 30 minutes.
2. Remove from the heat; allow to cool. Transfer the pears and liquid to a serving dish. Cover and refrigerate for 24 hours before serving.
Yield: 4 to 6 servings

IT'S ABOUT TIME WE ORGANIZED A PICNIC

Here's a medley of picnic fare. A crisp, chilled white would be ideal, perhaps one from Provence, such as Château Simone's Palette.

FLAMICHE AUX POIREAUX
Leek Tart

◆

PISSALADIÈRE
Onion, Anchovy, and Black Olive Tart

◆

TOURTE AUX BLETTES
Savory Swiss Chard Tart

◆

POIRES AU VIN ROUGE
Pears in Red Wine

◆

CAKE AU CITRON
Lemon Cake

PRUNEAUX AU VIN ROUGE

Prunes in Red Wine

As long as you think a bit ahead, it takes mere seconds to prepare this simple bistro dessert. In the wintertime, it's delicious as is. In the summer months, it can be transformed into a terrific outdoor dessert, by adding fresh, sliced strawberries just before serving. I generally don't pit the prunes, for I think they look prettier whole. But if the pits bother you, go ahead and get rid of them!

2 cups (about 1 pound; 500 g) dried prunes
1 cup (25 cl) full-bodied red wine, such as Gigondas
¼ cup (50 g) sugar
2 thin lemon slices, seeds removed
4 orange slices, seeds removed
2 cups (200 g) fresh strawberries, cored and sliced (optional)

1. The day before serving the dish, cover the prunes with water. Cover and marinate for 24 hours.

2. Drain the prunes, discarding the soaking liquid. In a nonreactive large saucepan, combine the prunes, wine, sugar, and lemon and orange slices. Bring to a boil over high heat. As soon as the liquid comes to a boil, remove from the heat and set aside to cool.

3. In season, add the strawberries just before serving.

Yield: 6 to 8 servings

BASICS

Pastries, Bread Dough, Sauces, and Stocks

PÂTE BRISÉE

Flaky Pastry

*1 to 1¼ cups (140 to 175 g) all-pur-
  pose flour (do not use unbleached)*
*7 tablespoons (3½ ounces; 105 g) un-
  salted butter, chilled and cut into
  pieces*
⅛ teaspoon salt
3 tablespoons ice water

1. Place 1 cup of flour, the butter, and salt in a food processor. Process just until the mixture resembles
coarse crumbs, about 10 seconds.
Add the ice water and pulse just until
the pastry begins to hold together,
about 6 to 8 times. Do not let it form
a ball. Transfer the pastry to waxed
paper; flatten the dough into a disk.
If the dough seems too sticky, sprinkle it with additional flour, incorporating 1 tablespoon at a time. Wrap
the pastry in waxed paper. Refrigerate for at least 1 hour.

2. On a lightly floured surface,
carefully roll out the dough to a 12-
inch (30 cm) circle. Transfer the
dough to a 10½-inch (27 cm) loose-
bottomed black tin tart pan. With
your fingertips, carefully press the
pastry into the pan and up the side,
trying not to stretch it. Trim the
overhang, leaving about a 1-inch (2.5

cm) edge. Tuck this overhang inside the pan, pressing gently against the side to create a sturdy, double-sided shell. If you build the pastry a bit higher than the height of the pan, you will have less problem with shrinkage. Prick the bottom of the shell. Chill for at least 20 minutes, or wrap well and chill for up to 24 hours.

3. Preheat the oven to 375°F (190°C).

4. Line the shell loosely with heavy-duty foil, pressing well into the edges so the pastry does not shrink while baking. Fill with baking weights, rice, or dried beans—making sure you get all the way into the edges—to prevent shrinkage.

5. *For a partially baked shell:* Bake just until the pastry begins to brown around the edges and seems firm enough to stand up by itself, about 20 minutes. Remove the weights and foil and continue baking until lightly browned all over, about 10 or more minutes. *For a fully baked shell:* Remove the weights and foil. Continue to bake for 20 more minutes. Watch the pastry carefully! Ovens vary tremendously and pastry can brown very quickly. Cool for at least 10 minutes before filling.

Yield: 1 partially baked or 1 pre-baked pastry shell

PÂTE SUCRÉE

Flaky Sweet Pastry

1 to 1¼ cups (140 to 175 g) all-pur-pose flour (do not use unbleached)
7 tablespoons (3½ ounces; 105 g) un-salted butter, chilled and cut into pieces
2 teaspoons sugar
⅛ teaspoon salt
3 tablespoons ice water

1. Place 1 cup of flour, the butter, sugar and salt, in a food processor. Process just until the mixture resembles coarse crumbs, about 10 seconds. Add the ice water and pulse just until the pastry begins to hold together, about 6 to 8 times. Do not let it form a ball. Transfer the pastry to waxed paper; flatten the dough into a disk. If the dough seems too sticky, sprinkle it with additional flour, incorporating 1 tablespoon at a time. Wrap the pastry in waxed paper. Refrigerate for at least 1 hour.

2. On a lightly floured surface, carefully roll out the dough to a 12-inch (30 cm) circle. Transfer the dough to a 10½-inch (27 cm) loose-bottomed black tin tart pan. With your fingertips, carefully press the pastry into the pan and up the side, trying not to stretch it. Trim the

overhang, leaving about a 1-inch (2.5 cm) edge. Tuck this overhang inside the pan, pressing gently against the side to create a sturdy, double-sided shell. If you build the pastry a bit higher than the height of the pan, you will have less problem with shrinkage. Prick the bottom of the shell. Chill for at least 20 minutes, or wrap well and chill up to 24 hours.

3. Preheat the oven to 375°F (190°C).

4. Line the shell loosely with heavy-duty foil, pressing well into the edges so the pastry does not shrink while baking. Fill with baking weights, rice, or dried beans—making sure you get all the way into the edges—to prevent shrinkage.

5. *For a partially baked shell:* Bake just until the pastry begins to brown around the edges and seems firm enough to stand up by itself, about 20 minutes. Remove the weights and foil and continue baking until lightly browned all over, about 10 more minutes. *For a fully baked*

shell: Remove the weights and foil. Continue to bake for 20 more minutes. Watch the pastry carefully! Ovens vary tremendously and pastry can brown very quickly. Cool for at least 10 minutes before filling.

Yield: 1 partially baked or 1 prebaked pastry shell

PÂTE SABLÉE

◆━━◆

Sweet Pastry

his is a classic French sweet pastry using confectioners' sugar and egg, to make for a very rich dough that goes particularly well with fruit tarts. When I make this dough, it brings up fond memories of the days I made sugar cookies with my mother. It is, however, a horror to roll out. I find that in the end, it's easier to just press out the pastry right after you remove it from the food processor.

1 cup (140 g) all-purpose flour (do
    not use unbleached)
6 tablespoons (3 ounces; 90 g) un-
    salted butter, chilled and cut into
    pieces
⅛ teaspoon salt
½ cup (70 g) confectioners' sugar
1 large egg, lightly beaten

1. Place the flour, butter, salt, and sugar in a food processor. Process just until the mixture resembles coarse crumbs, about 10 seconds. Add the egg and pulse just until the pastry begins to hold together, about 20 times. Transfer the pastry to waxed paper. Flatten the dough into a disk.

2. Dust your fingers with flour, then, working very quickly with just your fingertips, press the dough into a 10½-inch (27 cm) loose-bottomed black tin tart pan. Press the dough up the sides of the shell and crimp evenly. Cover carefully with plastic wrap or foil. Refrigerate for 2 to 3 hours.

3. Preheat the oven to 375°F (190°C).

4. Prick the bottom of the shell with the tines of a fork. Line the shell loosely with heavy-duty foil, pressing well into the edges so the pastry does not shrink while baking. Fill with baking weights, rice, or dried beans—making sure you get all the way into the edges—to prevent shrinkage. Bake just until the pastry begins to brown around the edges and seems firm enough to stand up by itself, about 20 minutes.

5. *For a partially baked shell:* Remove the weights and foil and continue baking until lightly browned all over, about 10 more minutes. *For a fully baked shell:* Remove the weights and foil. Bake for an additional 20 minutes. Watch the pastry carefully! Ovens vary tremendously and pastry can brown very quickly. Cool for at least 10 minutes before filling.

Yield: One 10½-inch (27 cm) pastry shell

PÂTE À PAIN

◆

Basic Bread Dough

This yeast dough can be used for a variety of purposes—bread tarts, pizzas, the ladder-like Provençal *fougasse,* or a basic white loaf. I often keep a batch in the refrigerator, for it will keep for several days in a sealed container. This recipe makes enough dough for two average-size tarts or pizzas, or one loaf of bread.

1 cup (25 cl) lukewarm water
1 tablespoon or 1 package active dry
   yeast
2¼ to 2½ cups (315 to 350 g) unbleached all-purpose flour
Pinch of sugar
1 teaspoon salt

1. In a large mixing bowl, combine the water, yeast, 1 cup of the flour, and the sugar. Stir until thoroughly blended. Set aside to proof for about 5 minutes.

2. Once proofed and foamy, add the salt, then begin adding more flour, little by little, until the dough is too stiff to stir. Place the dough on a lightly floured work surface and begin kneading, adding additional flour if the dough is too sticky. Knead until the dough is smooth and satiny, about 10 minutes.

3. Place the dough in a bowl. Cover and let rise at room temperature until doubled in bulk, about 1 hour.

4. Punch down the dough. Cover and let rise again until double in bulk, about 1 hour.

5. The dough is ready to use. If it is to be stored, place in a well-sealed container and refrigerate.

Yield: About 1 pound (500 g) of bread dough

PÂTE-DEMI FEUILLETÉE

Rough Puff Pastry

This is a less uncomplicated version of classic puff pastry. It still demands a bit of patience and clock-watching, but I find that when a recipe demands puff pastry, this is the version I'm more likely to make.

10 tablespoons (5 ounces; 150 g) unsalted butter, chilled
1¼ cups (160 g) unbleached all-purpose flour
½ teaspoon salt
6 to 7 (9 cl) tablespoons ice water

1. Divide the butter into 4 portions. Sift the flour onto a marble slab or cool work surface and make a well in the center. Add 1 portion of the butter, the salt, and 6 tablespoons of the ice water. Work the butter, salt, and water together with the fingertips of one hand until well mixed.

Gradually draw in the flour, working the dough into large crumbs using the fingertips of both hands. If the dough is dry, add the additional 1 tablespoon of ice water. Press the dough together firmly. It should be soft but not sticky. Wrap in plastic wrap and chill thoroughly in the refrigerator for at least 15 minutes.

2. Roll out the dough to a 6 × 15 inch (15 × 38 cm) rectangle on a lightly floured marble slab or cool work surface. Cut the second portion of chilled butter into small pieces. Sprinkle the bits onto two-thirds of the dough, leaving an empty square at one end. Fold the dough in thirds so that the butter divides each layer. (Fold the non-buttered third over the center third, then fold over the re-maining third of the pastry.) Press the ends with the rolling pin to seal. (This rolling and folding is called a "turn.") Wrap in plastic wrap and refrigerate again for at least 15 minutes.

3. Place the dough on the floured work surface, with the open edge toward you, and roll out again to a rectangle. Cut up and sprinkle on the third portion of chilled butter. Fold, as you did in Step 2, then wrap and refrigerate again for 15 minutes.

4. Repeat with the fourth and final portion of butter. If the dough looks streaky, chill it, then give it one more turn, folding it without adding more butter. Wrap in plastic wrap, and refrigerate until ready to use.

Yield: Pastry for one 10½-inch (27 cm) shell

HERBES DE PROVENCE

Mixed Herbs from Provence

This fragrant, heavenly herb mixture is used liberally in all French cooking, not just in Provence. It is essential in preparing a well-seasoned pork terrine and is also wonderful to have on hand to add to grilled meat marinades or to toss in green salads and vinaigrettes.

2 heaping tablespoons dried thyme
1 heaping tablespoon dried oregano
*1 heaping tablespoon dried summer
    savory*
2 heaping tablespoons dried marjoram

Mix together the herbs in a small bowl. Place in a jar and seal well. Store away from direct sunlight, if possible.

Yield: ½ cup (12.5 cl) herbs

SUCRE VANILLÉ

Vanilla Sugar

I don't know how others bake without a stash of vanilla-infused sugar in the larder. I seem to use up an awful lot of vanilla beans, and once they've been soaked or stewed, I allow them to dry thoroughly, then tuck them inside a big glass jar of sugar. In a very short time, you have a wonderfully fragrant blend for scenting custards, cakes, and tarts. As the sugar is used up, just keep adding more and you'll never be caught short again!

4 vanilla beans, split lengthwise
4 cups (800 g) sugar

Scrape out the seeds from the bean pods. Combine the bean pods, seeds, and sugar in a jar. Cover securely and allow to sit for several weeks to scent and flavor the sugar. Use the vanilla sugar in place of regular sugar when baking desserts.

Yield: 4 cups (800 g)

MAYONNAISE

There's no trick to a great mayonnaise, just be sure that all the ingredients are at room temperature when you begin. The emulsion—or suspension of the particles of oil within the egg yolk—will not take if the oil or the egg yolks are too cold. For best results, warm the mixing bowl with warm water, then dry well before you begin.

½ cup (12.5 cl) light olive oil
½ cup (12.5 cl) corn or peanut oil
3 large egg yolks, at room temperature
1 teaspoon imported Dijon mustard
1 tablespoon freshly squeezed lemon juice

Pinch of salt
Pinch of freshly ground white pepper
1 tablespoon white wine vinegar
1 tablespoon boiling water

1. Mix together the oils in a glass measuring cup with a pouring spout. Set aside.

2. In a medium-size bowl, whisk the egg yolks until light and thick. Whisk in the mustard, lemon juice, salt, and pepper, and continue beating steadily until the mixture is smooth and thick.

3. Gradually add just a few drops of oil, whisking until all the oil is incorporated. Do not add too much oil in the beginning, or the mixture will not emulsify. Once the mayonnaise begins to thicken, add the rest of the oil in a slow and steady stream, whisking continually.

4. Whisk in the vinegar and the boiling water. Taste the mayonnaise and adjust the seasonings. Cover and refrigerate, for up to 5 days.

Yield: 1½ cups (37.5 cl)

SAUCE TOMATE

Basic Tomato Sauce

T his recipe offers proportions for about 1 quart (1 l) of sauce, and ingredients can, of course, be multiplied to make a larger batch. Be sure to make some when the summer tomatoes are plentiful and can extra batches for when they're not.

2 tablespoons extra-virgin olive oil
4 medium onions, coarsely chopped
3 garlic cloves, coarsely chopped
4 pounds (2 kg) ripe tomatoes, quartered, or 3 large cans (each 28 ounces; 794 g) Italian plum tomatoes
1 imported bay leaf
A handful of fresh herbs, preferably basil, chervil, thyme, and flat-leaf parsley, stemmed and minced
½ teaspoon hot red pepper flakes (optional)
Grated zest of 1 orange (optional)
Salt and freshly ground black pepper

1. Heat the oil in a large skillet over medium heat. Add the onions and garlic and cook, stirring frequently, until soft but not brown. Increase the heat to medium-high and add the remaining ingredients, seasoning lightly with salt and pepper. Cook, uncovered, stirring frequently, over medium heat until thick, 30 to 45 minutes. Check the seasoning.

2. Press the mixture through a fine-mesh sieve or food mill. The sauce will keep in the refrigerator for several days or may be frozen for several months.

Yield: About 1 quart (1 l)

CRÈME FRAÎCHE

Crème fraîche is France's mature, slightly tangy cream. I prefer it to sour cream, which is blander and firmer in texture. Crème fraîche is easy to make, and is delicious served with fresh fruit, and great in sauces and salad dressings.

2 cups (50 cl) heavy cream
2 tablespoons buttermilk

1. Thoroughly mix the cream and buttermilk in a medium-size bowl. Cover with plastic wrap and let stand at room temperature overnight or until fairly thick.

2. Cover tightly and refrigerate at least 4 hours to thicken it even more. The cream may be stored for several days, as the tangy flavor continues to develop.

Yield: 2 cups (50 cl)

SAUCE GRIBICHE LA CAGOUILLE

La Cagouille's Vinaigrette with Capers and Eggs

I've always loved *sauce gribiche,* the zesty, bright French sauce that's perfect over grilled fish, with cooked leeks, tossed on a bed of greens. Chef Gérard Allemandou, of the fine Paris fish bistro, La Cagouille, serves this over warm *raie,* or skate. Prepare this the same day you will be serving it. Store the prepared sauce at room temperature.

*1 tablespoon best-quality red wine vin-
egar*
*1 tablespoon best-quality sherry wine
vinegar*
Salt
¼ cup (6 cl) extra-virgin olive oil
¼ cup (6 cl) diced red onion
2 tablespoons diced cornichons
2 teaspoons drained small capers
½ teaspoon imported Dijon mustard
Freshly ground black pepper
*2 hard-cooked eggs, yolks and whites
minced separately*

3 tablespoons minced flat-leaf parsley

1. Place the vinegars and a pinch of salt in a small bowl. With a wire whisk, whisk until the salt dissolves. Add the oil in a thin stream, whisking constantly until emulsified. Add the onion, cornichons, capers, and mustard; mix well. Season with salt and pepper to taste.

2. When serving, stir in the minced yolk, white, and parsley.

Yield: ¾ to 1 cup (25 cl)

FOND DE VOLAILLE

Chicken Stock

I consider the larder bare if there are not a few containers of chicken stock in my freezer. When I have time and know I'll be near the kitchen all day long, I make a stock out of fresh chicken necks and wings, which make it wonderfully gelatinous. When I'm in a hurry, I make stock in the microwave, using about 1 pound (500 g) cut-up raw or cooked chicken carcasses along with the traditional herbs and vegetables to 2 cups (50 cl) water. Cook at high power for 12 minutes and strain.

*4 pounds (2 kg) raw chicken parts or
raw or cooked carcasses*
4 carrots
2 large onions, 1 stuck with 2 cloves
1 rib celery
*1 leek (white and tender green parts),
halved lengthwise and well rinsed*
1 bouquet garni: 12 parsley stems, 8

*peppercorns, ¼ teaspoon thyme, ¼
teaspoon fennel seeds and 1 imported bay leaf tied in a double
thickness of cheesecloth*
Pinch of salt

1. Place the chicken pieces in a heavy stockpot and cover with cold water by at least 2 inches (5 cm). Bring to a boil over medium heat. Skim to remove the scum that rises to the surface. Continue skimming until the broth is clear, then add cold water to replace the water removed.

2. Add the vegetables and bouquet garni, burying them among the chicken pieces. Sprinkle in just a pinch of salt. Return the liquid to a boil over high heat. Reduce the heat and simmer gently for 2 hours. Skim and degrease the soup as necessary.

3. Line a large colander with a double layer of dampened cheesecloth and place the colander over a large bowl. Ladle the broth into the colander; discard the solids.

4. Refrigerate the stock. When it is cold, spoon off all traces of fat that rise to the surface. The stock may be safely refrigerated for 3 or 4 days, or can be frozen for up to 6 months.

Yield: 2 quarts (2 l) stock

FUMET DE POISSON

Fish Stock

5 pounds (2.5 kg) non-oily fish bones, heads, and trimmings (gills removed), well rinsed and cut up
2 onions, chopped
3 ounces (90 g) fresh mushrooms, washed and thinly sliced
Bouquet garni: 12 parsley stems, 8 peppercorns, ½ teaspoon thyme, ¼ teaspoon fennel seeds, and 1 imported bay leaf tied in a double thickness of cheesecloth
2 cups (50 cl) dry white wine
1 teaspoon freshly squeezed lemon juice

1. In a large nonreactive stockpot, combine all the ingredients and add 2 quarts (2 l) of cold water. Bring to a simmer, skimming frequently. Simmer, uncovered, skimming frequently, for 30 minutes.

2. Line a colander with a double layer of dampened cheesecloth and place the colander over a large bowl. Ladle the stock into the colander; discard the solids. Measure the fish stock and, if necessary, boil until it is reduced to 4 cups (1 l).

Yield: 1 quart (1 l)

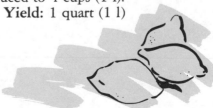

WHEN IN FRANCE

The following is a personal list of my favorite small bistros, small family restaurants, brasseries and wine bars, where authentic bistro cooking can be found in France:

PARIS:

ALLARD
41 Rue Saint-André-
des-Arts
75006 Paris
(43.26.48.23)

AMBASSADE
D'AUVERGNE
22 Rue du Grenier-
Saint-Lazare
75003 Paris
(42.72.31.22)

L'AMI LOUIS
32 Rue du Vertbois
75003 Paris
(48.87.77.48)

CHEZ ANDRÉ
12 Rue Marbeuf
75008 Paris
(47.20.59.57)

ARTOIS
13 Rue d'Artois
75008 Paris
(42.25.01.10)

L'ASSIETTE
181 Rue du Château
75014 Paris
(43.22.64.86)

ASTIER
44 Rue Jean-Pierre-
Timbaud
75011 Paris
(43.57.16.35)

BRASSERIE BALZAR
49 Rue des Ecoles
75005 Paris
(43.54.13.67)

BENOIT
20 Rue Saint-Martin
75004 Paris
(43.72.25.76)

LE BOEUF SUR LE TOIT
34 Rue du Colisée
75008 Paris
(43.59.83.80)

LA BOUTARDE
4 Rue Boutard
92200 Neuilly-sur-Seine
(47.45.34.55)

LA CAGOUILLE
10-12 Place Constantin-
Brancusi
75014 Paris
(43.22.09.01)

LE CAMÉLÉON
6 Rue de Chevreuse
75006 Paris
(43.20.63.43)

LA COUPOLE
102 Boulevard
Montparnasse
75014 Paris
(43.20.14.20)

CARTET
62 Rue de Malte
75011 Paris
(48.05.17.65)

CHARDENOUX
1 Rue Jules-Vallès
75011 Paris
(43.71.49.52)

AUX CHARPENTIERS
10 Rue Mabillon
75006 Paris
(43.26.30.05)

LE CLOS MORILLONS
50 Rue des Morillons
75015 Paris
(48.28.04.37)

LE BISTROT D'À CÔTÉ
10 Rue Gustave-
Flaubert
75017 Paris
(42.67.05.81)

LE BISTROT DE
L'ETOILE NIEL
75 Avenue Niel
75017 Paris
(42.27.88.44)

LA FERMETTE DU SUD-
OUEST
31 Rue Coquillière
75001 Paris
(42.36.73.55)

BRASSERIE FLO
7 Cour des Petites-
Ecuries
75010 Paris
(47.70.13.59)

LA FONTAINE DE MARS
129 Rue Saint-
Dominique
75007 Paris
(47.05.46.44)

CHEZ FRED
190 bis Boulevard
Péreire
75017 Paris
(45.74.20.48)

LA GALOCHE
D'AURILLAC
41 Rue de Lappe
75011 Paris
(47.00.77.15)

CHEZ GEORGES
1 Rue du Mail
75001 Paris
(42.60.07.11)

CHEZ GEORGES
273 Boulevard Péreire
75017 Paris
(45.74.31.00)

CHEZ GÉRAUD
31 Rue Vital
75016 Paris
(45.20.33.00)

LE GLOBE D'OR
158 Rue Saint-Honoré
75001 Paris
(42.60.23.37)

LES GOURMETS DES
TERNES
87 Boulevard de
Courcelles
75008 Paris
(42.27.43.04)

BRASSERIE DE L'ILE
SAINT-LOUIS
55 Quai de Bourbon
75004 Paris
(43.54.02.59)

CHEZ JENNY
39 Boulevard du
Temple
75003 Paris
(42.74.75.75)

JUVÉNILES
47 Rue Richelieu
75001 Paris
(42.97.46.49)

LESCURE
7 Rue Mondavi
75001 Paris
(42.60.18.91)

LOUIS XIV
1 bis Place des Victoires
75001 Paris
(40.26.20.81)

LA LOZÈRE
4 Rue Hautefeuille
75006 Paris
(43.54.26.64)

AUX LYONNAIS
32 Rue Saint-Marc
75002 Paris
(42.96.65.04)

CHEZ MAÎTRE PAUL
12 Rue Monsieur-le-
Prince
75006 Paris
(43.54.74.59)

MANUFACTURE
20 Esplanade de la
Manufacture
92130 Issy-les-
Moulineaux
(40.93.08.98)

LE PETIT MARGUERY
9 Boulevard de Port-
Royal
75013 Paris
(43.31.58.59)

MOISSONNIER
28 Rue des Fossés-
Saint-Bernard
75005 Paris
(43.29.87.65)

L'OULETTE
38 Rue Tournelles
75004 Paris
(42.71.43.33)

CHEZ PAULINE
5 Rue Villedo
75001 Paris
(42.96.20.70)

LE PERRAUDIN
157 Rue Saint-Jacques
75005 Paris
(46.33.15.75)

PHARAMOND
24 Rue de la Grande-
Truanderie
75001 Paris
(42.33.06.72)

AU PIED DE COCHON
6 Rue Coquillière
75001 Paris
(42.36.11.75)

PIERRE AU PALAIS
ROYAL
10 Rue de Richelieu
75001 Paris
(42.96.09.17)

CHEZ PHILIPPE
(Auberge Pyrénées-
Cevennes)
106 Rue de la Folie-
Méricourt
75011 Paris
(43.57.33.78)

CHEZ RENÉ
14 Boulevard Saint-
   Germain
75005 Paris
(43.54.30.23)

BRASSERIE STELLA
133 Avenue Victor-
   Hugo
75016 Paris
(47.27.60.54)

LE TOUR DE
   MONTLHÉRY
5 Rue Prouvaires
75001 Paris
(42.36.21.82)

CHEZ TOUTOUNE
5 Rue de Pontoise
75005 Paris
(43.26.56.81)

AU TROU GASCON
40 Rue Taine
75012 Paris
(43.44.34.26)

LE TRUMILOU
84 Quai de l'Hôtel-de-
   Ville
75004 Paris
(42.77.63.98)

VAUDEVILLE
29 Rue Vivienne
75002 Paris
(42.33.39.31)

CHEZ LA VIEILLE
   (CHEZ ADRIENNE)
37 Rue de l'Arbre-Sec
75001 Paris
(42.60.15.78)

WILLI'S WINE BAR
13 Rue des Petits-
   Champs
75001 Paris
(42.61.05.09)

BRITTANY AND NORMANDY:

L'ETRAVE
Place de l'Eglise
Cléden-Cap-Sizun
29113 Audierne
(98.70.66.87)

CHEZ JACKY
29124 Riec-sur-Belon
(98.06.90.32)

LE PAVÉ D'AUGE
Beuvron-en-Auge
14430 Douzlé
(31.79.26.71)

LA MÈRE POULARD
50116 Le Mont-Saint-
   Michel
(33.60.14.01)

BRASSERIE LES
   VAPEURS
160 Boulevard Fernand-
   Moureaux
14360 Trouville-sur-
   Mer
(31.88.15.24)

SOLOGNE AND THE LOIRE:

JEANNE DE LAVAL
54 Rue Nationale
Les Rosiers
49350 Gennes
(41.51.80.17)

AUBERGE ALPHONSE
   MELLOT
16 Nouvelle Place
18300 Sancerre
(48.54.20.53)

HÔTEL TATIN
5 Avenue de Vierzon
41600 Lamotte-Beuvron
(54.88.00.03)

ILE DE FRANCE:

L'ESTURGEON
6 Cours du 14-Juillet
78300 Poissy
(39.65.00.04)

BRASSERIE DU
   THÉÂTRE
15 Rue des Réservoirs
78000 Versailles
(39.50.03.21)

ALSACE:

LES ALISIERS
5 Le Faudé
68650 Lapoutroie
(89.47.52.82)

L'AMI SCHUTZ
1 Ponts-Couverts
67000 Strasbourg
(88.32.76.98)

HÔTEL AU BOEUF
67117 Ittenheim
(88.69.01.42)

CAVEAU D'EGUISHEIM
3 Place du Château-
   Saint-Léon
68420 Eguisheim
(89.41.08.89)

LA GRANGE DU
   PAYSAN
8 Rue Principale
67260 Hinsingen
(88.00.91.83)

TIRE-BOUCHON
5 Rue des Tailleurs-de-
Pierres
67000 Strasbourg
(88.32.47.86)

FERME-AUBERGE
ZUEM DORFWAPPE
3 Rue Principale
67340 Weiterswiller
(88.89.48.19)

BURGUNDY AND LYON:

LA BOUZEROTTE
Bouze-les-Beaune
21200 Beaune
(80.26.01.37)

AUBERGE DU CEP
Place de l'Eglise
69820 Fleurie-en-
Beaujolais
(74.04.10.77)

CAFÉ DES
FÉDÉRATIONS
8 Rue du Major-Martin
69001 Lyon
(78.28.26.00)

CAFÉ DU JURA
25 Rue Tupin
69002 Lyon
(78.42.20.57)

LÉON DE LYON
1 Rue Pleney
69001 Lyon
(78.28.11.33)

CHEZ LILY ET GABY
76 Rue Mazenod
69003 Lyon
(78.60.47.98)

BISTROT DE LYON
64 Rue Mercière
69002 Lyon
(78.37.00.62)

LA MEUNIÈRE
11 Rue Neuve
75001 Lyon
(78.28.62.91)

GRAND CAFÉ DES
NÉGOCIANTS
1 Place Francisque-
Régaud
69002 Lyon
(78.42.50.05)

CHEZ ROSE
4 Rue Rabelais
69003 Lyon
(78.60.57.25)

CHEZ TANTE
PAULETTE
2 Rue Chavanne
75001 Lyon
(78.28.31.34)

LA VOÛTE (CHEZ LÉA)
11 Place Antonin-
Gourju
69002 Lyon
(78.42.01.33)

JURA/RHÔNE ALPS:

RESTAURANT
CHARTRON
Avenue Gambetta
26260 Saint-Donat
(75.45.11.82)

RELAIS DE CHAUTAGNE
73310 Chindrieux
(79.54.20.27)

LE FRANÇAIS
7 Avenue Alsace-
Lorraine
01000 Bourg-en-Bresse
(74.22.55.14)

FERME-AUBERGE
RENÉ LARACINE
01510 Ordonnaz
(74.36.42.38)

FERME-AUBERGE LE
POELE
Fourcatier-et-Maison-
Neuve
25370 Les Hôpitaux-
Neufs
(81.49.90.99)

PROVENCE:

AUBERGE D'AILLANE
Plan d'Aillane
Rue A. Messmer
13290 Les Milles
(42.24.24.49)

LA BEAUGRAVIÈRE
Route Nationale 7
84430 Mondragon
(90.40.82.54)

MAURICE BRUN
Aux Mets de Provence
18 Quai Rive-Neuve
13007 Marseilles
(91.33.35.38)

FERME-AUBERGE
DOMAINE DE SAINT-
LUC
La Baume de Transit
26790 Saint-Paul-Trois-
Châteaux
(75.98.11.51)

CHEZ FONFON
140 Vallon des Auffes
13007 Marseilles
(91.52.14.38)

CHEZ GILBERT
Quai Baux
3260 Cassis
(42.01.71.36)

LE BISTROT DU
  PARADOU
Avenue de la Vallée-
  des-Baux
13120 Paradou
(90.97.32.70)

MOULIN DE TANTE
  YVONNE
Rue Benjamin-Raspail
13410 Lambesc
(42.92.72.46)

CÔTE-D'AZUR:

BARALE
39 Rue Beaumont
06000 Nice
(93.89.17.94)

L'ESTAMINET DES
  REMPARTS
24 Rue Honoré-Henri
06250 Mougins-Village
(93.90.05.36)

AUBERGE DE LA
  MADONE
Peillon-Village
06440 L'Escarène
(93.79.91.17)

LA MÈRE BESSON
13 Rue des Frères-
  Pradignac
06400 Cannes
(93.39.59.24)

LA MÉRENDA
4 Rue de la Terrasse
06000 Nice
(No telephone)

TÉTOU
Avenue des Frères-
  Roustan
06220 Golfe-Juan
(93.63.71.16)

TOCELLO
6 Rue Sainte-Reparate
06300 Nice
(93.62.10.20)

THE LANGUEDOC:

LA CAMARGUE
19 Rue de la
  République
30220 Aigues-Mortes
(66.53.86.88)

LA CÔTE BLEUE
34140 Bouzigues
(67.78.30.87)

LA FREGATE
24 Quai de l'Amirauté
66190 Collioure
(68.82.06.05)

L'HOSTAL
Castelnou
66300 Thuir
(68.53.45.42)

AUVERGNE:

FERME-AUBERGE DU
  BRUEL
Saint-Illide
15130 Cernin
(71.49.72.27)

LES MOUFLONS
Route de Super Besse
63610 Besse-en-
  Chandesse
(73.79.51.31)

A LA REINE MARGOT
19 Guy-de-Veyre
15000 Aurillac
(71.48.26.46)

GASCONY, TOULOUSE, QUERCY:

AUBERGE DE LA
  BRAISE
31340 Villematier
(61.35.35.64)

LA BELLE GASCONNE
Poudenas
47170 Mezin
(53.65.71.58)

LE RELAIS
  D'ARMAGNAC
Luppé Violles
32110 Nogaro
(62.08.95.22)

RIPA ALTA
3 Place de l'Eglise
32160 Plaisance
(62.69.30.43)

BASQUE COUNTRY:

ARRANTZALEAK
Avenue Jean-Poulou
64500 Ciboure
Saint-Jean-de-Luz
(59.47.10.75)

EUZKADI
Espelette
64250 Cambo-les-Bains
(59.29.91.88)

AUBERGE DE LA GALUPE
Urt
64240 Hasparren
(59.56.21.84)

ITHURRIA
Aïnhoa
64250 Cambo-les-Bains
(59.29.92.11)

LES PYRÉNÉES
19 Place du Général-de-Gaulle
64220 Saint-Jean-Pied-de-Port
(59.37.01.01)

THE DORDOGNE:

CRO-MAGNON
24620 Les Eyzies-de-Tayac
(53.06.97.06)

LA FERME
Caudon-de-Vitrac
24200 Montfort-Caudon
(53.28.33.35)

LA PESCALERIE
46330 Cabrerets
(65.31.22.55)

BORDEAUX AND THE ATLANTIC COAST:

LE CHAT BOTTÉ
2 Rue Mairie
17590 Saint-Clement-Les-Baleines
(46.29.42.09)

CHEZ DIEGO
Centre Captal
33260 La Teste
(56.54.44.32)

LE MARTRAY
17590 Ars-en-Ré
(46.29.40.04)

CHEZ PHILIPPE
1 Place du Parlement
33000 Bordeaux
(56.81.83.15)

LA TUPIÑA
6 Rue Porte-de-la-Monnaie
33000 Bordeaux
(56.91.56.37)

LES VIVIERS
Port de Larros
33470 Gujan-Mestras
(56.66.01.04)

INDEX

of greens, headcheese, eggs, and tomatoes, Brasserie du Théâtre's, 59–60
of ham, walnuts, and duck gizzards,
L'Oulette's, 64–65
herring and potato, La Meunière's, 54–
55
marinated squid, 166–67
mixed summer, La Mère Besson's, 55–
56
Niçoise, La Mère Besson's, 43–44
potato, warm poached sausage with, 7
quick dressings for, 65
of Roquefort, walnuts, and Belgian endive, Chardenoux's, 44–45
sausage, cheese, and endive, Chez Jenny's, 45–46
sausages preserved in olive oil, 51–52
seasoned couscous, 11
smoked duck breast, Cro-Magnon's, 42–
43
smoked haddock and spinach, L'Aquitaine's, 52–54
tossed green, with vinaigrette, Tante
Yvonne's, 63–64
warm potato, with herbed vinaigrette,
106–7
of white beans and smoked sausages,
Quai d'Orsay's, 58–59
Salmon:
cooked with its skin, Chardenoux's,
145–46
fresh roasted, with olive oil, 144–45
Salt:
adding to beaten eggs, 245
adding to vinaigrette, 42
adding to water for pasta or vegetables,
68
Brittany sea, giant shrimp grilled with,
Chez Géraud's, 164–66
-cured duck with cabbage, Le Petit Marguery's, 189–90
Salt cod:
gratin, 134–35
with herbed tomato sauce, Le Caméléon's, 136–37
purée of garlic, cream and, Madame
Cartet's, 138–39
and vegetables (grand aïoli), 135–36
Sandwiches:
"bathed" Provençal, 15
of beef and confit of tomatoes, Juvé-
nile's, 13

ham and blue cheese, Les Bacchantes',
14
Sauces:
basil and garlic, 77
tartar, 159, 160
wilted sorrel, 85
see also Tomato sauces
Sauge, ravioles à la crème du laurier et de la,
78–79
Sausage(s):
cheese, and endive salad, Chez Jenny's,
45–46
curly endive salad with bacon and, Aux
Lyonnais', 38–39
poached, with potato salad, warm, 7
pork, lentil soup with, 34–35
pork, with mustard sauce, 8
preserved in olive oil, 51–52
smoked, salad of white beans and, Quai
d'Orsay's, 58–59
spicy chorizo, and blood sausage with
red beans, 219–21
spicy, oysters and, from Happy Oyster
Restaurant, 157–58
Sautéed:
chicken livers, salad of fresh spinach
and, 60–62
chicken with shallots, 176–77
potatoes with garlic and walnut oil,
111–12
potato quarters in their skins, 113–14
veal with carrots, La Boutarde's, 204–5
Sauternes, civet de canard au, 187–88
Sauternes, duck stew in, 187–88
Savory Swiss chard tart, 129–31
Savoy cabbage:
skate wing with spring onions and,
L'Ambroisie's, 148–49
smoked haddock with, Chez la Vieille's,
139–40
Savoy, Guy, fall leg of lamb from, 213–14
Scallops:
with garlic, tomatoes, basil, and thyme,
162–63
oven-roasted, La Tupina's, 163–64
Seasoned couscous salad, 11
Sel de Guérande, gambas grillé au, Chez Gér-
aud, 164–66
Shallots, chicken sautéed with, 176–77
Shapiro, Maggie, 89
Shellfish, 150–67